2ND **Edition**

BEST ⛺ TENT
Camping

NEW JERSEY

YOUR CAR-CAMPING GUIDE TO SCENIC BEAUTY, THE SOUNDS
OF NATURE, AND AN ESCAPE FROM CIVILIZATION

Best Tent Camping: New Jersey

Published by Menasha Ridge Press
Printed in the United States of America
Distributed by Publishers Group West
Second edition, first printing

Library of Congress Cataloging-in-Publication Data for this book is available at catalog.loc.gov.
ISBN: 978-1-63404-098-3; eISBN: 978-1-63404-099-0

Project editor: Ritchey Halphen
Cover and interior design: Jonathan Norberg
Maps: Steve Jones and Matt Willen
Photos: Matt Willen except as noted
Copy editor: Scott Alexander Jones
Proofreader: Vanessa Lynn Rusch
Indexer: Meghan Miller Brawley/Potomac Indexing

MENASHA RIDGE PRESS
An imprint of AdventureKEEN
2204 First Ave. S., Ste. 102
Birmingham, AL 35233

Visit menasharidge.com for a complete listing of our books and for ordering information. Contact us at our website, at facebook.com/menasharidge, or at twitter.com/menasharidge with questions or comments. To find out more about who we are and what we're doing, visit blog.menasharidge.com.

Front cover: A campsite among the dogwoods at Belleplain State Park (see Campgrounds 39 and 40, pages 136 and 140); photo: Matt Willen. *Cover inset and opposite page:* Lake view at Turkey Swamp Park (see Campground 31, page 108); photo: Mike Klein.

2ND Edition

BEST ⛺ TENT
Camping

NEW JERSEY

YOUR CAR-CAMPING GUIDE TO SCENIC BEAUTY, THE SOUNDS
OF NATURE, AND AN ESCAPE FROM CIVILIZATION

Matt Willen

MENASHA RIDGE PRESS
Your Guide to the Outdoors Since 1982

New Jersey Campground Locator Map

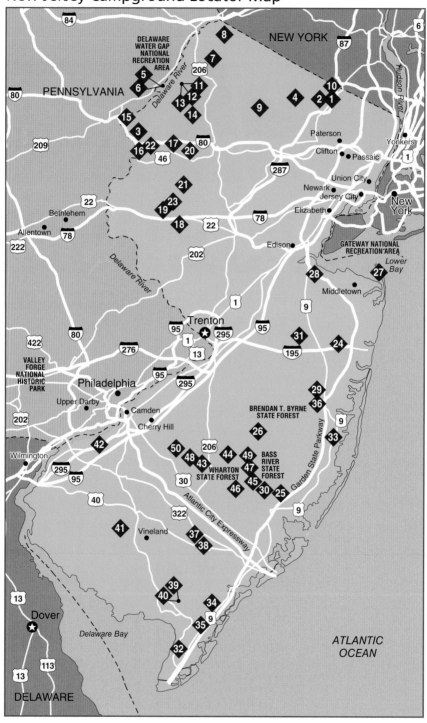

TABLE OF CONTENTS

Map Legend

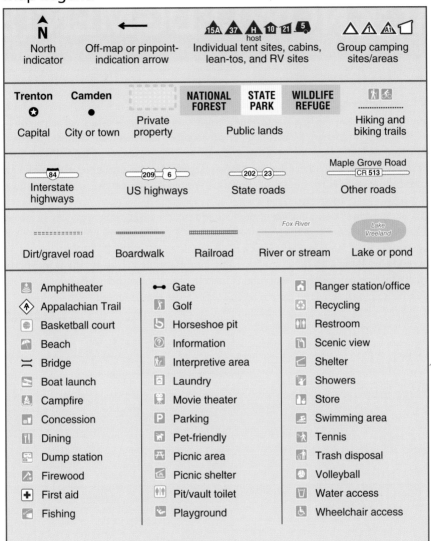

N North indicator

Off-map or pinpoint-indication arrow

Individual tent sites, cabins, lean-tos, and RV sites

Group camping sites/areas

Trenton ✪ Capital

Camden ● City or town

Private property

NATIONAL FOREST | STATE PARK | WILDLIFE REFUGE

Public lands

Hiking and biking trails

Interstate highways

US highways

State roads

Maple Grove Road CR 513
Other roads

Dirt/gravel road

Boardwalk

Railroad

Fox River
River or stream

Lake Vreeland
Lake or pond

Amphitheater	Gate	Ranger station/office
Appalachian Trail	Golf	Recycling
Basketball court	Horseshoe pit	Restroom
Beach	Information	Scenic view
Bridge	Interpretive area	Shelter
Boat launch	Laundry	Showers
Campfire	Movie theater	Store
Concession	Parking	Swimming area
Dining	Pet-friendly	Tennis
Dump station	Picnic area	Trash disposal
Firewood	Picnic shelter	Volleyball
First aid	Pit/vault toilet	Water access
Fishing	Playground	Wheelchair access

ACKNOWLEDGMENTS

While I was gathering the information for the second edition of this book, I met and spoke with numerous representatives of individual campgrounds and public-land agencies: Michele Buckley of the New Jersey Department of Environmental Protection, Kathy Hackney of Atlantic County Parks, Jean Taylor of Camp Taylor, and Ira Alexander of Triple Brook Camping Resort, among many others. I am extremely grateful for the assistance of everyone who took the time to answer my questions, show me around, and direct me to places of interest that I wouldn't have discovered otherwise.

Thanks to Marie Javins, author of the first edition, for giving this non–New Jerseyan a solid foundation upon which to create the second; to Tim Jackson for inviting me to do this project; to Ritchey Halphen, Steve Jones, Scott Jones, and Vanessa Rusch for working with me to produce a book with timely and accurate information; to Jackson Galloway for showing up at a few campgrounds so that I didn't have to camp alone; and to all of my friends and family who graciously covered for me when I was on the road working on this book.

—Matt Willen

PREFACE

When I began working on the second edition of *Best Tent Camping: New Jersey,* my familiarity with the state and the lay of its public lands was somewhat limited. Because of the hiking and camping I had done in the area in recent years, I was well acquainted with that part of the state through which the Appalachian Trail passes (along the Delaware River north of I-80 and along the New York–New Jersey state line south of I-84). When I was young, during the 1970s, I visited Ocean City for a week each year for a Collins family reunion (the Collinses were my mother's side of family). Finally, I had read what John McPhee had written about the Pine Barrens.

With the above being the extent of my knowledge, I found the prospect of working on a book on camping in New Jersey a little daunting at first—but it was also quite inviting. I've always wanted to learn the geography of new places, to become familiar with the shape of the land, the different ecosystems supported, the way the light falls across the landscape at different times of day and during different seasons. So in the summer of 2016, I began the project of familiarizing myself with the Garden State.

Because I was traveling often to southern New England during the last half of 2016, I decided to begin my work for the book with the northern section of the state, visiting several campgrounds on each of the trips I made across I-84 or I-287. As fall passed into winter, I focused on the central part of New Jersey, as it was easily accessible from my home in Pennsylvania. And during the spring of 2017, I made two extended trips during which I covered the southern part of the state and whatever else remained. I knew that the Jersey Shore area would get busy after Memorial Day. Because I typically rely on a fair bit of serendipity to guide me through my travels, I thought that finishing the work before the first holiday weekend of summer would allow me to travel without worrying about having to reserve campsites in advance. That was a sound idea, though I discovered that some campgrounds were still closed before Memorial Day.

One of the best aspects of learning a new place is the surprises—those moments when your assumptions are turned on their heads. I had several of those moments when I visited the campgrounds. Most notably, I learned how friendly (without exception) everyone was, campers and park/campground staff alike. New Jersey is a small state packed with a lot of people, and I had assumed that lots of those people would be too busy to talk with me. On the contrary, I often found myself in the awkward position of having to exit a long, friendly conversation because I had work to do.

I was also surprised at how much the state values its green spaces and public lands. New Jersey is densely populated, but its natural areas are so thoughtfully designed that in many cases you really get the feeling that you're away from it all, even though there might be a busy highway a mile or two from camp. Even along the Jersey Shore, a place enshrined in popular culture thanks to the eponymous MTV reality show, there are natural areas, parks, and wildlife preserves that provide some respite from the busyness of the coastal communities. Drive a few miles inland to some of the campgrounds, and you're in a different world.

And then there are the Pine Barrens, with their sandy soil, tea-colored creeks and rivers, conifer forests, and historic sites, encompassing 1.1 million acres of remote wild land within a couple of hours of the metropolitan New York City–New Jersey area. I would have liked to spend several more weeks exploring this magical place.

At 8,729 square miles, New Jersey is the 47th-largest state in the union—not one of the big ones, or even medium-sized. But its public lands are big on diversity and character. And in spite of the state's proximity to several of the country's major population centers, you can still immerse yourself in nature and all it has to offer—only a short drive from home.

—M. W.

BEST
CAMPGROUNDS

BEST FOR BIKING

BEST FOR BOATING

BEST FOR FAMILIES

BEST FOR FAMILIES *(continued)*

BEST FOR FISHING

BEST FOR HIKING

BEST FOR HIKING *(continued)*

BEST FOR SCENERY

BEST FOR SOLITUDE

BEST FOR SOLITUDE *(continued)*

BEST FOR SWIMMING

BEST FOR WILDLIFE VIEWING

INTRODUCTION

Welcome to New Jersey, where you'll find unexpectedly beautiful campgrounds that rival any in the United States. This is a densely populated state, with the vast majority of its people crammed into the urban northeast and the cities; it's also a small state, where you're never more than a few hours from the Atlantic Ocean, the Appalachian Trail, or the solitude of the Pinelands. Whether you enjoy fishing, surfing, mountain biking, canoeing, or just staring at the stars from a remote campsite, New Jersey will surprise you with its state forests, its public parks, and the occasional private-but-wooded campground.

New Jersey has unique features that may appeal to more than the outdoors-oriented members of the family. To many, camping is about relaxing in serene wilderness, but to others, it's an economic choice that offers affordable accommodation. Travelers bound for Philadelphia on a budget should check out Philadelphia South/Clarksboro KOA Campground, while visitors en route to Manhattan will want to focus on the campgrounds profiled in the Northern New Jersey chapter. Beach and casino lovers should turn first to the Jersey Shore profiles.

Those looking for more-natural environments where they can hike, canoe, and bike through the woods have the most choices. Every chapter describes vast parks and rivers waiting to be explored. The western side of the state features canoe-in sites along the Delaware River and hike-in sites along the Appalachian Trail. Campgrounds in southern New Jersey sit under the tall trees of the Pinelands National Reserve, which encompasses miles of forest and winding streams. Central New Jersey offers a campground for every interest, from the historic village of Allaire State Park to the multiuse path that runs through Sandy Hook National Recreation Area. Even northern New Jersey offers pockets of woodlands and outdoor-education centers.

One advantage of camping in such a small but highly developed state is that you're never far from businesses and stores. Even though your tent may be the only one in sight, with the odd frog or deer as your sole companion, you can still easily rent a canoe or swim in a lake with a lifeguard on duty. So grab your tent and head outside!

HOW TO USE THIS GUIDEBOOK

Menasha Ridge Press welcomes you to *Best Tent Camping: New Jersey.* Whether you're new to camping or you've been sleeping in your portable shelter over decades of outdoor adventures, please review the following information. It explains how we have worked with the author to organize this book and how you can make the best use of it.

Some text on the following pages applies to all books in the Best Tent Camping series. Where this isn't the case, such as in the descriptions of weather and wildlife, the author has provided information specific to the area covered in this particular book.

THE RATING SYSTEM

As with all books in the Best Tent Camping series, the author personally experienced dozens of campgrounds and campsites to select the top 50 locations in New Jersey. Within that universe of 50 sites, the author then ranked each one according to the six categories described below.

Each campground is superlative in its own way. For example, a site may be rated only one star in one category but perhaps five stars in another category. Our rating system allows you to choose your destination based on the attributes that are most important to you. Although these ratings are subjective, they're still excellent guidelines for finding the perfect camping experience for you and your companions.

Below and following we describe the criteria for each of the attributes in our five-star rating system:

★★★★★　　The site is **ideal** in that category.

★★★★　　The site is **exemplary** in that category.

★★★　　The site is **very good** in that category.

★★　　The site is **above average** in that category.

★　　The site is **acceptable** in that category.

INDIVIDUAL RATINGS

Each campground description includes ratings for **beauty, privacy, quiet, spaciousness, security,** and **cleanliness;** each attribute is ranked from one to five stars, with five being the best. Yes, these ratings are subjective, but we've tried to select campgrounds that offer something for everyone.

BEAUTY

In the wilds of northwest New Jersey, five-star campgrounds sit among protected forests, their beauty obvious to tent campers who value thick greenery, craggy mountains, and wild animals. But beauty in the southern forest is defined differently, with the Pinelands' scrubby underbrush, cranberry bogs, and sandy ground—features that combine to make an ecosystem that is unique worldwide. After the surprise at this environmental shift wears off, the beauty of the Pinelands reveals itself.

PRIVACY

For those who seek wooded solitude, relatively few New Jersey campgrounds have sites spaced very far apart. Some campgrounds offer wide-open spaces as buffer zones, while others use natural barriers such as hedges and undergrowth to provide the illusion of privacy. In general, public campgrounds offer more seclusion than private campgrounds. Those who wish to be truly alone should seek out the wilderness camping areas listed in this book, where campers often have entire campgrounds to themselves.

SPACIOUSNESS

When it comes to tent camping, space needs vary depending on the size of your group. But even a solo camper needs room to move around and not feel cramped—nobody wants their tent too close to the fire pit, picnic table, or parking spot. In general, the more rustic the campground, the more spacious the site.

Unlike the privately owned campgrounds in this book, those in New Jersey state parks do not provide RV hookups: sites are either tent-only or suitable for both tents and camping trailers. If you have a trailer, check with the park before you go to make sure it's not too long for the site—while some campgrounds list specific length limits, others do not.

QUIET

Let's face it: *quiet* isn't a word that often springs to mind regarding New Jersey campgrounds. Happily, there are exceptions—campgrounds that are cleverly located and designed so that the only non-natural noises might come from canoe paddles breaking the water or cyclists whizzing by. To increase your chances for serenity, avoid summer weekends, and set up camp midweek. Again, the very quietest sites are found in wilderness camping areas.

SECURITY

On the face of it, a wilderness campsite seems safer than, say, a large RV resort "down the shore." (After all, who would hike 3 miles to steal a can of propane?) On the other hand, the larger and less remote the campground, the more likely your neighbors are to notice sketchy activity around your site, and the more likely there is to be a security guard or park ranger on patrol. Thus, even at remote campsites, common sense should still guide you: leave valuables at home, and keep other tempting items locked in the trunk of your vehicle.

CLEANLINESS

Most of New Jersey's state parks provide garbage bags at contact stations, and visitors are encouraged to pack out everything they packed in. Dumpsters are usually located near bathhouses, with allowances made for bearproofing. Nevertheless, rubbish can accumulate after busy weekends. Popular parks are cleaned quickly, so busy doesn't necessarily equal dirty. Remote sites are less fastidiously maintained, but littering typically isn't a big problem. A low cleanliness rating should not necessarily discourage you from visiting a campground—in many cases, the lower the rating, the wilder the site.

THE CAMPGROUND PROFILE

Each profile contains a concise but informative narrative of the campground and individual sites. In addition to the property, the recreational opportunities are also described—what's in the area and perhaps suggestions for touristy activities. This descriptive text is enhanced with three helpful components: Ratings, discussed previously; Key Information; and Getting There (accurate driving directions that lead you to the campground from the nearest major roadway, along with GPS coordinates).

CAMPGROUND LOCATOR MAP AND MAP LEGEND

Use the New Jersey Campground Locator Map, opposite the Table of Contents on page iv, to assess the exact location of each campground. The campground's number appears not only on the overview map but also in the table of contents and on the profile's first page.

A map legend that details the symbols found on the campground layout maps appears immediately following the Table of Contents, on page vii.

CAMPGROUND LAYOUT MAPS

Each profile includes a map showing campsites, roads, facilities, and other key elements.

GPS CAMPGROUND ENTRANCE COORDINATES

Readers can easily access all campgrounds in this book by using the driving directions and maps, which generally show/indicate at least one major road leading into the area. But for those who enjoy using GPS technology to navigate, the book includes coordinates for each campground's entrance in latitude and longitude, expressed in degrees and decimal minutes.

To convert GPS coordinates from degrees, minutes, and seconds to the above degrees–decimal minutes format, the seconds are divided by 60. For more on GPS technology, visit usgs.gov. *Tip:* Check whether your wireless carrier has coverage in the area you want to camp in. If service is poor, a dedicated GPS unit is a safer bet than a smartphone.

If you're visiting from out of state, from outside of the Northeast in particular, know that toll roads are a fact of life in New Jersey. The three biggies to be aware of are the **New Jersey Turnpike,** the **Garden State Parkway,** and the **Atlantic City Expressway,** but they're not the only ones. If you're unfamiliar with tolls, don't get caught off-guard: check the sources in Appendix B (page 176), and perhaps invest in an **E-ZPass** (ezpassnj.com). Using the GPS coordinates and a mapping tool such as Google Maps, you can also create your own toll-free alternative routes.

WEATHER

New Jersey is a four-season state for the outdoors, and many of the campgrounds in this book are open year-round. Most readers will likely be out sometime between Memorial Day weekend and Labor Day weekend, the height of camping season in New Jersey. Summer provides the benefits of warm days and long nights; temperatures in the 80s are not uncommon or unpleasant. While camping during the summer can be quite nice, the weather can be very hot and humid later in the season, in which case you'd do well to choose campgrounds with access to drinking water and places to swim on-site or nearby, be they man-made or natural.

Fall is probably the best time for camping. The cooler temperatures and drier air make for days as crisp as the changing leaves, which can be spectacular, especially in northern New Jersey. Plus, the bugs have finished doing their buggy thing, and you can put away the insect repellent. Nights and mornings can get chilly, however. As the days grow shorter and creep toward winter, temperatures around or even below freezing are not uncommon.

Winter is probably the most daunting and challenging season for camping. While New Jersey winters tend to be moderate in terms of cold and snow, every year brings along at least one of what meteorologists benignly call a weather event. Temperatures in the low teens (or lower) and heavy snow are uncommon but also not unusual. If you come prepared, though, there's nothing like the still of a winter morning right after a snowfall.

With spring, things start to come to life. The snows melt, and the rain falls. By April, the flowers are in bloom, then the trees, and suddenly it seems like every cave and crack and crevice has some critter or other ducking in and out of it. This can be a great season for camping, with daytime temperatures in the 60s and nights dropping into the 40s—perfect for sleeping! March and April can be damp, though, with regular rain, so the forest can become muddy. But what a great time of year to see wildlife.

The following chart lists average temperatures and precipitation by month for New Jersey. For each month, "Hi Temp" is the average daytime high in degrees Fahrenheit, "Lo Temp" is the average nighttime low, and "Rain/Snow" is the average precipitation in inches.

NEW JERSEY Average Daily Temperatures and Precipitation						
	JAN	**FEB**	**MAR**	**APR**	**MAY**	**JUN**
HI TEMP	39°F	42°F	51°F	62°F	72°F	82°F
LO TEMP	24°F	27°F	34°F	44°F	53°F	63°F
RAIN/SNOW	3.5"	2.87"	4.17"	4.17"	4.06"	4.02"
	JUL	**AUG**	**SEP**	**OCT**	**NOV**	**DEC**
HIGH	86°F	84°F	77°F	65°F	55°F	44°F
LOW	69°F	67°F	60°F	48°F	39°F	30°F
RAIN/SNOW	4.72"	3.7"	3.82"	3.58"	3.62"	3.78"

Source: USClimateData.com

FIRST AID KIT

A useful first aid kit may contain more items than you might think necessary. These are just the basics. Prepackaged kits in waterproof bags (Atwater Carey and Adventure Medical make them) are available. As a preventive measure, take along sunscreen and insect repellent. Even though quite a few items are listed here, they pack down into a small space:

- Ace bandages or Spenco joint wraps

- Adhesive bandages

- Antibiotic ointment (Neosporin or the generic equivalent)

- Antiseptic or disinfectant, such as Betadine or hydrogen peroxide

- Aspirin, acetaminophen (Tylenol), or ibuprofen (Advil)

- Butterfly-closure bandages

- Comb and tweezers (for removing ticks from your skin)

- Diphenhydramine (Benadryl, in case of allergic reactions)

- Epinephrine (EpiPen) in a prefilled syringe (for severe allergic reactions to outdoor mishaps such as bee stings)

- Gauze (one roll and six 4-by-4-inch compress pads)

- LED flashlight or headlamp

- Matches or lighter

- Moist towelettes

- Moleskin/Spenco 2nd Skin

- Pocketknife or multipurpose tool

- Waterproof first aid tape

- Whistle (for signaling rescuers if you get lost or hurt)

WATCHWORDS FOR FLORA AND FAUNA

PLANTS

FIREWOOD Nearly all of the parks and forests in this book have restrictions on bringing firewood into campgrounds. These restrictions have arisen to control the transportation of invasive insect species from one forest to another. In recent years, some New Jersey forests have succumbed to infestations of a variety of pests; transporting firewood simply exacerbates the problem and puts the forests at risk.

Generally speaking, it's best to buy or collect firewood on-site. If a campground allows you to bring your own, do so *only* from within the county or forest within which you're camping, and burn it all before you leave. Check firewood policies and availability with the campground or managing agency before you go.

POISON IVY This natural nuisance is abundant throughout New Jersey, especially near perennial streams and ponds. Recognizing the plant and avoiding contact with it are the most effective ways to prevent its painful, itchy rash. Poison ivy (*right*) ranges from a thick, tree-hugging vine to a shaded ground cover, 3 leaflets to a leaf. Urushiol, the plant's oily sap, is responsible for the rash. Usually within 12–14 hours of exposure (but sometimes much later), raised lines and/or blisters will appear, accompanied by a terrible itch. Try not to scratch: dirty fingernails can cause an infection, and in the best case you'll spread the rash to other parts of your body.

Photo: Tom Watson

Wash the rash with cold water and a mild soap or cleanser such as Tecnu, and dry it thoroughly, applying calamine lotion or a topical cortisone cream to help soothe the itch; if the rash is painful or blistering is severe, seek medical attention. Note that any oil that gets on clothing, boots, and the like can keep spreading its misery for at least a year if you don't thoroughly clean it off, so wash everything that you think could have urushiol on it, including pets.

CRITTERS

PETS In recent years, the New Jersey State Park Service has begun experimenting with the idea of pet-friendly camping, and numerous campgrounds now have entire loops or selected sites designated for campers with pets. Nonetheless, the practice is not universal, and many campgrounds—public and private—require that you provide evidence of vaccination if you bring Fido along. Note also that a few privately owned campgrounds prohibit certain dog breeds. Although I've identified campgrounds with pet-friendly areas and policies, it's worth checking ahead of your trip for the latest information.

BEARS In case you weren't aware, New Jersey has an overpopulation of black bears. Most avoid humans, but some associate humans with food and have lost their fear of people. (See page 10 for ways to bearproof your food.)

If you should have an unexpected black bear encounter, stand upright and back away slowly. Speak in a calm voice. If you spot a bear as you hike, stay far away from it, and make enough noise so that it's aware of your presence—*never surprise a bear.* Likewise, never get between a mother bear and her cub. Always contact the forest office after a bear encounter.

Photo: Jane Huber

SNAKES New Jersey is home to 22 varieties of snakes. Most of them are benign, copperheads and the timber rattlesnake being the exceptions. The copperhead is found throughout the state, in both urban and suburban areas, while the timber rattler is found primarily in the mountainous regions of central and northwestern New Jersey.

To avoid encountering these snakes, stick to well-used trails, and wear over-the-ankle boots and loose-fitting long pants when hiking. Rattlesnakes like to bask in the sun and won't bite unless threatened. In general, the heads of both species are more triangular than their nonvenomous cousins. Don't step or put your hands where you cannot see, and avoid wandering around in the dark. Step *up* onto logs and rocks, never over them, and be especially careful when climbing rocks or gathering firewood. Avoid walking through dense brush or willow thickets whenever possible. Hibernation season is November–April.

TICKS The bane of camping trips, ticks are abundant throughout the Mid-Atlantic states and tend to lurk in the brush, leaves, and grass that grow alongside trails. April–mid-July is the peak period for ticks in New Jersey, but you should be tick-aware all year round.

Ticks, which are related to spiders, need a host to feast on in order to reproduce. The ones that light onto you will be very small, sometimes so tiny that you won't be able to spot them until you feel the itchiness of their bite. Primarily of two varieties, deer ticks (which can carry Lyme disease) and wood ticks, both need a few hours of actual attachment before they can transmit any illness they may harbor, so the quicker you remove them the better. Ticks may settle in shoes, socks, or hats and may take several hours to actually latch on.

Wearing light-colored clothing makes ticks easier to spot; tucking the cuffs of your pants into your socks, though geeky-looking, helps keep them from latching on; and using an insect repellent with DEET helps keep them away. Visually check yourself for ticks throughout the day while you're out in the woods, and do an even more thorough check of your entire body when you're in your tent/cabin or taking a posthike shower.

If a tick should bite you, don't freak out. Use tweezers to remove it—grab as close to the skin as possible, and firmly pull the tick loose without crushing it, making sure to remove the entire head. Then wash the area well with warm, soapy water.

Keep an eye on the bite for several days afterward to ensure that it doesn't get infected and that a rash doesn't develop. The telltale sign of Lyme infection is a bullseye-shaped rash that forms around the site of the bite; be aware, however, that you could be infected even if the rash doesn't develop. If you start experiencing flulike symptoms within a couple of weeks of getting bitten, see your doctor.

TIPS FOR HAPPY CAMPERS

Few things are more disappointing than a bad camping trip—the good news is, it's really easy to have a great one. Here are a few things to consider as you prepare for your trip:

- **PLAN AHEAD.** Know your equipment, your ability, and the area where you'll be camping—and prepare accordingly. Be self-sufficient at all times; carry the necessary supplies for changes in weather or other conditions.

  In the same vein, reserve your site in advance when that's an option, especially if it's a weekend or holiday or if the campground is extremely popular. Also do a little research on what the campgrounds have to offer. Park employees and volunteers can be extremely helpful in suggesting things to do and places to go. Information on all New Jersey state parks can be found at state .nj.us/dep/parksandforests. Finally, consider the accessibility of supplies before you go—it's a pain to have to get in the car and make a long trek in search of hot dog buns or bug spray.

- **USE CARE WHEN TRAVELING.** Stay on designated roadways. Be respectful of private property and travel restrictions. Familiarize yourself with the area you'll be traveling in by picking up a map that shows land ownership.

- **WHEN SELECTING A CAMPGROUND OR CAMPSITE, CONSIDER YOUR SPACE REQUIREMENTS.** In general, choose a single site if your group consists of 8 people or fewer, a double site for groups of up to 16 people, a triple site for groups of up to 24, or a group camping area for groups larger than 24.

- **PLAY BY THE RULES.** If you're unhappy with the site you've selected, check with the campground host for other options. Don't just grab a seemingly empty site that looks more appealing than yours—it could be reserved.

- **PICK YOUR CAMPING BUDDIES WISELY.** Make sure that everyone is on the same page regarding expectations of difficulty (amenities or the lack thereof, physical exertion, and so on), sleeping arrangements, and food requirements.

- **DRESS FOR THE SEASON.** Educate yourself on the temperature highs and lows of the specific part of the state you plan to visit. It may be warm at night in the summer in your backyard, but up in the mountains it will be quite chilly.

- **PITCH YOUR TENT ON A LEVEL SURFACE,** preferably one covered with leaves, pine straw, or grass. Use a tarp or specially designed footprint to thwart ground moisture and to protect the tent floor. Before you pitch, do some site cleanup, such as picking up small rocks and sticks that can damage your tent floor and make sleep uncomfortable. If you have a separate rainfly but aren't sure you'll need it, keep it rolled up at the base of your tent in case it starts raining late at night.

- **CONSIDER PACKING A SLEEPING PAD** if sleeping on bare ground makes you uncomfortable. A wide range of pads in varying sizes and thicknesses is sold at outdoor stores. Inflatable pads are also available—don't try to improvise with a home air mattress, which conducts heat away from the body and tends to deflate as you sleep.

- **DON'T HANG OR TIE CLOTHESLINES, HAMMOCKS, AND EQUIPMENT ON OR TO TREES.** Even if you see other campers doing this, be responsible and do your part to reduce damage to trees and shrubs.

- **IF YOU TEND TO USE THE BATHROOM MULTIPLE TIMES AT NIGHT, PLAN AHEAD.** Leaving a comfy sleeping bag and stumbling around in the dark to find a place to heed nature's call—be it a vault toilet, a full restroom, or just the woods—is no fun. Keep a flashlight and any other accoutrements you may need by the tent door, and know exactly where to head in the dark.

- **WHEN YOU CAMP AT A PRIMITIVE SITE, KNOW HOW TO GO.** Bringing large jugs of water and a portable toilet are the easiest and most environmentally friendly solutions. A variety of portable toilets are available from outdoor-supply catalogs; in a pinch, a 5-gallon bucket fitted with a toilet seat and lined with a heavy-duty plastic trash bag will work just as well. (Be sure to pack out the trash bag.)

    A second, less desirable method is to dig an 8-inch-deep cathole. It should be located at least 200 yards from campsites, trails, and water, in an inconspicuous location with as much undergrowth as possible. Cover the hole with a thin layer of soil after each use, and *don't burn or bury your toilet paper*—pack it out in resealable plastic bags. If you plan to stay at the campsite for several days, dig a new hole each day, being careful to replace the topsoil over the hole from the day before.

In addition to the plastic bags, your outdoor-toilet cache should include a garden trowel and toilet paper or wet wipes. Select a trowel with a well-designed handle that can also double as a toilet paper dispenser.

- **IF YOU WON'T BE HIKING TO A PRIMITIVE CAMPSITE, DON'T SKIMP ON FOOD.** Plan tasty meals, and bring everything you'll need to prep, cook, eat, and clean up. That said, don't duplicate equipment such as cooking pots among the members of your group.

- **KEEP A CLEAN KITCHEN AREA,** and avoid leaving food scraps on the ground both during and after your visit. Maintain a group trash bag, and be sure to secure it in your vehicle at night. Many sites have a pack-in/pack-out rule, and that means everything: no cheating by tossing orange peels, eggshells, or apple cores in the shrubs.

- **DO YOUR PART TO PREVENT BEARS FROM BECOMING CONDITIONED TO SEEKING HUMAN FOOD.** The constant search for food influences every aspect of a bear's life, so when camping in bear country, store food in your vehicle or in bearproof containers. Keep food (including canned goods, soft drinks, and beer) and garbage secured, and don't take food with you into your tent. You'll also need to stow scented or flavored toiletries such as deodorant, toothpaste, and lip balm, as well as cooking grease and pet food. Common sense and adherence to the simple rules posted in the campgrounds will help

A view from the Appalachian Trail just above Culvers Gap, about a 5-minute drive from Harmony Ridge Campground (see page 32)

keep both you and the bears safe and healthy. (See page 7 for what to do if you encounter a bear.)

- **USE ESTABLISHED FIRE RINGS, AND BE AWARE OF FIRE RESTRICTIONS.** Make sure that your fire is totally extinguished whenever you leave the area. If you cook with a Dutch oven, use a fire pan and elevate it to avoid scorching or burning the ground. Don't burn garbage in your campfire—trash fires smell awful and often don't burn completely, and fire rings fill with burned litter over time.

  Check ahead to see whether bringing your own firewood is allowed or if firewood is sold at the campground. If bringing your own is against the rules, buying it on-site (if available) is preferable to gathering deadfall: in my experience, wood found near camp is nearly always green and/or wet.

- **DON'T WASH DISHES AND LAUNDRY OR BATHE IN STREAMS AND LAKES.** Food scraps are unsightly and can be potentially harmful to fish, and even biodegradable dish soap can be harmful to fragile aquatic environments.

- **BE A GOOD NEIGHBOR.** Observe quiet hours, keep noise to a minimum, and keep your pets leashed and under control.

- **MOST OF ALL, LEAVE YOUR CAMP CLEANER THAN YOU FOUND IT.** Pick up all trash and microlitter in your site, including in your fire ring. Disperse leftover brush used for firewood.

VENTURING AWAY FROM CAMP

If you decide to go for a hike, bike, swim, or paddle, here are some safety tips.

- **LET SOMEONE AT HOME OR AT CAMP KNOW WHERE YOU'LL BE GOING AND HOW LONG YOU EXPECT TO BE GONE.** Also let him or her know when you return.

- **SIGN IN AND OUT OF ANY TRAIL REGISTERS PROVIDED.** Leave notes on trail conditions if space allows—that's your opportunity to alert others to any problems you encounter.

- **DON'T ASSUME THAT YOUR PHONE WILL WORK ON THE TRAIL.** Reception may be spotty or nonexistent, especially on a trail embraced by towering trees.

- **ALWAYS CARRY FOOD AND WATER, EVEN FOR A SHORT HIKE.** And bring more water than you think you'll need.

- **ASK QUESTIONS.** Public-land employees are on hand to help.

- **STAY ON DESIGNATED TRAILS.** If you become disoriented, assess your current direction, and then retrace your steps to the point where you went astray. Using a map, compass, and/or GPS unit, and keeping in mind what you've passed thus far, reorient yourself and trust your judgment on which way to continue. If you become absolutely unsure of how to continue, return to your vehicle the way you came in. Should you become completely lost, remaining in place and waiting for help is most often the best option for adults and always the best option for children.

- **CARRY A WHISTLE.** It could save your life if you get lost or injured.

- **BE ESPECIALLY CAREFUL WHEN CROSSING STREAMS.** Whether you're fording a stream or crossing on a log, make every step count. If you have any doubt about maintaining your balance on a log, ford the stream instead: use a trekking pole or stout stick for balance, and *face upstream as you cross.* If a stream seems too deep to ford or the current seems too strong, turn back.

- **BE CAREFUL AT OVERLOOKS.** While these areas provide spectacular views, they're also potentially hazardous. Stay back from the edge of outcrops, and be absolutely sure of your footing.

- **STANDING DEAD TREES AND DAMAGED LIVING TREES POSE A SIGNIFICANT HAZARD TO HIKERS.** These trees may have loose or broken limbs that could fall at any time. While walking beneath trees, and when choosing a spot to rest or enjoy your snack, *look up.*

- **KNOW THE SYMPTOMS OF SUBNORMAL BODY TEMPERATURE, OR HYPOTHERMIA.** Shivering and forgetfulness are the two most common indicators. Hypothermia can occur at any elevation, even in the summer—especially if you're wearing lightweight cotton clothing. If symptoms develop, get to shelter, hot liquids, and dry clothes as soon as possible.

- **LIKEWISE, KNOW THE SYMPTOMS OF ABNORMALLY HIGH BODY TEMPERATURE, OR HYPERTHERMIA.** Lightheadedness and weakness are the first two indicators. If you feel these symptoms, find some shade, drink some water, remove as many layers of clothing as practical, and stay put until you cool down. Marching through heat exhaustion leads to heatstroke—which can be fatal. If you should be sweating and you're not, that's the signature warning sign. If you or a hiking partner is experiencing heatstroke, do whatever you can to get cool and find help.

- **BE SAFE IN THE WATER.** Always wear a flotation device when boating or paddling. Know proper paddling technique, especially as it relates to recovering from spills. At the beach, swim only in designated areas supervised by lifeguards, and obey any posted current or shark warnings. Never swim alone. Make sure that young children and nonswimmers wear life jackets, and keep a watchful eye on kids in the water. Have everyone wear sunscreen/sunblock with an SPF of 15 or higher, and reapply it frequently.

- **MOST IMPORTANT, TAKE ALONG YOUR BRAIN.** Think before you act. Watch your step. Plan ahead.

NORTHERN NEW JERSEY

Early-morning light on the Delaware River

⛺ Campgaw Mountain Campground

Beauty ★★★ / Privacy ★★★ / Spaciousness ★★★★ / Quiet ★★ / Security ★★★ / Cleanliness ★★★

Campgaw's accessibility means a weekend camping expedition can start as late as Saturday afternoon.

Famed for its ski resort rather than its camping, Campgaw Mountain County Reservation takes a lot of heat in winter. Detractors are quick to point out that the trails are easy and the slopes are mild. Supporters defend Campgaw with stories of learning to ski there, in a friendly environment that helped them build confidence in snow and the outdoors. Families take their children to Campgaw to teach them skiing or snowboarding in a nonthreatening environment, while parents appreciate the chance to practice close to home.

The campsites at Campgaw generate similar reactions. Some wilderness buffs scoff at this urban forest, smack in the middle of northern Jersey and less than 30 miles from Manhattan. The steady drone of traffic on nearby I-287 is always audible from the campground, reminding you that civilization is just past the nearest row of trees. But Campgaw's biggest handicap is also its major strength. A weekend camping expedition can begin as late as Saturday afternoon. The accessibility of Campgaw means that families can show their kids how to sleep outdoors, but it also means they can break camp and drive home if the tots become grumpy and refuse to sleep.

Rustic sites line both sides of a dead-end road. Some have parking but most are hike-in sites, although the hikes are little more than 40 feet. Visitors can leave their cars in one of three central parking areas. Four shelters dot the campground, and site borders are not

The tent sites at Campgaw Mountain County Reservation are mixed with lean-to sites.

KEY INFORMATION

ADDRESS: 200 Campgaw Road, Mahwah, NJ 07430

OPERATED BY: Bergen County Department of Parks

CONTACT: 201-327-3500, tinyurl.com /campgawcamping

OPEN: April 1–November 30

SITES: 18 (4 have shelters)

EACH SITE HAS: Picnic table, fire ring

WHEELCHAIR ACCESS: None

ASSIGNMENT: Call ahead to check site availability when filling out your camping permit (see below)

REGISTRATION: Download permits in advance at the website above; then print and mail to Bergen County Department of Parks, 1 Bergen County Plaza, Hackensack, NJ 07601

FACILITIES: Water, flush and vault toilets

FEES: $10/night

PARKING: At lots near sites

RESTRICTIONS:

PETS: On leash

FIRES: Permit required

ALCOHOL: Prohibited

VEHICLES: Not applicable (hike-in sites)

OTHER: 14-night stay limit; 6-person site limit; campers must bring plastic bags and carry out all trash

clearly delineated. There are no privacy hedges and little understory, but sites are spacious and shaded. A few portable toilets line the road. Running water facilities are located in restrooms in the nearby cul-de-sac, near a grassy picnic area.

You must obtain a permit before setting up camp. A downloadable PDF form is available at tinyurl.com/campgawcamping (click "Permits & Fees," then "Camping Application").

Campgaw Mountain is also home to a county-owned 28-station field archery range. Additionally, 18-hole Darlington Golf Course is located across from the entrance on Campgaw Road. If you're visiting from out of town and wish to take a day trip into New York City, park your car 3 miles away at the Ramsey train station. Catch the New Jersey Transit train to New York's Penn Station with a quick transfer at Secaucus Junction.

A small pond sits by the ski area, but swimming and boating are forbidden. Fishing is catch-and-release only. Additionally, hiking and bridle trails lace the 1,373-acre reservation. Nearby Saddle Ridge Riding Center (saddleridgeridingcenter.com) sits atop Campgaw Mountain and is accessible from nearby Franklin Lakes. They offer horseback riding lessons, trail rides, and accommodations for birthday parties. Some of its offices and stables were originally built in the 1950s as part of the control area of Nike Battery NY–93/94, a program designed to launch guided surface-to-air missiles in the event of a Cold War Soviet attack. The launch site was located a mile north and has since been razed and turned into housing developments. New Jersey housed 14 sites for the Nike missile program—named for the Greek goddess, not the athletic company—that were meant to protect New York and Philadelphia. The only one that was not destroyed is in Livingston, where the barracks and command center are preserved and open to the public at Riker Hill Park.

Campgaw Reservation features four easy and three moderate hiking trails. Only one, Old Cedar Trail, is more than a mile long. Combine this 2.1-mile trail with the Rocky Ridge Trail to form a longer 3-mile loop, which will take you to the top of the ski slope. Immediately after the trail crosses two stone walls near a ski slope building, you'll see a white-blazed trail. Follow this a short way for panoramic views of the surrounding area. On clear days, you can see the Palisades and beyond to the Manhattan skyline. On humid summer days, don't expect to see much through the haze.

Access to Campgaw Mountain is easy for city and suburban dwellers. As such, its mission is different than that of true wilderness campgrounds. Campgaw provides local families with great recreational activities and even a chance to view small wildlife (and possibly a few black bears), along with its access to the interstate.

Campgaw Mountain Campground

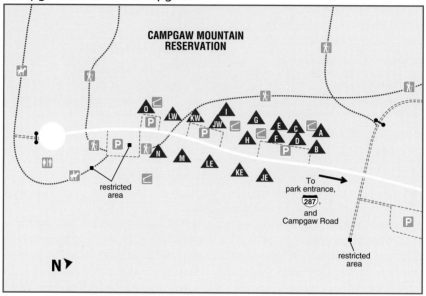

GETTING THERE

From I-287 South, take Exit 66. Continue onto NJ 17 South, and drive just 0.3 mile; then turn right to exit onto US 202 South. Drive 1.7 miles to Darlington Avenue, and turn left. Drive 0.3 mile; then turn right onto Campgaw Road, and drive 1.1 miles. The park entrance will be on the right.

From I-287 North, take Exit 59 for US 208 South/Franklin Lakes, and continue on US 208 South for 1.3 miles. Take the Summit Avenue exit, and keep left off the exit ramp to get onto Summit Avenue going northeast. In 0.4 mile, turn left onto Franklin Avenue; then drive 0.5 mile. Turn right onto Pulis Avenue, and drive 1.5 miles. Turn left onto Campgaw Road, and drive 1.6 miles. The park entrance will be on the left.

GPS COORDINATES: N41° 03.606' W74° 10.998'

Camp Glen Gray

Beauty ★★★ / Privacy ★★★ / Spaciousness ★★ / Quiet ★★★ / Security ★★★ / Cleanliness ★★

A former Boy Scout camp, Glen Gray helped generations of boys learn to boat, fish, and respect nature on its 750 wooded acres.

Rustic and conveniently located, Bergen County's newest campground is also its oldest. Camp Glen Gray was established in 1917 and developed over the next decade. For the next 85 years, it operated as a Boy Scouts of America camp. Generations of boys learned to boat, fish, respect nature, and cooperate on its 750 wooded acres.

Bergen County acquired the camp from the Boy Scouts in 2002 with help from the Trust for Public Land and a group of volunteers. The county provides mosquito control and snow removal, but for the most part, Camp Glen Gray is self-funded and managed by the Friends of Glen Gray Camp Operating Committee.

Ramapo Valley County Reservation is only 4.5 miles from Camp Glen Gray, and while both are wooded, primitive environments with great hiking trails, they serve different needs and different clienteles. Ramapo Valley is the top dog-walking and dog-camping destination in the region, and hundreds of people take their dogs through the park every day. Camp Glen Gray, however, does not allow visitors to bring dogs. Also, campsites at Ramapo are located near the entrance to the park, so every hiker passes by them. Wilderness camping at Camp Glen Gray is usually done in the North Quad, where campers who leave the trail are unlikely to see another human for the entire weekend. Ramapo Valley sites are well manicured, whereas Camp Glen Gray sites are more rugged.

A rainy, misty fall day at Camp Glen Gray.

KEY INFORMATION

ADDRESS: 200 Midvale Mountain Road, Mahwah, NJ 07430

OPERATED BY: Friends of Glen Gray Camp Operating Committee

CONTACT: 201-327-7234, glengray.org; reservations: glengray.org/camping-reservation-request.html

OPEN: Year-round, only on weekends

SITES: 6 tent sites, 8 lean-tos, 14 cabins; backcountry area

EACH SITE HAS: Picnic table, fire ring, some platforms; no amenities in wilderness sites

WHEELCHAIR ACCESS: None

ASSIGNMENT: By reservation

REGISTRATION: By phone or online

FACILITIES: Toilets, showers, water (limited in winter)

FEES: $8 per person for weekend

PARKING: Central lot; sites are hike-in

RESTRICTIONS:

PETS: Prohibited

FIRES: By permit only

ALCOHOL: Prohibited

VEHICLES: Not applicable (hike-in sites)

OTHER: Use dumpster near office; no hunting; no bikes; weekend stays only (check out Sunday by 11 a.m.)

All camping at Camp Glen Gray is hike-in, and the North Quad wilderness sites are ideal for solo campers or those hiking with a partner. Campers must leave their cars at the headquarters and hike to the backcountry along Old Guard Trail; it's also possible to hike in from other public lands via Cannonball Trail. Campers must check in and buy a permit at the headquarters. Wilderness camping at Glen Gray offers no amenities, so campers must familiarize themselves with the basics of backcountry etiquette and bear behavior. Food should be carefully stored away from tents and campsites, either in a bearproof container or hanging from a tree in a food bag. Inquire at the office about the current bear population. All gear and garbage must be packed in and out.

Regular family camping is available on nonorganized (no workshops or classes) weekends. The camp has six designated tent-camping areas, each of which has tent platforms, latrines, and water nearby. Campers stay in shady clearings that hold several tents. North Brook Campsite is one of the most popular clearings. It has two tent platforms and is suitable for up to 10 people. It sits near the lake, close to amenities and under hemlock trees on a bubbling stream. Swimming is prohibited unless a certified swim instructor is present. Rowboats are available to rent, but personal boats cannot be transported to the lake. With advance notice, special transportation arrangements can be made for disabled campers. Located about twice as far from parking as North Brook are the Howard Tober and Ramapo Campsites. Howard Tober has 4 tent platforms (suitable for up to 16 campers) and Ramapo has 12 platforms (suitable for up 24 campers). Both are wooded and about a 20-minute walk from the car. The other three tenting areas (Bobcat Hollow, Hawk Ridge, and Stag Run) are designed for groups of up to 30 campers.

Glen Gray also has eight lean-to campsites. Located on the banks of Lake Vreeland and very close to the parking area, the Waterfront lean-to accommodates four people. The Scott Gaipa lean-to accommodates up to six people and is located in a wooded area near the amphitheater on the far side of Lake Vreeland from the parking lot. The Mothercroft lean-to is quite large, suitable for up to 16 campers, and is almost cabinlike. It has loft space for sleeping and a floor large enough to pitch several tents. The other five lean-tos accommodate from 26 to 32 people and would be better suited for large groups. Unlike campsites, lean-tos are rented for a flat fee for the entire weekend.

Several marked hiking trails wind through and across camp and offer diverse experiences of the Glen Gray countryside. A short half-mile hike takes in the shore of Lake Vreeland. The white-blazed, 2-mile Millstone Trail is the most central. Easily accessed from the lake or office, it loops around camp, providing nice views from the top of Millstone Hill. Slightly longer, the Matapan Rock hike has led many novice hikers to their first high point and overlook. Those looking for a real challenge will appreciate the Ten Mile hike and the 9.8-mile History of the Glen hike. Both lead hikers through historic parts of Glen Gray and into the nearby backcountry of the Ramapo Mountains. Patches for most of these hikes are available for purchase at the camp store.

Camp Glen Gray rents out its facilities to groups year-round. It has almost unlimited space for medium-sized groups but limited parking and is at the end of a private road. Campers are encouraged to stay at camp all weekend rather than constantly drive in and out. Bear in mind that the facilities are not new. Campers seeking a rustic outdoors experience will be pleased here, but those who require modern plumbing and drive-in sites will be better served setting up tents at nearby Campgaw Mountain Reservation (see previous profile).

Camp Glen Gray

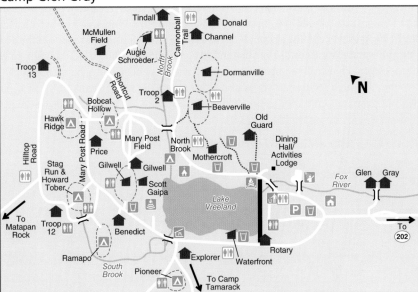

GETTING THERE

From I-287, take Exit 58 and turn onto US 202 North. Drive 1.9 miles to Glen Gray Road. Turn left and drive 0.4 mile, over the steel bridge; Glen Gray Road veers right and becomes Midvale Mountain Road. Continue 0.6 mile to the camp entrance.

GPS COORDINATES: N41° 03.675' W74° 14.028'

⛺ Camp Taylor

Beauty ★★★★★ / Privacy ★★★★ / Spaciousness ★★★★★ / Quiet ★★★★★ / Security ★★★★★ /
Cleanliness ★★★★

What distinguishes Camp Taylor from the pack is its own pack—that is, an on-site wolf preserve.

Set on a remote hillside on the ridge of the Kittatinny Mountains, this private campground offers an unusual and appealing mix of attractions. Camp Taylor's wooded hillside tenting area, with primitive sites that are both spacious and shaded, is only part of its appeal. The remote location is another draw; the 350-acre camp is adjacent to 70,000-acre Delaware Water Gap National Recreation Area, which is quite large for a backyard. Most campers who visit Camp Taylor come to take advantage of this proximity and to enjoy the remote setting. Nonetheless, Camp Taylor offers organized activities for both kids and adults, including a miniature golf course, a swimming area, and a game room. But what truly distinguishes Camp Taylor from the pack is its own pack—that is, an on-site wolf preserve.

Lakota Wolf Preserve features four wildlife pens dispersed over 10 acres. Three of the football field–sized pens house adult timber, tundra, and arctic wolves; the fourth pen houses foxes, bobcats, and wolf pups. The animals have all been raised in captivity and are habituated to humans, so they do not hide when visitors stop by. Wolf watches (which include feedings) happen twice daily, although there is no guarantee that you will see the wolves playing and wandering around. They do tend to come out at feeding times, though, so you'll have an excellent chance of seeing them eat. Wolf watches and feedings happen at 10:30 a.m. year-round. Through lectures, visitors also learn about the social structure of wolf packs, the wolves' daily lives, and their eating habits. Reservations are necessary for weekday wolf

The sites at Camp Taylor are wooded and offer some privacy.

KEY INFORMATION

ADDRESS: 85 Mount Pleasant Road, Columbia, NJ 07832

OPERATED BY: Private

CONTACT: 908-496-4333 or 800-545-9662, camptaylor.com; reserve by phone Monday–Thursday, 9 a.m.–6 p.m. Eastern time, Friday and Saturday, 9 a.m.–9 p.m.

OPEN: Mid-April–October, off-season by reservation

SITES: 114, including 20 primitive tent sites (sites 47–49 and 81–98)

EACH SITE HAS: Picnic table, fire ring, trash can

WHEELCHAIR ACCESS: None

ASSIGNMENT: First-come, first-served or by reservation (recommended)

REGISTRATION: On arrival or by phone (2-day minimum for weekend reservations)

FACILITIES: Water, restrooms, showers, store

PARKING: At campsites or in lot

FEES: $32/night for 2 people; $12/night for each additional adult; $4/night for children ages 2–17

RESTRICTIONS:

PETS: On leash, 1 pet/site; prohibited near wildlife pens

FIRES: In fire rings only

ALCOHOL: Permitted at campsites only

VEHICLES: Up to 38 feet

OTHER: No stay limit specified; quiet hours 11 p.m.–9 a.m.; check-in 3 p.m. or later

watches, but no appointments are necessary on weekends. Pets are prohibited from going on wolf watches. The nearby Blairstown Animal Hospital (908-362-6430) may be available to board pets during your wolf watch; inquire at the office. Noncampers can also visit and view the wolves on wolf-watch walks.

Wolf walks involve a 0.5-mile hike through the forest. Transportation is available if visitors cannot walk that distance; inquire at the office for details. Photographers should note that a chain-link fence sits between wolves and visitors. Professional photographers can schedule private photo sessions for a fee.

The wolves eat between 30,000 and 40,000 pounds of meat a year. They get a lot of local roadkill—New Jersey has an abundance of deer that wander onto roadways. But the bulk of their food comes from Space Farms Zoo on County Route 519 in Sussex County. The private zoo, originally a general store, began as a roadside attraction in 1927. Goliath, a 12-foot-tall Alaskan brown bear and its star attraction for many years, is now stuffed and on display in the gift shop.

Camp Taylor gets busy on summer weekends, and they require a two-night minimum for reservations, which are highly recommended. The campsites are open from mid-April to October, but year-round camping is possible with advance reservations. Three trailer toilets service the tent-camping area, and flush toilets and showers are available at the office. Although all of the tent sites are quite spacious, some provide more under-story and privacy than others, so arrive early and

One of the wolves at Lakota Wolf Preserve, on the property of Camp Taylor

choose carefully. All sites feature shade. The usual warnings about camping in bear country apply: use bearproof containers, and never take food into or near your tent. (See the Introduction for more information on how to camp safely in bear country.) Camp Taylor provides trash containers at each site, as well as centrally located recycling barrels.

Fishing is prohibited at the campground, but swimming is allowed in the 2-acre lake. Nonswimmers must stay in the immediate beach area and must be accompanied by an adult swimmer at all times. Paddleboats and kayaks are available for rent. Anglers enjoy nearby Delaware and Paulinskill Rivers.

Campers who tire of the game room, volleyball court, and organized activities can take to the trails. Mountain Trail leaves Camp Taylor property behind the farthest wildlife pen and meets up with a fire road right inside public lands. Hike to the left for 2.2 miles to reach the Delaware Water Gap National Recreation Area and the trail up Mount Tammany. Take a right, and the same length hike will take you to Yards Creek, where walking trails surround a power facility. You can also access the Appalachian Trail from Yards Creek.

Even without the wolf preserve, Camp Taylor stands on its own as a decent campground. Sites are wooded, and campers will find plenty of activities to keep both children and adults occupied. But the wolf preserve elevates this campground from a nicely wooded private area to an experience unlike any other in New Jersey.

Camp Taylor

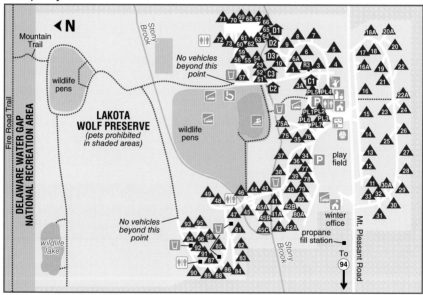

GETTING THERE

From I-80, take Exit 4, following the signs for NJ 94 North. Merge onto NJ 94 North, and drive 2.6 miles. Turn left onto Mt. Pleasant Road, and drive 1.6 miles. The campground entrance will be on the left.

GPS COORDINATES: N40° 58.256' W75° 04.330'

Camp Wyanokie

Beauty ★★★ / Privacy ★★★★ / Spaciousness ★★★ / Quiet ★★★★ / Security ★★ / Cleanliness ★★★★

Camp Wyanokie provides an ideal setting for a youngster's first overnight camping trip.

With only 150 acres, Camp Wyanokie is definitely a small recreation area. Yet its four wooded tent sites provide an ideal setting for a youngster's first overnight camping trip. And it's a nice place for the more seasoned camper to get away from the hustle and bustle of civilized life. The sites at Camp Wyanokie are clean, spacious, and level. The cleanliness is due in part to the fact that all campers are encouraged to perform a bit of service by picking up trash, straightening the facilities, and so forth. In this manner, users of the park learn that stewardship involves caring for public lands, not just using them.

Each tent site is situated in a clearing among the woods far enough from the other sites to provide the feel of a backcountry experience, yet no site is more than a 5-minute walk from the car, from latrines, or from water. In addition to the tent sites, the camp has five lean-tos, a 5-acre pond in which fishing is allowed (sunfish being the prominent "game fish"), and picnic facilities.

Each campsite has its own character. Two of the sites, Northeast Campsite and East Campsite, are quite secluded. To reach both of these, walk across the dam and follow the trail along the lakeside. Northeast Campsite is uphill from the lake to your left at the fork in

This old concrete dam that forms Boy Scout Lake also provides access to the sites across the lake.

KEY INFORMATION

ADDRESS: 572 Snake Den Road, West Milford, NJ 07480

OPERATED BY: Towns of Caldwell, Fairfield, North Caldwell, Roseland, and West Caldwell

CONTACT: 973-228-6432, campwyanokie.com

OPEN: Year-round

SITES: 4 tent sites, 5 lean-tos

EACH SITE HAS: Picnic table, fire ring

WHEELCHAIR ACCESS: None

ASSIGNMENT: Call ahead to check site availability when filling out your camping permit (see below).

REGISTRATION: Download permits in advance at campwyanokie.com/html /permits.html; then print and mail to North Caldwell Recreation Office, Gould Avenue, North Caldwell, NJ 07006.

PARKING: In designated lot

FEES: No charge for residents of Caldwell, Fairfield, North Caldwell, Roseland, and West Caldwell; nonresidents: $5/person/night, plus $10 registration fee

---

RESTRICTIONS:

PETS: On leash

FIRES: Permit required (see below); camp stoves permitted

ALCOHOL: Prohibited

VEHICLES: No formal restrictions

OTHER: No stay limit; fire permits must be obtained from the District Fire Warden, 842 Macopin Road, West Milford, NJ 07480; 973-697-9389.

---

the trail. East Campsite is a few minutes farther along the trail, making it the most remote from the parking area. Lean-to #2 at East Campsite sits aside the trail overlooking the pond, and there is ample level space for tents in the woods behind it. With several tent platforms, West Campsite is the most spacious; it sits on a hill above the parking area. South Campsite abuts private land, and seems a little more cramped than the other.

The camp is owned collectively by the towns of Caldwell, Fairfield, North Caldwell, Roseland, and West Caldwell, and the primary caveat associated with the use of the area is that residents of those towns get first dibs on the use of the facilities. Both residents and nonresidents need to apply for a camping permit at least two weeks in advance of their planned trip. Permit application forms for both residents and nonresidents are available online. All campers have to sign a Hold Harmless Agreement and provide evidence of insurance in the event of a mishap; information on both is available online. Nonresidents also have to pay a fee to use the facilities. At $5 per person per night, though, camping here is as inexpensive as it gets.

In addition to getting a little bit of wilderness-like camping without having to travel too far from home, one of the great benefits of camping at Camp Wyanokie is the access it provides to the southern sector of Norvin Green State Forest, which is adjacent to the camp. From Camp Wyanokie, hikers can follow the Wyanokie Circular Trail into the state forest. In spite of what its name suggests, Wyanokie Circular Trail does not form a loop, although from it you can hop onto several different trails that make loops of various lengths back to camp. A popular hike is to follow Circular Trail out to the top of Wyanokie High Point (about 2 miles). From there you can continue east along the Highlands Trail for an additional 1.5 miles to the view point above Wanaque Reservoir. The Highlands Trail is more than 150 miles long and extends from the Delaware River across New Jersey to Storm

King Mountain above the Hudson River in New York. Ten miles of the Highlands Trail pass through Norvin Green State Forest.

Camp Wyanokie is located on colorfully named Snake Den Road, which intersects West Brook Road at two locations. Campers coming from the east who inadvertently turned on the first Snake Den Road will have discovered that the road doesn't continue all the way through to the camp. However, at the top of the first Snake Den Road are two gems of the area that campers should definitely visit. The first of these is the Highlands Natural Pool, a spring-fed Olympic-size pool that is carved into the side of the hill (highlandsnaturalpool.org). There are no chemicals used in the pool, and its cool waters provide some respite from the heat on muggy summer days.

The other destination is the New Weis Center for Education, Arts & Recreation. Originally a farm dating back to the 1800s, the land was acquired and converted into Camp Midvale in the early 20th century. Since then, the land has been preserved by different parties for the purposes of promoting outdoor recreation. The pool was originally part of the camp. In 2014, the center came under the ownership of the Highlands Nature Friends, Inc., which hosts a variety of arts and environmental programs that are open to the public. Visit their website (highlandsnaturefriends.org) for information on programming.

Camp Wyanokie

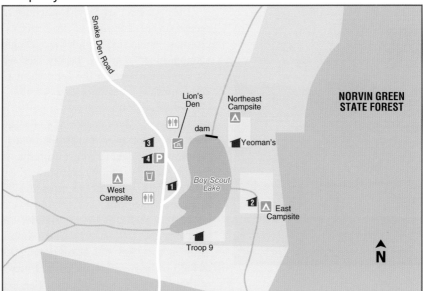

GETTING THERE

From I-287, take Exit 55 for Wanaque/Pompton Lakes. Head north on Ringwood Avenue for 4 miles to West Brook Road. Turn left and drive 4.4 miles; then turn left onto Snake Den Road (this is the second intersection of Snake Den Road with West Brook Road). Drive about 0.8 mile to the campground.

GPS COORDINATES: N41° 04.445' W74° 20.856'

Delaware Water Gap National Recreation Area: CANOE-IN CAMPSITES

Beauty ★★★★ / Privacy ★★★ / Spaciousness ★★ / Quiet ★★★ / Security ★★ / Cleanliness ★★

More than 100 free canoe-in campsites dot the river in Delaware Water Gap National Recreation Area. Thirty-four of these sites are located within New Jersey.

The shallow, gentle Delaware River hardly seems powerful enough to wash away a sandbar, much less a chunk of mountain. But centuries ago, this unassuming body of water carved a 1,100-foot-deep, 3-mile-long gorge out of the solid rock of the Kittatinny Ridge.

Canoeists have used this part of the Delaware for travel since the days of the Lenape Indian Tribe, but today's boaters are more interested in scenery and recreation than in transportation. Mount Tammany rises above the river on the Jersey side, and Mount Minsi overshadows it on the Pennsylvania side. The Delaware Water Gap National Recreation Area (DWGNRA) stretches north from the gap for 40 miles, encompassing 70,000 acres of land along both sides of the river in both New Jersey and Pennsylvania.

Sunset along the Delaware River

The National Park Service administers the recreation area and runs no developed campgrounds within its boundaries. (Dingmans Campground, a private facility, lies within the recreation area on the Pennsylvania side and is profiled in my book *Best Tent Camping: Pennsylvania.*) Those with cars or trailers must use the sites at Worthington State Forest (see page 56) or nearby private campgrounds. But for campers willing to rough it on the water, leaving cars, RVs, and the heaviest amenities behind, there are plenty of campsites in the Delaware Water Gap.

More than 100 canoe-in primitive campsites dot the Delaware between Kittatinny Point at the Gap and Mashipacong Island at the northern end of the park. Thirty-four of these sites are located within New Jersey. Many sites are inaccessible without a boat. And even if you have a boat, you can't just canoe in, camp, and then canoe back to your car at the nearest boat ramp. Nor is it acceptable for campers to leave their cars by the side of the road and hike to a campsite. The DWGNRA canoe-in sites are meant for boaters who are on what the park service terms "bona fide overnight trips," meaning trips that cover a long enough distance to merit an overnight stop.

One-night trips that are defined as bona fide are trips that extend for at least 14 miles for a one-night trip, 26 miles for two nights, or 34 miles for three nights. Popular one-night

KEY INFORMATION

ADDRESS: Delaware Water Gap National Recreation Area Headquarters, River Road off Route 209, Bushkill, PA 18324. See description for locations of individual sites and Getting There for put-in location.

OPERATED BY: National Park Service

CONTACT: 570-588-2452, tinyurl.com /dwgnrarivercamping

OPEN: Year-round

SITES: 34 sites in New Jersey distributed through 6 camping areas

EACH SITE HAS: Fire ring (some sites), vault toilet (some sites)

WHEELCHAIR ACCESS: None

ASSIGNMENT: First-come, first-served; no reservations

REGISTRATION: None

FEE: Camping is free, but there is a $5 vehicle fee at Milford Beach, Smithfield Beach, Bushkill, and Dingmans Ferry.

RESTRICTIONS:

PETS: On short leash

FIRES: In fire rings only; okay to collect downed wood

ALCOHOL: Prohibited while boating and from Depew Island to Dupue Island

VEHICLES: Not applicable

OTHER: Camp only at designated sites; carry out all trash; no cutting of live trees; wash away from water sources; bury pet and human waste 6 inches underground and at least 300 feet from water; quiet hours 10 p.m.–6 a.m.; 1-night stay as part of multiday river trip where length is too long to paddle in a single day

excursions go from Milford Beach to Eshback (or farther), Dingmans Ferry or Eshback to Smithfield Beach (or farther), and Bushkill to Kittatinny Point (or farther). Two-night trips that merit camping are from Milford Beach to Smithfield Beach (or farther) and Dingmans Ferry to Kittatinny Point (or farther). The only trip requiring three nights of camping along the way begins at the northernmost access point at Milford Beach and goes the length of the park to Kittatinny Point. All this assumes you've arranged a shuttle between access points (see next page for more information). Camping is limited to one night per site.

The sites in New Jersey are situated at the following locations: **Mashipacong Island,** site 1, suitable for up to 4 people (N41° 20.633' W74° 45.002'); **Namanock Island,** sites 14–17, each suitable for up to 6 people (N41° 15.899' W74° 50.638'); **Sandyston,** sites 18–23, each suitable for up to 6 people (N41° 14.933' W74° 51.331'); **Ratcliffs,** sites 52–54, each suitable for up to 6 people (N41° 06.748' W74° 58.395'); **Peters,** sites 56–68, each suitable for up to 6 people (N41° 05.609' W74° 59.390'); and **Quinns,** sites 73–79, each suitable for up to 6 people (N41° 05.768' W74° 58.057').

Some sites are on islands, while others are located on the banks on either the New Jersey or Pennsylvania side of the river. Several are isolated individual sites, while others are clustered together. Some have vault toilets, while others have no facilities at all, which means you'll need to dig a cathole (see Introduction for guidelines). Drinking water is unavailable at most sites, and river water is not recommended for drinking; bring your own. Carry out all garbage. Remember that bears live in the area, so use bearproof containers, and never take food into or near your tent.

Alcohol is prohibited at all times while paddling in Worthington State Forest and between Depew Island and Dupue Island on the Pennsylvania side of the park. Canoeists should remember that alcohol and canoeing can be a deadly combination. Rangers can remove you from the river if you appear intoxicated.

The National Park Service does not offer shuttles or canoe rentals, but many liveries are licensed to rent gear and transport boaters between access points (see nps.gov/dewa /planyourvisit/liveries.htm for more information). Children under 12 years old are required to wear life jackets, and people of all ages are encouraged to wear them. The Delaware River has no difficult rapids, and access points appear every 8–10 miles. Visit during a shoulder season or midweek if you can, as the river gets crowded on summer weekends.

Delaware Water Gap National Recreation Area: Canoe-in Campsites

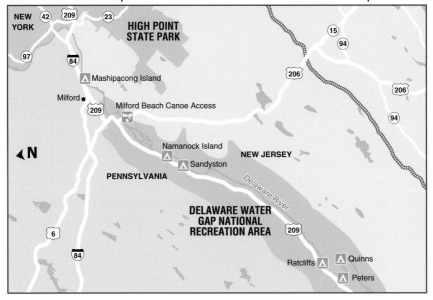

GETTING THERE

From I-80 at the Delaware Water Gap, boat launches are accessible from points north along Old Mine Road (New Jersey side; take Exit 1) and US 209 (Pennsylvania side; take Exit 309). A popular launch is from Milford Beach Road, on the Pennsylvania side of the river: from Exit 309 off of I-80, drive 30.5 miles north on US 209; then turn right onto Milford Beach Road, just north of the intersection with US 206. Or, from I-84 in Pennsylvania, take Exit 46, drive south on US 6 for 2.8 miles, and then turn left onto Milford Beach Road.

GPS COORDINATES: MILFORD BEACH PUT-IN: N41° 18.627' W74° 47.759' (see description for coordinates of individual camping areas)

Delaware Water Gap National Recreation Area Campground:
APPALACHIAN TRAIL DISPERSED CAMPING

Beauty ★★★★★ / Privacy ★★★ / Spaciousness ★★★ / Quiet ★★★★★ / Security ★★★ /
Cleanliness ★★★★

Free primitive camping along this section of the Appalachian Trail is reserved for hikers on trips requiring an overnight stop.

Setting up camp in the Delaware Water Gap along the Appalachian Trail isn't something you do on a whim. You can't park your car nearby, lug your gear up a hill, drag along the cooler, and erect a tent. Instead, camping along the Appalachian Trail (AT) in New Jersey's heavily used Delaware Water Gap National Recreation Area (DWGNRA) is limited to designated areas and reserved exclusively for hikers on trips that require an overnight stop.

As most hikers know, the Appalachian Trail traverses mountain ridges and valleys for 2,100 miles as it winds its way across 14 states. The Garden State, although this term seems a misnomer on the craggy Kittatinny Range, is crossed by 73.6 of those miles. The Delaware Water Gap's 27.3 miles get a lot of use, particularly on weekends, when urban refugees leave New York City and North Jersey behind and take to the remote trails.

Hikers have created some unusual rock formations on the shore of Sunfish Pond.

Some states allow dispersed backcountry camping along the AT. New Jersey, however, is one of three states that precisely designates where hikers can and cannot camp. The other two states are New York and Connecticut, both heavy-use states. Hikers are reminded to obey these rules, both to preserve the natural environment and to avoid stumbling onto private property.

New Jersey State Parks is particular about where hikers can camp in state forests, but the National Park Service is a little more relaxed. You will find only one spot where trailside camping is allowed in Worthington State Forest, and that is the backpacker's site about 2 miles along the trail from the Dunnfield Creek Trailhead near I-80. Stokes State Forest welcomes campers with a sign forbidding them to camp for the next 4 miles. In between state property is federal land, part of the Delaware Water Gap National Recreation Area, and hikers are allowed to set up tents within 100 feet of the trail, but there are rules to follow.

KEY INFORMATION

ADDRESS: Delaware Water Gap National Recreation Area Headquarters, River Road off US 209, Bushkill, PA 18324

OPERATED BY: National Park Service

CONTACT: 570-588-2452, tinyurl.com/dwgnrabackcountrycamping

OPEN: Year-round

SITES: Wilderness camping in designated areas vs. specific sites

EACH SITE HAS: No amenities

WHEELCHAIR ACCESS: None

ASSIGNMENT: Pick an available spot within the designated area

REGISTRATION: None

FACILITIES: None

PARKING: At designated lots; hike in to sites

FEE: None

RESTRICTIONS:

PETS: On leash only

FIRES: Prohibited

ALCOHOL: Prohibited

VEHICLES: Prohibited

OTHER: No camping within 200 feet of other campers; 1-night limit per campsite; carry out all trash; camping restricted to those hiking 2 or more days; camp within 100 feet of trail

If you want to camp along the trail, you must begin and end your hike at different locations, and you must be hiking for two or more consecutive days. Hikers must not camp within 100 feet of a water source or within 200 feet of another party. Camping is prohibited within a half mile of a roadway and from a half mile south of Blue Mountain Lake to 1 mile north of Crater Lake. Hikers may not start ground fires but may use camp stoves.

Day hikers use the 4 miles from the Dunnfield Creek Trailhead to Sunfish Pond heavily. Nevertheless, enough distance hikers stop at the single campsite within the Worthington State Forest section that the site is often crowded. But those who begin their hikes at the Dunnfield parking area typically don't use the site. Sites farther on, past the Worthington boundary and within the DWGNRA lands, are numerous, rarely as much as a mile between each. Some sites are utilitarian and best for the exhausted, while others are scenic and private, requiring short side hikes. Your best bet for locating sites is to consider how far you would like to go and keep your eyes open along the trail.

The boundary between Worthington State Forest and Delaware Water Gap lands (N41° 00.837' W75° 02.649') is in the area of the significant power line cut about 2.5 miles beyond Sunfish Pond, and the boundary between Water Gap and Stokes State Forest lands (N41° 08.670' W74° 51.229') is about 1 mile north of Rattlesnake Mountain and 4.6 miles south of Culvers Gap at US 206. Possible excursions for overnight trips beginning at the Dunnfield Creek Trailhead lead to County Road 602 (13 miles) and to US 206 (27 miles).

Remember that bears live in the area, so use bearproof containers, and never take food into or near your tent. See the Introduction for more information on how to camp safely in bear country.

Snakes inhabit the woods but are shy and seldom encountered by people. Avoid them if you see them. Few snakebites have been reported along the AT. Hikers should take precautions against ticks, as many of them carry Lyme disease. Some mosquitoes transmit West Nile virus. Wear insect repellent and long sleeves, if practical.

National Park Service regulations state that hikers must carry enough water for their entire hike within the Delaware Water Gap. You will find water along the trail, but it is unreliable and often contaminated. With advance research, campers can learn of water sources, but you must chemically treat the water, boil it for 5 minutes before drinking, or use a water filter. All trash must be carried out. Campers are reminded that these campsites are for overnight hikers, which means you must familiarize yourself with not only the rules of the AT but also with the basics of overnight hikes. Read some books on AT hiking, visit the official AT website (appalachiantrail.org), and talk to staff at the New York–New Jersey Trail Conference (nynjtc.org) before setting out for your first overnight hike.

Delaware Water Gap National Recreation Area: Appalachian Trail Dispersed Camping

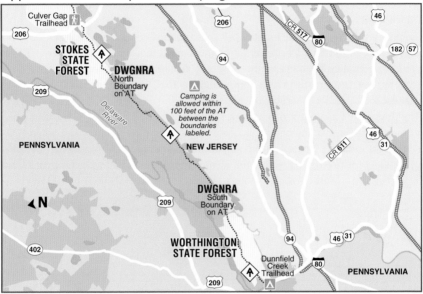

GETTING THERE

From I-80 heading west toward the New Jersey–Pennsylvania border, take Exit 1, and follow the signs to the ranger station and then to the Dunnfield Creek parking area. Or exit to the parking area before Exit 1—the rest stop immediately after mile marker 1—when heading west.

Parking at the northern end of this AT stretch is at the Culvers Gap parking area, outside the DWGNRA. From I-80 West, take Exit 34B (NJ 15 North/Jefferson/Sparta). Drive 16.6 miles; then continue onto US 206 North and drive 6.2 miles. Turn right onto Upper North Shore Road, and turn left almost immediately into the lot.

GPS COORDINATES:
DUNNFIELD CREEK TRAILHEAD: N40° 58.297′ W75° 07.534′
US 206/CULVERS GAP TRAILHEAD: N41° 10.812′ W74° 47.286′

Harmony Ridge Campground

Beauty ★★★ / Privacy ★★ / Spaciousness ★★★ / Quiet ★★ / Security ★★★★ / Cleanliness ★★★★

Harmony Ridge is perfect for families who want to explore nearby natural areas.

Only a few private campgrounds in northern Jersey offer tent camping, and fewer still actually designate entire sections for tents only. Many private campgrounds cater to RV and trailer camping because tent campers require fewer services and expect to pay less for sites. Conversely, public campgrounds are often geared toward tents, with trailer camping being an afterthought.

Family-run Harmony Ridge is a rare private campground that encourages tent camping. Section O and its 28 tent sites are set off by themselves in a shaded, level grove. The small dirt road discourages RV owners; that said, the RV sites are spacious and not crammed together as they are at many private campgrounds. The entire campground has been carefully landscaped and is impeccably maintained.

The three rustic campgrounds of Stokes State Forest (see pages 44–52) are nearby, and some may wonder what the benefit is of staying at a private campground when $20 tent sites are right over the ridge past the Appalachian Trail (AT). Camping can be different things to different people. For some, the ideal campsite is a small wooded clearing with a

Looking northwest toward the Poconos from the clearing beneath the Culver fire tower

KEY INFORMATION

ADDRESS: 23 Risdon Drive, Branchville, NJ 07826

OPERATED BY: Private

CONTACT: 973-948-4941, harmonyridge .com; reserve by phone daily, 9 a.m.– 5 p.m. Eastern time

OPEN: Year-round

SITES: 173 total, 28 tent sites

EACH SITE HAS: Picnic table, fire ring

WHEELCHAIR ACCESS: None

ASSIGNMENT: First-come, first-served or by reservation

REGISTRATION: On arrival or by phone

FACILITIES: Water (May–October), flush toilets, showers, laundry room

PARKING: At campsites

FEES: Adults, $17.50/night; under age 16, $5/night; see website for additional rates and fees

---

RESTRICTIONS:

PETS: On leash; prohibited in rental trailers and cabins

FIRES: In fire rings only

ALCOHOL: Permitted at campsites only

VEHICLES: Up to 40 feet

OTHER: 2-night minimum stay; seasonal sites available for extended stays; check-in/ checkout: 5 p.m.

pit toilet and no neighbors in sight. For others, particularly those with families, the best campsites come with organized activities and amenities. Harmony Ridge, with its game room, pool, and shady tent sites, provides the best mixture for families needing some modern conveniences along with their forests and hiking trails. And at $17.50 a night for adults, Harmony Ridge's rates for tent sites are actually cheaper than those at Stokes.

Head up to Section H to find the hiking trail. From the last RV site, it's less than a mile's walk to the AT and the Culver (Normanook) fire tower. A favorite walk of many local hikers is the trail section that goes from the fire tower to Sunrise Mountain. Hike up to the fire tower and enjoy the view to the northwest from its picnic table (climbing the fire tower is forbidden). Then walk about 3.5 miles north to 1,653 feet at Sunrise Mountain. Relax at the summit in the pavilion built in the 1930s by the Civilian Conservation Corps (CCC) and take in the panorama of surrounding Sussex County. Hike early if recent days have been hazy. Several of the trails nearby continue into Stokes State Forest, while the AT goes north from Stokes through High Point State Park, eventually reaching Maine.

After breaking in your hiking shoes, you can relax back at Harmony Ridge's pool or beach. Fish (catch-and-release) for largemouth bass, catfish, or bluegill in one of the three stocked lakes. Play basketball, shuffleboard, bocce, horseshoes, miniature golf, or volleyball (on sand brought north from Cape May). Or simply sit at a campfire and just chill.

The old Culver fire tower. Although climbing it is forbidden, the view from the clearing beneath it is marvelous.

Ed and Doris Ann Risdon opened Harmony Ridge with just 10 campsites in 1966. Today there are almost 20 times as many sites on the 160-acre property, as well as several more Risdons. The family still manages and oversees the operation, which includes organized activities in addition to recreational facilities. Harmony Ridge offers RV and cabin rentals in addition to tent and trailer camping.

Campers receive an informational booklet at check-in, which includes campground policies, a guide to local restaurants and attractions, activity descriptions, and a guide to local wildlife. Hand-drawn raccoons, beavers, deer, turkeys, birds, and foxes are some of the animals shown. Campers can check off the wildlife they see as they hike the nearby trails.

For families wishing to experience outdoor living, there are times when a secluded campsite on New Jersey public property is not enough. Only a few private campgrounds can satisfy both outdoorsy people and those looking for activities and structure. Harmony Ridge, with its idyllic setting on the Kittatinny Ridge, is the perfect home base for families who want to explore nearby Tillman Ravine, High Point State Park, or Stokes State Forest while still keeping Fido in tow and giving children some community recreation at the same time.

Harmony Ridge Campground

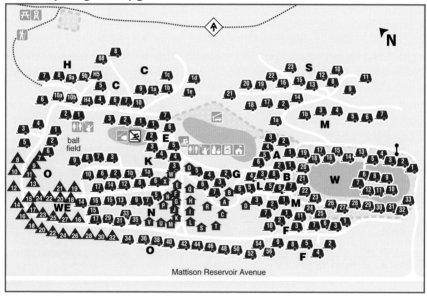

GETTING THERE

From I-80 West, take Exit 34B (NJ 15 N/Jefferson/Sparta). Drive 16.6 miles; then continue onto US 206 North, and drive 4 miles. After milepost 118, turn right onto Ridge Road. At the end of Ridge Road, go left for 1 block to Mattison Reservoir Avenue, and turn right. Drive 1.2 miles, and the campground entrance is on the left.

GPS COORDINATES: N41° 11.506' W74° 44.865'

High Point State Park:
SAWMILL LAKE CAMPING AREA

Beauty ★★★★ / Privacy ★★★ / Spaciousness ★★★★ / Quiet ★★★ / Security ★★★★ / Cleanliness ★★★★

You might see your neighbors in this tent campground, but they won't be close enough for conversation.

High Point State Park sits at the top of New Jersey in just about every way. Its 1,803-foot-tall mountain is the state's highest, and the park sits at the northernmost tip of the state, with the closest highway being in New York. The nearest large town is Port Jervis, a New York town 4 miles to the north at the junction of New York, New Jersey, and Pennsylvania. Port Jervis, long a transportation and rail center, has a commuter train that makes daily 90-minute trips to New York City. Campers wishing to tour Manhattan can use this train for day trips to New York City, while city dwellers can use this train in combination with taxi services to access the Appalachian Trail (AT).

High Point's camping area is not near the contact station near Lake Marcia; that's the swimming and day-use area. The campground is farther north up NJ 23, off Sawmill Road. Many sites are open, especially those right on Sawmill Lake, but there's plenty of space between these sections of prime real estate. You might see your neighbors at High Point State Park, but they won't be near enough to chat with.

Sites 46–50 are particularly appealing, as they lie secluded at the end of the loop. They're set back in the woods, like the other sites on the outer loop. Some aren't level, but large wooden tent platforms have been built. Some sites directly on the lake are walk-in, but the walks are manageable for those carrying standard tent-camping gear. Remember that your

Sawmill Lake with the 220-foot-tall High Point Monument in the background

KEY INFORMATION

ADDRESS: Sawmill Road south of NJ 23, Sussex, NJ 07461

OPERATED BY: New Jersey State Park Service

CONTACT: 973-875-4800, njparksandforests .org/parks/highpoint.html; reservations: camping.nj.gov

OPEN: April 1–October 31

SITES: 50; all tent-only except sites 9, 16, 17, 19, 26, 46, 47, 49, and 50

EACH SITE HAS: Picnic table, fire ring, lantern hook

WHEELCHAIR ACCESS: None

ASSIGNMENT: First-come, first-served or by reservation (minimum 2 nights)

REGISTRATION: On arrival or online

FACILITIES: Water, flush toilets

PARKING: At campsites or lots; 2-vehicle limit

FEES: New Jersey residents, $20/night; nonresidents, $25/night; $5/night pet fee

---

RESTRICTIONS:

PETS: On leash, sites 29–50 only, 2 pets/site; pet permit and proof of current vaccinations required. See njparksandforests.org /parks/pet_friendly_camping.html for more information.

FIRES: In fire rings only

ALCOHOL: Prohibited

VEHICLES: No RV hookups at tent/trailer sites

OTHER: Quiet hours 10 p.m.–6 a.m.; 14-night stay limit; 6-person/2-tent site limit

cooler must always remain in your car in bear country, so consider the number of walks you'll make to the car when choosing a site. Only a few sites at Sawmill Lake are large enough for trailers, and there are no hookups or dump stations. Two rental cabins on the eastern shore of nearby Steenykill Lake (also in the park) are available May–October.

Sawmill Lake is one of three public lakes at High Point. No swimming is allowed in Sawmill or Steenykill Lakes, but you can launch boats at both (electric motors and non-motorized boats only). Fishing with a license is permitted in all three lakes, although boats are prohibited in Lake Marcia. Sawmill is stocked with trout, and all three lakes are home to perch, bass, catfish, and sunfish. Fishing licenses are available at some nearby businesses; check with the park office for details. There are no canoe concessions within High Point State Park, but three private firms rent canoes on the nearby Delaware River.

Spring-fed Lake Marcia offers the only swimming area at High Point. The sandy beach, along with its bathhouse and food concession, is open in summer when lifeguards are on duty. There are no trash cans at Lake Marcia—visitors are given plastic bags at the contact station and are required to carry out all garbage. This not only contributes to a cleaner park but also reduces conflicts between wildlife and trash.

You'll have access to nearly a dozen hiking trails in 14,218-acre High Point State Park, in addition to an 18-mile stretch of the AT. Campers can hike from the campground to the AT on the rugged 0.4-mile Blue Dot Trail.

The Monument Trail is a popular 3.7-mile hiking loop that connects the day-use area to High Point Monument. The 220-foot-high granite obelisk, built in 1928, is a memorial to New Jersey veterans and marks the highest point in the state The area around the monument offers sweeping vistas of the nearby mountains and can easily be reached by car from Monument Drive, but the hiking trail offers unique views of the three surrounding states of New York, New Jersey, and Pennsylvania. Most of the trail is uphill and was built in the 1930s by FDR's Civilian Conservation Corps. The Appalachian Trail does not pass High

Point Monument, but AT hikers can detour to the monument via Scenic Drive and the Monument Trail.

Part of the Monument Trail crosses Cedar Swamp, the highest-elevated swamp of its kind in the world, within High Point's 800-acre Dryden Kuser Natural Area. Pick up a booklet at park headquarters to take a self-guided nature walk along the bog trail.

Mountain biking and horseback riding are allowed on eight of High Point's trails. Additionally, some trails allow cross-country skiing, dogsledding, and snowmobiling in winter. High Point Cross Country Ski Center, open during winter months, provides winter-sports-equipment rental as well as hot food. Artificial snow is manufactured for many of the trails.

High Point isn't just the highest point in New Jersey; it's also one of the state's most rural and scenic spots. Don't miss the trip to the summit of the Kittatinny Ridge, even if you don't camp at placid Sawmill Lake.

High Point State Park: Sawmill Lake Camping Area

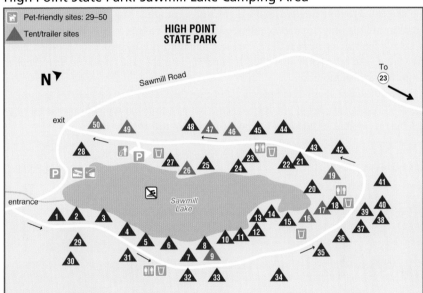

GETTING THERE

From I-287, take Exit 52 to NJ 23 North, and drive about 27 miles. Turn left on Loomis Avenue, and then make an immediate right onto Mill Street/NJ 23 North. Drive about 8.5 miles, and the park office will be on your left. From I-84 in New York, take Exit 1 and turn onto NJ 23 South. Drive about 4 miles to the park office on your right.

To reach the campground, travel north from the park office on NJ 23 for about 0.2 mile; then turn left onto Sawmill Road, following the signs for the campground.

GPS COORDINATES: N41° 17.478' W74° 41.372'

Mahlon Dickerson
Reservation Campground

Beauty ★★★ / Privacy ★★★★ / Spaciousness ★★★★★ / Quiet ★★★★ / Security ★★★ / Cleanliness ★★★★

Mahlon Dickerson features plenty of accessible natural recreation close to an urban environment.

Mahlon Dickerson Reservation, best known for its multiuse trails, recreational facilities, and undeveloped wilderness areas, has the only public campground in Morris County. Surprisingly few people are aware of this rustic jewel of a campground, tucked away just north of Lake Hopatcong between two wildlife management areas in the northwestern corner of the county.

The eight tent sites are located on a dead-end singletrack road—a spur that juts out from a loop dedicated to four shelters ($16 a night) and a campfire ring. Two portable toilets and a dumpster are the only luxuries on offer, but a modern restroom with flush toilets and hot showers is a short drive away at the RV area, where there are 18 sites. (Restrooms are heated in the winter.) All of the RV sites offer 30- and 50-amp electrical hookups as well as water hookups in warmer months.

The tent sites are shaded and private, and most are sprawling estates by camping standards. Not all sites are level, but each has a 12-by-12-foot flat wooden platform. Site 2 is wheelchair accessible, as is one of the porta-potties in the area.

The campground at Mahlon Dickerson Reservation has a few rustic lean-tos in addition to the beautiful tent campsites.

KEY INFORMATION

ADDRESS: 955 Weldon Road,
Lake Hopatcong, NJ 07849

OPERATED BY: Morris County Park
Commission

CONTACT: 973-697-3140, tinyurl.com
/mdickersoncamping, mdrcamping
@morrisparks.net; reserve in person or
by phone Wednesday–Friday, 1–6 p.m.,
Saturday, 10 a.m.–6 p.m., and Sunday,
1–6 p.m. (An online reservation system
was in development but was not yet func-
tional at press time.)

OPEN: Year-round

SITES: 8 tent sites, 18 RV sites, 4 lean-tos

EACH SITE HAS: Picnic table, fire ring,
tent platform

WHEELCHAIR ACCESS: Site T2, Shelter S1,
and 1 portable toilet are accessible

ASSIGNMENT: First-come, first-served or
by reservation

REGISTRATION: On arrival or by phone

FACILITIES: Vault and flush toilets, water,
showers at RV sites across Weldon Road

PARKING: At campsites (2-vehicle limit) or
designated lot

FEES: $14/night, $84/week

RESTRICTIONS:

PETS: On leash

FIRES: Permit required

ALCOHOL: Prohibited

VEHICLES: Up to 35 feet

OTHER: 14-night stay limit; 2-night minimum
stay on holiday weekends; 4 people/site
($5/extra person)

For would-be campers who don't have tents of their own, Mahlon Dickerson offers a limited number of rental tents as well as the four shelters near the campfire ring. The shelters are popular in autumn and winter. Mahlon Dickerson's campsites are open year-round, but few people set up tents once ice-skating and cross-country skiing season begins.

Reserve a site ahead if you can, although sites are usually available on nonholiday weekdays and in the off-season. To register on arrival, go to the visitor center or campground office (May–October). After hours, register with the camp host at the trailer area or at the "quick registration" board at the entrance to the trailer area. If you've prepaid, you may proceed straight to your campsite, which will be marked with your name and the date.

A multiuse trail starts from the cul-de-sac at the tent camping area, right beside site 8. Follow this path straight to the yellow trail (bike and foot traffic only), turning right to cut over to the teal-blazed Highlands Trail. To the left on the Highlands Trail are two viewpoints. Both offer panoramic views of the area, but the second one, Headley Overlook, is more popular as it is easier to access from Weldon Road.

The Highlands Trail traverses 150 miles between the Delaware River in Central New Jersey and the Hudson River in New York's Hudson Valley. It is a cooperative conservation effort by state and local governments, local businesses, and the New York–New Jersey Trail Conference. The Mahlon Dickerson section enters the park in the south near NJ 15 and exits north of the trailer area.

Follow Highlands Trail north, crossing Weldon Road. From there, several trails branch off heading north or west. Find your way to the western section of Pine Swamp Trail to reach the highest point in Morris County at 1,395 feet.

The Morris County Park System prides itself on its dedication to multipurpose parks and spectacular settings. Nowhere is this more evident than at Mahlon Dickerson, where mountain bikers and equestrians are treated with the same consideration given to foot hikers.

Mahlon Dickerson's 20 acres of multiuse trails include bike trails that are regarded as the best bike trails in Morris County, but they're not for beginners. Novices might consider practicing on the Morris County section of the Patriots' Path, which is smoother. Mahlon Dickerson's mountain biking is technical with some steep climbs. A yellow-blazed 5.3-mile multiuse trail that begins at the Saffin Pond Area is quite popular and offers nice views of the pond. Also popular is the 2.5-mile Ogden Mine Railroad Path, which follows an old rail bed. Trail maps are available at the Saffin Visitor Center and at information points around the park.

Saffin Pond offers fishing and canoeing. For those who want to try more-active watersports, Lake Hopatcong, with its waterskiing and swimming, is just a few miles away. Only a small percentage of Mahlon Dickerson Reservation is developed. A hike or bike ride may take you past deer or beaver as well as many smaller mammals. With more than 3,000 acres of near wilderness, Mahlon Dickerson features plenty of accessible natural recreation close to an urban environment.

Mahlon Dickerson Reservation Campground

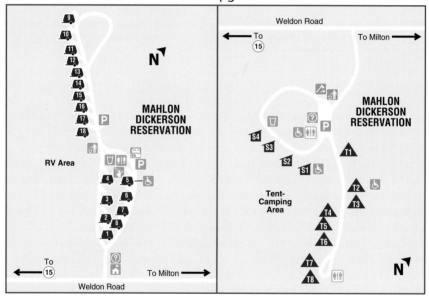

GETTING THERE

From I-80, take Exit 34 for NJ 15 North. Drive about 5 miles on NJ 15 North; then turn left onto Weldon Road. Drive about 3.5 miles; the camping office is at the entrance to the RV loop, which will be on your left. Continue a short distance farther on Weldon Road, and you'll see the tent-camping area on your right.

GPS COORDINATES: N41° 00.800' W74° 32.184'

Ramapo Valley County Reservation Campground

Beauty ★★★ / Privacy ★★ / Spaciousness ★★★★ / Quiet ★★★ / Security ★★ / Cleanliness ★★★

Signs warn of bears, but you're more likely to encounter throngs of happy mutts straining at their leashes.

Bergen County, with 933,500 people, has the largest human population of any of New Jersey's counties. Its canine population cannot be far behind, and you will see a large cross-section of both as people and dogs enjoy the trails and ponds of Ramapo Valley County Reservation.

Five tent campsites surround 22-acre Scarlet Oak Pond. All sites are hike-in only because the park's entire 3,313 acres are closed to vehicles. The hike from the parking area to Scarlet Oak Pond is a short 200 yards. The restrooms, with sinks and flush toilets, are located near the parking area. There are no showers.

All sites are adjacent to trails traveled by day hikers, but site 7, located the farthest from the parking area on the north side of the pond, provides slightly more privacy. Ramapo Valley County Reservation closes a half hour after sunset, and the crowds disperse, leaving behind a bucolic scene where campers sleep on spacious grassy areas under the stars, the silence broken only by the sound of the gurgling river.

You cross this small stream upon entering Ramapo Valley County Reservation.

KEY INFORMATION

ADDRESS: 584 Ramapo Valley Road, Mahwah, NJ 07430

OPERATED BY: Bergen County Department of Parks

CONTACT: 201-327-3500, tinyurl.com /ramapocamping

OPEN: April 1–November 30

SITES: 5

EACH SITE HAS: Picnic table, fire ring

WHEELCHAIR ACCESS: None

ASSIGNMENT: Call ahead to check site availability when filling out your camping permit (see below)

REGISTRATION: Download permits in advance at the website above; then print and mail to Bergen County Department of Parks, 1 Bergen County Plaza, Hackensack, NJ 07601

FACILITIES: Water, flush toilets

PARKING: Lots near sites

FEE: $10/night

RESTRICTIONS:

PETS: On leash

FIRES: Permit required

ALCOHOL: Prohibited

VEHICLES: Not applicable (hike-in sites)

OTHER: 14-night stay limit; carry out all trash (dumpster in parking lot); licensed fishing only; no hunting, swimming, or boating

---

Early morning brings back the urban refugees. Join the fisherfolk by pulling on rubber waders and fly-fishing or casting for trout in the seasonally stocked Scarlet Oak Pond or Ramapo River. Catfish, panfish, perch, and bass are also present. Signs indicate when trout stocking occurs and whether it is taking place in the pond, river, or both. New Jersey fishing licenses are required for those over age 16.

Fifteen miles of moderately difficult trails wind through this hilly former farmland. The New York–New Jersey Trail Conference, whose offices are located next door to the reservation, has recently developed a host of trails. Stop by for information and maps about the hiking trails at the reservation and elsewhere in New York and New Jersey.

The steep yellow-blazed Vista Loop Trail, which begins at the reservation parking lot and passes along the west side of Scarlet Oak Pond, is recommended for its access to three overlooks. The first, Hawk Rock, is a ledge featuring outstanding views of Bergen County and Manhattan. Go early on humid summer days to avoid the haze that can descend over New York City. A second lookout named Cactus Ledges is just beyond. Near the intersection of the Vista Loop Trail and the blue-blazed Ridge Trail is a third lookout, Ridge Overlook, which provides a view of Campgaw Mountain and Manhattan.

Three trails—Cannonball, Hoeferlin, and Crossover—are maintained by volunteers from the New York–New Jersey Trail Conference. These continue through Ringwood State Park and the Ramapo Mountains.

Camping and fires are allowed by permit only, and anyone arriving late without a permit is forbidden to camp. Vehicles left in the parking area without permits may be towed. All campers are required to pack out their garbage. New Jersey has an overpopulation of black bears, so be careful not to leave food or waste products. Bicycles aren't allowed on the trails, so leave them behind on the bike rack in the parking lot.

A downloadable permit form is available at tinyurl.com/ramapocamping (click "Permits & Fees," then "Camping Application"). Plan ahead for busy summer weekends, as sites fill up fast—a key reason being that Ramapo is in demand with dog owners. (New Jersey state campgrounds have only recently begun to implement pet-friendly sites on a limited basis.)

As you leave your site for your day's activities, keep in mind that hundreds of people may pass your tent during the day. Tent burglary is not a problem at Ramapo Valley County Reservation, and enough people are around to discourage would-be thieves, but consider locking valuables in your car as a preventive measure. The camping area is only occasionally patrolled by the Bergen County Park Security Department.

Only 35 miles from Manhattan, Ramapo Valley County Reservation caters to thousands as a wilderness area adjacent to an urban environment. Urban refugees, anxious for a green hike, populate its hiking trails. Signs warn of bears, but you're more likely to encounter throngs of happy mutts straining at their leashes.

Ramapo Valley County Reservation Campground

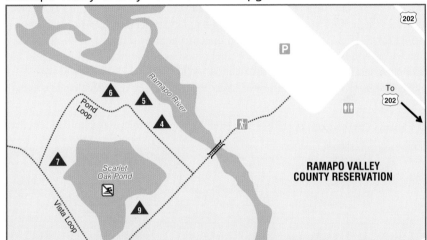

GETTING THERE

From I-287 South, take Exit 66, and turn left onto US 202 South. Drive 1.8 miles to the park entrance, on the right. From I-287 North, take Exit 58 onto US 202 North, and drive 5 miles to the park entrance, on the left.

GPS COORDINATES: N41° 04.672' W74° 11.146'

Stokes State Forest:
LAKE OCQUITTUNK CAMPING AREA

Beauty ★★★★ / Privacy ★★★ / Spaciousness ★★★ / Quiet ★★★★ / Security ★★★ / Cleanliness ★★★

Set up camp alongside what some anglers call one of New Jersey's finest rivers.

More scenic than Shotwell Camping Area (see next profile) but less rustic than Steam Mill Camping Area (page 50), Lake Ocquittunk Camping Area provides the best of both worlds in Stokes State Forest, combining a remote natural setting with modern plumbing facilities. Sites are spread throughout three areas, with a separate section dedicated to cabin camping.

Most picturesque is Big Flatbrook Loop. Sites 15–19 sit along the pleasantly bubbling creek. Sites are private, near restrooms, and sit under tall hardwoods. Sites 13 and 14 are isolated at the other end of the brook. Both have tent platforms, and while they lack restrooms, they offer total seclusion. Sites 1–12 are on the entry road and closest to the showers. Sites 8, 9, and 10 would be good to reserve together if you were camping with a group of friends or a couple of families. If you prefer seclusion, sites 25 and 26 are located near the cabin area along Big Flatbrook below the outflow of Lake Ocquittunk. The distance that separates these

A picnic pavilion on the shore of Lake Ocquittunk

ADDRESS: 5 Skellenger Road, Branchville, NJ 07826

OPERATED BY: New Jersey State Park Service

CONTACT: 973-948-3820, njparksandforests .org/parks/stokes.html; reservations: camping.nj.gov

OPEN: Year-round

SITES: 26 tent sites, 13 cabins

EACH SITE HAS: Picnic table, fire ring

WHEELCHAIR ACCESS: None

ASSIGNMENT: First-come, first-served or by reservation (minimum 2 nights)

REGISTRATION: On arrival or online

FACILITIES: Water, flush toilets, showers

PARKING: At campsites; 2-vehicle limit

FEES: New Jersey residents, $20/night; nonresidents, $25/night

---

RESTRICTIONS:

PETS: Prohibited here but allowed at Shotwell Camping Area (see next profile)

FIRES: In fire rings only

ALCOHOL: Prohibited

VEHICLES: Up to 24 feet; no RV hookups

OTHER: Quiet hours 10 p.m.–6 a.m.; 14-night stay limit; 6-person/2-tent site limit; no gas motors or swimming in Lake Ocquittunk

two large sites offers ample privacy in a quiet setting among large trees. You'll have only a pit toilet and water in this area, but the showers are close by.

Some anglers have called Big Flatbrook one of New Jersey's finest rivers. It's really more a creek than a river, and the tumbling of water over rocks fills the river with oxygen. The river and lake are both stocked with trout, but other fish call them home too. Only fish are allowed to swim in Big Flatbrook and 8-acre Lake Ocquittunk, although boating is allowed in the latter. People must drive or hike to the day-use area at Stony Lake to swim, and then in the summer only, when a lifeguard is on duty.

Two dozen trails crisscross Stokes State Forest. Blue Mountain Trail, an easy 1.4-mile route, is the closest trail to the campground. It links with Kittle Road to provide you with a hiking or bicycle route to the swimming area at Stony Lake. Tinsley Trail heads southeast from the campground for 2.8 miles and offers a challenging hike up to the Appalachian Trail.

For some scenic walks that aren't on the trail map, take a ride over to Tillman Ravine, at the most southwestern point of Stokes State Forest. Follow the park map to get there, or just head west on Strubble Road off US 206. Leave your car in the parking lot and follow the trail into the evergreens. Tillman Brook carves the ravine out of sandstone and shale as it descends from the Kittatinny Ridge. When it hits the bottom of the ravine, the water creates a bowl-like area, nicknamed The Teacup. Hikers like to relax under the forest canopy, put their feet in the cold waters of the pothole, and watch the brook cascade down the hill. Note that there are no facilities at Tillman Ravine.

A pleasant waterfall, Buttermilk Falls, is near Tillman Ravine. Exit the parking lot to the left on Brink Road and continue to dirt Mountain Road. Go left for 2 miles to Buttermilk Falls. If you stay on Brink Road just a little longer, you'll enter Walpack Center. Almost a ghost town now, Walpack Center was a thriving farming community more than a hundred years ago. Today it is a designated historic district that is slowly being restored by volunteers from the Walpack Historical Society and the National Park Service. Many old buildings in the region were destroyed during the planning stages for a massive dam that was to be built on the Delaware River. Local residents fought the dam in the 1970s, but many buildings had already been destroyed by the time the project was abandoned. Eleven buildings in the village center survived.

Just north of Walpack Center is the Walpack Inn, an acclaimed restaurant. The sign out front declares that they feed deer as well as people, and the dining room looks out over lush green fields where deer often snack.

Continue northeast on County Road 615 for 3.2 miles, and you'll reach the Kuhn Road turnoff for Peters Valley School of Craft. The center is dedicated to craft education in several disciplines: blacksmithing, ceramics, fine metals, photography, surface design, weaving, and woodworking. Additional special topics such as wearable art, mosaic design, and culinary sculpture are sometimes added. The on-site store and gallery is open daily May–December, 10 a.m.–6 p.m., and features work by local and national artists. Additionally, the school has a craft fair once a year and it hosts occasional open houses, lectures, and presentations.

Creekside spots at Lake Ocquittunk Camping Area are some of the nicest sites in the region, so call ahead for summer weekends. Remember to bring your fishing pole, hiking boots, and a map of regional attractions.

Stokes State Forest: Lake Ocquittunk Camping Area

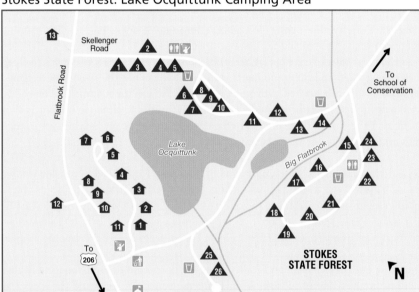

GETTING THERE

From I-80, take Exit 34B for NJ 15 North. After 17.2 miles, NJ 15 North becomes US 206 North; in another 6.7 miles, turn right onto Coursen Road at the top of the mountain to pay for camping at the visitor center. Turn right, back onto US 206 North, and drive about 2 miles. Turn right onto Flatbrook Road, and drive 2.4 miles. Turn right into the campground entrance on Skellenger Road.

GPS COORDINATES: N41° 13.855' W74° 45.774'

Stokes State Forest:
SHOTWELL CAMPING AREA

Beauty ★★★★ / Privacy ★★★ / Spaciousness ★★★ / Quiet ★★★★ / Security ★★★ / Cleanliness ★★★

Stokes's inaccessibility before the completion of I-80 preserved it from development for more than 100 years.

Shotwell Camping Area, just down the road from the forest office, is the most accessible of the three Stokes State Forest campgrounds. Heading straight from the entrance will take you into a maze of sites; only five of these are suitable for tent campers. The other sites contain lean-to shelters that rent for $35 and $45 a night. Tent sites, three at the end of the road and two on the return loop, have wooden platforms. Sites 103, 104, and 105 are sheltered from through traffic.

The best tent sites are located along the spur road that veers left off the main thoroughfare. These spacious sites are more secluded and rustic, offering a semblance of privacy. Sites 131–135 sit on a grassy field and require a brief walk from a central parking area. All sites have lantern posts in addition to picnic tables and fire rings, and some are situated on pleasant Shotwell Pond (*note:* no swimming allowed). Campers at the end of the spur will have to take hearty walks to reach the flush toilets, although abundant pit toilets are provided along the road.

Shotwell Pond

KEY INFORMATION

ADDRESS: Shotwell Road, Sandyston, NJ 07826

OPERATED BY: New Jersey State Park Service

CONTACT: 973-948-3820, njparksandforests .org/parks/stokes.html; reservations: camping.nj.gov

OPEN: Year-round

SITES: 27 tent sites, 9 lean-tos

EACH SITE HAS: Picnic table, fire ring

WHEELCHAIR ACCESS: None

ASSIGNMENT: First-come, first-served or by reservation (minimum 2 nights)

REGISTRATION: On arrival or online

FACILITIES: Water, pit and flush toilets

PARKING: At campsites; 2-vehicle limit

FEES: New Jersey residents, $20/night; nonresidents, $25/night; $5/night pet fee

---

RESTRICTIONS:

PETS: On leash, sites 101–137 only, 2 pets/ site; pet permit and proof of current vaccinations required. See njparksandforests .org/parks/pet_friendly_camping.html for more information.

FIRES: In fire rings only

ALCOHOL: Prohibited

VEHICLES: Up to 24 feet; no RV hookups

OTHER: Quiet hours 10 p.m.–6 a.m.; 14-day stay limit; 6-person/2-tent site limit; no tents allowed on lean-to sites; no swimming in Shotwell Pond

Stokes State Forest and the surrounding area were considered remote prior to the completion of I-80 in the 1970s. Its inaccessibility preserved it from development back in 1907, when the first 5,000 acres were purchased by the state of New Jersey and added to 500 acres bequeathed by Edward C. Stokes, then governor of New Jersey. The governor's greatest legacy was not in providing stiffer penalties for Sunday liquor sales but in creating water and forest commissions. Today, Stokes State Forest covers 15,947 acres, including 2,900 acres recently added through New Jersey's public Green Acres Program.

Nine of the Appalachian Trail's 2,000 miles cut through Stokes State Forest. Those who dream of being thru-hikers can test their mettle on the 5-mile walk from US 206 to Sunrise Mountain. Follow the white blazes and pretend you've been walking for months!

Three shelters provide camping for hikers on AT trips that require overnight stops, but day hikers must use one of the three developed campgrounds within Stokes. The Ladder, Acropolis, Tower, Stony Brook, Tinsley, Cartwright, and Howell Trails, as well as Sunrise Mountain Road, provide access to the AT from Stokes. Hikes to the Culver Fire Tower and the Acropolis are especially worthwhile undertakings, with the hike to the fire tower providing spectacular views. The fire tower is closed to the public, but a picnic table at its base provides an excellent view. To the east are the Jersey Highlands, and to the west are the Poconos. The rolling hills of Sussex County lie all around. The area is popular with birders, particularly in late August and September.

For a short geology lesson, follow Tinsley Trail from Sunrise Mountain Road to the Kittatinny Glacial Geology Trail. This self-guided trail is short and easy, although a little rocky in places. Fifteen numbered posts along the way correspond to numbered paragraphs in the trail brochure, which explains how the region transformed into the Kittatinny Ridge over the years after being a vast inland seacoast.

Remember that bears live in the area, so always use bearproof containers, and never take food into or near your tent. See the Introduction for more information on how to camp safely in bear country.

Nearby Stony Lake in the day-use area is open to campers. Swimming is allowed in Stony Lake during summer, provided that lifeguards are on duty. A food concession operates when the swimming beach is open. The bathhouse and Civilian Conservation Corps–constructed picnic area, with grills and a pavilion, is always open. Fishing is also allowed in Stony Lake, and there is a playground nearby. For people who enjoy the outdoors, there's something for everyone at Stokes State Forest.

Stokes State Forest: Shotwell Camping Area

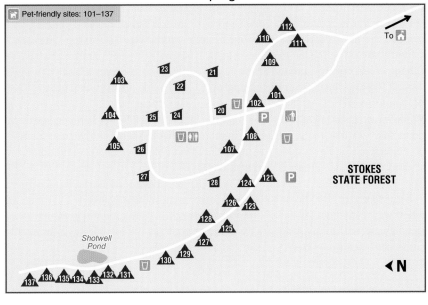

GETTING THERE

From I-80, take Exit 34B for NJ 15 North. After 17.2 miles, NJ 15 North becomes US 206 North. After 6.7 miles, turn right onto Coursen Road at the top of the mountain. Follow the signs past the visitor center to Shotwell Campground.

GPS COORDINATES: N41° 11.687′ W74° 48.009′

Stokes State Forest:
STEAM MILL CAMPING AREA

Beauty ★★★★ / Privacy ★★ / Spaciousness ★★★ / Quiet ★★★ / Security ★★ / Cleanliness ★★

You're unlikely to have many neighbors here, at least of the human variety.

Steam Mill Camping Area, set back in the woods 5 miles from US 206, is the most remote and primitive of the Stokes State Forest campgrounds. It's also the least popular—meaning it's also the most likely to have an open site even during high season. Sites are wide open, with little or no foliage to act as privacy barriers. But you're unlikely to have many neighbors, at least of the human variety. If you really want to ensure a bit of privacy, sites 207 and 209 are set back from the campground loop a fair distance and are surrounded by tall hemlocks.

Wildlife casually strolls nearby as you set up your tent. Trailers fit here too but are more suited to Lake Ocquittunk (see page 44). Remember that bears live in the area, so use bear-proof containers, and never take food into or near your tent. See the Introduction for more information on how to camp safely in bear country.

The nearest neighbor to Steam Mill is a former Civilian Conservation Corps camp built in the 1930s by Franklin D. Roosevelt's "army with shovels." One of FDR's first acts as president was to create a system of camps that employed young men in rural conservation projects. Today, the camp's residents have similar goals, as the New Jersey School of Conservation has taken up residency on the 240-acre property.

All of the sites at Steam Mill are quite wooded and offer a nice mix of shade and sun.

ADDRESS: Crigger Road, Sussex, NJ 07461

OPERATED BY: New Jersey State Park Service

CONTACT: 973-948-3820, njparksandforests .org/parks/stokes.html; reservations: camping.nj.gov

OPEN: Year-round

SITES: 27

EACH SITE HAS: Picnic table, fire ring

WHEELCHAIR ACCESS: None

ASSIGNMENT: First-come, first-served or by reservation (minimum 2 nights)

REGISTRATION: On arrival or online

FACILITIES: Water, vault toilets

PARKING: At campsites; 2-vehicle limit

FEES: New Jersey residents, $20/night; nonresidents, $25/night

RESTRICTIONS:

PETS: Prohibited here but allowed at Shotwell Camping Area (see previous profile)

FIRES: In fire rings only

ALCOHOL: Prohibited

VEHICLES: Up to 24 fee; no RV hookups

OTHER: Quiet hours 10 p.m.–6 a.m.; 14-day stay limit; 6-person/2-tent site limit

The New Jersey School of Conservation, run by Montclair State University, is the oldest university-operated environmental-education center in the nation. It became an environmental-education center in 1949 but did not become state-operated until 1972. In addition to offering programs in environmental science and ecology, it offers astronomical research at its observatory and short environmental workshops for elementary- and secondary-school students. Gifted young musicians attend a two-week workshop in music ecology in the summer, and young adults attend fly-fishing classes on the 12-acre lake.

Stokes State Forest is a hiker's dream destination, with more than 40 miles of trails. Fall is a great time to visit—the foliage turns, and bears wander around hunting food as they fatten up for their winter hibernation.

Parker Trail begins right across from Steam Mill Camping Area and follows Parker Brook for 2.3 miles through neighboring High Point State Park. Its winding hills are classified as moderately difficult. Parker Brook is a wild trout stream. Anglers planning to fish in Parker Brook should familiarize themselves with New Jersey fishing regulations, as certain wild-trout restrictions are in effect year-round.

The Appalachian Trail (AT) and the dramatic panorama from 1,600-foot Sunrise Mountain are less than 2 miles from the campground. The most direct route, the Cartwright Trail, is classified as difficult. It rises dramatically over 0.9 mile, but seasoned hikers will make relatively short work of its winding slopes. Be aware that the streambed running along the path is not the trail. Cartwright Trail can be accessed from Swenson Trail off Sunrise Mountain Road. Turn right from the campground, or you could walk along the road for the entire distance. Driving to Sunrise Mountain is tempting, but Sunrise Mountain Road is one-way from US 206 to the campground—in the wrong direction.

Swenson Trail offers a moderate 3.8-mile hike at an elevation of 1,000 feet through a rocky ravine and several streams. The reward is the swimming and day-use area at Stony Lake, which lies at the end of the trail. From Sunrise Mountain, you can also follow the AT to the Tower Trail, where you can get a view of the surrounding area if the fire tower is unmanned, before descending to Stony Lake.

The less ambitious can take an easy walk along 0.8-mile Steam Mill Trail. This route ends at the conservation school, where a road continues to Lake Ocquittunk. From here, you can circle back around to Steam Mill Camping Area by following the mostly level road. See njparksandforests.org/parks/stokes.html for a downloadable trail map and trail guide (see "Trails" at the bottom of the page).

Steam Mill is designated a carry-in/carry-out area. Remove your trash, leaving it in bearproof dumpsters at the cabin contact station by Lake Ocquittunk. And drive carefully as you leave—bears, chipmunks, turkeys, and deer are used to having the right of-way.

Stokes State Forest: Steam Mill Camping Area

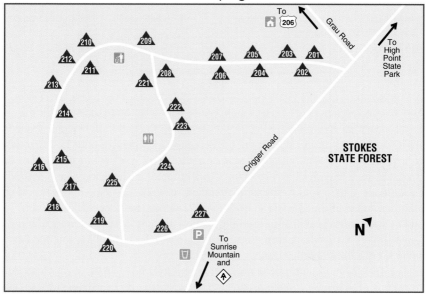

GETTING THERE

From I-80, take Exit 34B for NJ 15 North. After 17.2 miles, NJ 15 North becomes US 206 North. After 6.7 miles, turn right onto Coursen Road at the top of the mountain to pay for camping at the visitor center. Turn right, back onto US 206 North, and drive about 2 miles. Turn right onto Flatbrook Road, and drive 4.7 miles to the end of the road, where it intersects Crigger Road. Turn right onto Crigger Road, and follow it to the campground entrance on the right.

GPS COORDINATES: N41° 14.505' W74° 44.030'

Swartswood State Park Campground

Beauty ★★★ / Privacy ★★ / Spaciousness ★★★ / Quiet ★★★ / Security ★★★ / Cleanliness ★★★

Freshwater Swartswood Lake has been a resort area since the 1900s.

Families pour into Swartswood State Park Campground on warm summer weekends, and with good reason. Swartswood Lake and its junior sibling, Little Swartswood Lake, feature swimming, boating, and fishing. Highlights of the forested trails include biking, hiking, and horseback riding. Picnicking and birding are also popular, along with the clean, modern bathhouse; playground; laundry room; and choice of wooded or open campsites.

The grassy, open sites are the largest of the two loops and closer to the bathhouse. Choose these if you want to sacrifice privacy for space and community; they're popular with families and groups who want to stay in adjacent areas. The sites closest to the campground entrance will have constant traffic rolling by, so use caution when setting up camp near the entrance. The sites on the inside of the main loop would be good to reserve for a couple of families.

Two wooded loops are set against forested areas, where the tangled understory gives an illusion of privacy. Sites are spacious for one large tent, but some can become cramped if

A small gaggle of geese enjoys a New Jersey sunset on Swartswood Lake.

KEY INFORMATION

ADDRESS: 1091 E. Shore Road, Swartswood, NJ 07877

OPERATED BY: New Jersey State Park Service

CONTACT: 973-383-5230, njparksandforests .org/parks/swartswood.html; reservations: camping.nj.gov

OPEN: Sites 1–21, year-round; Sites 22–65, April 1–October 31

SITES: 65; 10 are tent-only (sites 28, 43–45, 50–53, 55, 56)

EACH SITE HAS: Picnic table, fire ring, lantern post

WHEELCHAIR ACCESS: Restrooms

ASSIGNMENT: First-come, first-served or by reservation (minimum 2 nights)

REGISTRATION: On arrival or online

FACILITIES: Water, flush toilets, showers

PARKING: At campsites; 2-vehicle limit

FEES: New Jersey residents, $20/night; nonresidents, $25/night

---

RESTRICTIONS:

PETS: On leash, sites 42–45 only, 2 pets/site; pet permit and proof of current vaccinations required. See njparksandforests.org /parks/pet_friendly_camping.html for more information.

FIRES: In fire rings only

ALCOHOL: Prohibited

VEHICLES: No RV hookups at tent/trailer sites

OTHER: Quiet hours 10 p.m.–6 a.m.; 14-day stay limit; 6-person/2-tent site limit; check-in at noon

two tents are set up. The small one-way roads can be filled with children on bicycles. Children should wear helmets, as required by New Jersey state law. A boat launch exclusively for campers is located directly across from site 65.

Six yurts are set off on a loop by themselves. They have their own bathhouse, which might be worth the walk if you get tired of waiting to use the shower on the main loop.

A protected swimming beach is across the park entrance road from the campground, but campers can also reach it on a lakeside multiuse trail. Lifeguards staff the beach Memorial Day weekend–Labor Day; note that the beach is closed when no lifeguards are on duty. Facilities include a refreshment stand, first aid room, and a bathhouse.

Swartswood is famed for its fishing opportunities. Both freshwater lakes are stocked with trout in the spring, and other fish are present throughout the year. Swartswood has been called one of the best walleye spots in New Jersey and is sometimes known as a great largemouth bass spot, but anglers have occasionally complained about the size of the lake, the wind, and the rule that powerboats are limited to electric motors. At around 500 acres of surface water, Swartswood Lake is one of the largest natural lakes in the state. Most of it is more than 10 feet deep (over 50 feet deep near Pike Rock).

In addition to electric powerboats, small privately owned watercraft may be launched from three free public ramps. Rowboats, canoes, paddleboats, kayaks, and small sailboats can be rented at the park from a concessionaire near the swimming area. Parking by the boat launch areas is limited, but there is plenty of parking by the swimming beach. You must wear a life jacket when boating or sailing.

Nearly 11 miles of multiuse trails are located throughout the park. The most popular is the 0.6-mile-long Duck Pond Trail, a paved path accessible to wheelchairs, strollers, skateboards, cyclists, and skaters. The path features a bird blind as well as exhibits that explain natural features along the route. Branching off at the southern end of the Duck Pond is the 2.8-mile moderately difficult Spring Lake Trail. Follow it through varied forest habitats before passing both Spring Lake and Frog Pond and then looping back to Duck Pond. Follow 0.8-mile Bear Claw Trail for an easier option. Because hunting is allowed in this section, be cautious and wear bright clothes during hunting season.

Hikers can reach 1.5-mile Grist Mill Trail from the southwestern end of the lake, near the dam area off West Shore Drive (County Route 521); it's inaccessible from the campground without transportation. Grist Mill Trail is difficult but rewards hikers with views of the lake. Keen's Grist Mill, at the tip of the lake, was built in 1838 on the site of earlier mills.

Swartswood Lake got its name from Captain Anthony Swartwout, a British military officer who lived on the lake with his family in the 1700s. He incurred the wrath of American Indians through his service during the French and Indian Wars and, in 1756, was killed by some of his enemies. The lake became a weekend resort in the early 1900s, with the advent of the railroad through Blairstown. It's still a weekend retreat today, although visitors are more likely to stay in tents than in inns or boarding houses.

Swartswood State Park Campground

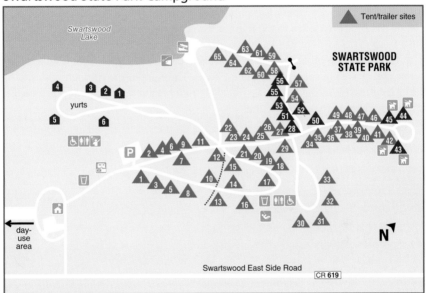

GETTING THERE

From I-80, take Exit 25 for US 206 North (Stanhope/Newton). Drive 11.8 mile on US 206 North. Turn left onto Spring Street to stay on US 206 North, and drive just 0.1 mile. Turn left onto Mill Street, and drive 0.4 mile. Turn left onto Swartswood Road, which quickly becomes Newton Swartswood Road, and drive 4.3 miles. Turn left onto Swartswood East Side Road, and drive 0.6 mile. The park entrance will be on your right.

GPS COORDINATES: N41° 04.413' W74° 49.114'

Worthington State Forest Campground

Beauty ★★★ / Privacy ★★★ / Spaciousness ★★★★ / Quiet ★★★ / Security ★★★ / Cleanliness ★★★★

Worthington State Forest Campground offers the only public developed sites within Delaware Water Gap National Recreation Area.

Nearly five million people visit the Delaware Water Gap National Recreation Area every year. Fortunately, these visitors are spread out over 40 miles of river and 70,000 acres of land across two states. Still, you should reserve your campsite ahead of time on summer weekends, because Worthington State Forest Campground offers the only public developed sites within the park's boundaries.

The campground stretches along the Delaware River for 2 miles and is situated just north of the Delaware Water Gap itself. Kittatinny Mountain, part of the Appalachian Range, rises above the camping area. Sites to the right of the central forest office are sunnier; most surround a treeless field where RVs have to camp. If you prefer shade to sun, the 23 tent-only sites to the left of the office are situated under a tall forest. These sites offer understory between sites as well as spacious, level tent areas. Throughout the campground, sites close to the river are level. Sites on the grassy field are more suitable for trailers, but there are no hookups anywhere in the campground.

A fall day along Flat Brook in the Delaware Water Gap National Recreation Area in New Jersey

KEY INFORMATION

ADDRESS: 2 Old Mine Road, Columbia, NJ 07832

OPERATED BY: New Jersey State Park Service

CONTACT: 908-841-9575, njparksandforests .org/parks/worthington.html; reservations: camping.nj.gov

OPEN: Sites 1–4, second Friday in May–October 31; sites 5–23, second Friday in April–October 31; sites 29–77, April 1–December 31

SITES: 73; sites 1–23 are tent-only

EACH SITE HAS: Picnic table, fire ring, lantern hook

WHEELCHAIR ACCESS: Restrooms near sites 29–77

ASSIGNMENT: First-come, first-served or by reservation (minimum 2 nights)

REGISTRATION: On arrival or online

FACILITIES: Water and vault toilets in tent-camping area; water, flush toilets, and showers near sites 29–77

PARKING: At campsites; 2-vehicle limit

FEES: New Jersey residents, $20/night; nonresidents, $25/night

RESTRICTIONS:

PETS: Prohibited

FIRES: In fire rings only

ALCOHOL: Prohibited

VEHICLES: No RV hookups at tent/trailer sites

OTHER: Quiet hours 10 p.m.–6 a.m.; 14-day stay limit; 6-person/2-tent site limit; carry out trash in bags provided

Worthington State Forest Campground is well appointed when it comes to amenities, including plenty of fresh water and well-situated toilets. Three bathhouses include multiple shower facilities and bicycle racks. Two playgrounds and a basketball court are nearby. All toilets near sites 29–77 (the field sites) are modern, flushable, and ADA-accessible. The toilets near sites 1–23 are more primitive yet sturdy vault toilets, although the main bathhouse is modern. There are vending machines next to the bathhouse by the entrance road.

Seventy-two miles of the famed Appalachian Trail (AT) traverse New Jersey, with 7.8 of those miles in Worthington State Forest. The scenic walk from the Delaware Water Gap to Worthington's Sunfish Pond is the most popular section in the state and gets crowded on summer weekends. Ambitious campers can avoid the AT day-hiker crowds and hike up the 1.1-mile Turquoise Trail to Sunfish Pond. Unfortunately, while the Turquoise Trail provides pleasant views as it passes waterfalls and follows a bubbling creek, this most direct route rises 900 feet within a mile. Douglas Trail provides a 2.5-mile moderate alternative. It leaves from the campground and rises 900 feet over 2 miles before intersecting the AT. Follow the white blazes of the AT left to Sunfish Pond, passing the backpacker's campsite en route.

Sunfish Pond is a clear glacial lake formed during the last ice age. Swimming in the lake is illegal, although the beavers don't seem to be aware of this restriction. Few fish live in the 41-acre lake, as its acidic waters only support a few sturdy species. Hikers like to sit on its rocky shore for a rest or picnic lunch; an especially nice spot is along the Turquoise Trail as it passes the lake. You can make a nice loop of Sunfish Pond by following the Turquoise Trail along its northeast edge to a substantial forest road. Turn right and follow the forest road southwest to the AT, which you'll follow along the northwest edge of the lake back to the Turquoise Trail.

You should remove all trash from Sunfish Pond and take it back to camp with you. All of Worthington State Forest is designated carry-in/carry-out. Bags are provided throughout the forest, and a dumpster is situated by the forest office at the entrance to the campground.

This policy is not just about environmental responsibility; a large population of black bears lives in the area (see the Introduction for more information on how to camp safely in bear country). Rattlesnakes and ticks also call the area home, so be prepared.

Other popular hikes go to Mohican Point at the northern end of the forest and Mount Tammany at the southern end. Both are renowned for their scenic vistas, which afford panoramic views of the surrounding region.

Fishing, hunting, and boating are also popular in Worthington. Some anglers have reported that the fishing in the vicinity is the best on the Delaware River; the area is known for its spring shad run as well as its summer bass population. A small boat launch is near the forest office; campers can also fish in waders or from the river's edge. Up on the Kittatinny Ridge, Dunnfield Creek is famed for its natural brook trout fishery. Special wild-trout-stream regulations apply.

In the 1890s, millionaire Charles Worthington began purchasing land in the area. He bought 8,000 acres, including the village of Brotmanville, where the campground sits today. He made much of it into a private preserve and reintroduced deer and pheasant, but he didn't destroy the village (that happened later, during a flood in 1955). New Jersey began purchasing the land from Worthington's heirs in 1954. Today, Worthington's former home covers 6,200 wooded acres of land and features one of the most popular campgrounds on the Delaware River.

Worthington State Forest Campground

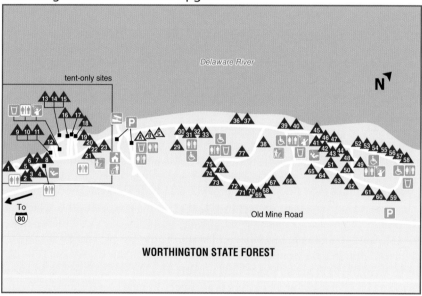

GETTING THERE

From I-80 at the New Jersey–Pennsylvania border, take Exit 1 (Millbrook/Flatbrookville). Go north on Old Mine Road for 3 miles; the forest office will be on your left.

GPS COORDINATES: N41° 00.592' W75° 05.303'

WEST CENTRAL NEW JERSEY

The Musconetcong River flows through Stephens State Forest. The campground is on top of the hillside in the back. (See page 73 for campground profile.)

Delaware River Family Campground

Beauty ★★★ / Privacy ★★ / Spaciousness ★★★ / Quiet ★★ / Security ★★★ / Cleanliness ★★★

The river is the star attraction here, offering boating, tubing, and fishing from its banks.

Tucked away in the northwestern corner of this private riverside RV park are 121 grassy tent-only sites. Don't be deceived by the rows of trailers you must pass to get there, and don't be put off by the clambakes, barbecues, or bingo. There are two secluded, wooded state parks nearby for those who prefer more scenic, wilder experiences. But for families with children, for those wishing to bring along the family pet, or for those who like to consume a beer with their freshly caught fish, Delaware River Family Campground is a well maintained, friendly option. It's also one of the rare private campgrounds that don't give short shrift to tent campers.

In fact, the best sites in the campground—those right on the river—are reserved for tents. Many of the RV sites are closer to the main road, which make them noisier than the tent sites. The campground does try to control the noise; no motorized scooters, motorbikes, or chainsaws are allowed.

The Delaware River is the star attraction here, and the camp offers rafting, canoeing, tubing, and kayaking, in addition to allowing fishing from its banks. You can launch boats

The campground does quite a business with canoe and raft rentals on the river. They'll provide you with shuttle service as well.

KEY INFORMATION

from the campground, as well as sit-down Jet Skis (you must bring your own). Stand-up Jet Skis are not permitted on the Delaware. Swimming is allowed in the pool only and is not permitted on the beach or near the boat launch.

Eight-mile rafting, canoeing, and kayaking trips are offered, with shuttle transportation included. Tubing trips are 4 miles long. Trips leave on the hour from 9 a.m. to 3 p.m. daily. Shuttles drop off tubers upstream, and the current brings them back. Canoes and motor-ized boats can also be rented for daily use. Fishing is not allowed from rafts, and life vests must always be worn. There is a three-beer-per-adult limit on the river, and US park rangers have been known to enforce it.

Pets are welcome, but be aware of the following rules and regulations: Dogs must be leashed and attended, and waste must be cleaned up immedi-ately. Barking dogs are not tolerated. Finally, all dogs must be up to date on their rabies vaccines.

The experience of camping in a private camp-ground is distinctly different from that of setting up a tent in a pristine, secluded wilderness. But there are benefits to camping in an organized environment,

Campers can fish at this idyllic spot along the river.

particularly for those looking to entertain children. The campground offers a safe environ-ment for kids to ride bicycles (helmets required) or swim in the pool. There is a playground, miniature golf course, basketball court, game room, and sand volleyball court. Activities suit-able for kids and adults are scheduled for every summer weekend as well as Labor Day and Columbus Day weekends.

Delaware River Family Campground is centrally located for those wishing to make the climb up Mount Tammany at the Delaware Water Gap. Tear the kids away from tubing and swimming long enough to drive up to the Dunnfield Creek parking area, near the Delaware Water Gap National Recreation Area Visitor Center off I-80. Hike along the Red Dot Trail (also known as the Mount Tammany Trail) for 1.5 miles, rising 1,250 feet to the summit. The walk is rocky and moderately strenuous. You'll see dramatic views of the Gap and of Mount Minsi in Pennsylvania before hiking back down along the Blue Dot Trail.

The campground has its own "distinctly Delaware" rules. Firewood must be purchased on-site. Wristbands must be worn at all times, identifying campers as paying members of the community; gate cards must be rented or tokens purchased to get in and out of the campground. The only thing you're allowed to wear over your bathing suit in the pool is a white T-shirt. And you must leave your chainsaws and pit bulls at home, even if they seem like part of the family. But when it comes to riverside camping with on-site river trips and no restrictions against having a beer in the evening, Delaware River can't be beat.

Delaware River Family Campground

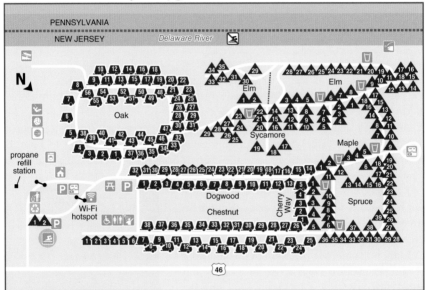

GETTING THERE

From I-80, take Exit 4B for US 46 East. Merge onto US 46 East, and drive 3.2 miles. The campground entrance will be on the right.

GPS COORDINATES: N40° 53.161' W 75° 03.672'

Jenny Jump State Forest Campground

Beauty ★★★★★ / Privacy ★★★★★ / Spaciousness ★★★ / Quiet ★★★★ / Security ★★★ / Cleanliness ★★★

Private, wooded, lofty sites, along with modern plumbing, make Jenny Jump unrivaled throughout the state.

For campers seeking both forested solitude and indoor plumbing, campsites at Jenny Jump State Forest fill the bill. And for those who are less excited by the thought of flushing toilets and warm showers, Jenny Jump offers three lofty wilderness sites (9–11) that are slightly more remote, higher up, and even more secluded.

Developed sites at Jenny Jump are mostly level clearings, well spaced from each other, and encircled by trees and understory. Nine sites are designated walk-in, but six of these require only brief walks from parking areas. These six sites (22, 23, 26, 27, 34, 35) are located in the main camping area along East Road, close to restrooms and trails.

Campers will find the three wilderness sites in the woods above the eight shelters. You must carry your gear up a hill to the primitive sites, but the rustic perch is worth the effort. These sites have no plumbing but do provide a gentle breeze on all but the warmest of days. Modern restrooms are located down the hill by the cabins, but hiking along the rocky path is not recommended after dark.

Jenny Jump State Park is quite a bit higher than the surrounding area. This view, to the southeast, is from near the observatory just outside of the park.

KEY INFORMATION

ADDRESS: 289 State Park Road, Blairstown, NJ 07825

OPERATED BY: New Jersey State Park Service

CONTACT: 908-459-4366, njparksandforests .org/parks/jennyjump.html; reservations: camping.nj.gov

OPEN: April 1–October 31

SITES: 30 (including 8 shelters); sites 9–11, 22, 23, 34–36 are tent-only

EACH SITE HAS: Picnic table, fire ring, lantern post

WHEELCHAIR ACCESS: Bathrooms are accessible, and most sites are hardened soil and gravel

ASSIGNMENT: First-come, first-served or by reservation (minimum 2 nights)

REGISTRATION: On arrival or online

FACILITIES: Water, flush toilets, showers

PARKING: Drive-in sites, 2-vehicle limit; walk-in sites, nearby lots

FEES: New Jersey residents, $20/night; nonresidents, $25/night

RESTRICTIONS:

PETS: Prohibited

FIRES: In fire rings only

ALCOHOL: Prohibited

VEHICLES: Up to 25 feet; no RV hookups at tent/trailer sites

OTHER: Quiet hours 10 p.m.–6 a.m.; 14-day stay limit; 6-person/2-tent site limit

---

The terrain in Jenny Jump State Forest was gouged out 21,000 years ago at the end of the Wisconsin Ice Age. Advancing glaciers halted a few miles away, leaving debris and sediment, and carving out chunks of rock. The result was dramatic, leaving jagged boulders, rocky mountains, and valleys. Some of the man-made features can be attributed to the Civilian Conservation Corps, which built roads and the picnic area in the 1930s.

Columbine grows on the side of a boulder in the campground.

Other man-made features include a variety of legends and local folklore regarding the name of the road that goes to the Ghost Lake boat launch. The sinister tall tales that explain how Shades of Death Road and Ghost Lake were named run the gamut from the believable (an 1850 malaria epidemic) to the absurd (a deerskin-bedecked American Indian guards the road and will chase you). Jenny Jump itself has a disturbing legend behind its moniker: the myth claims that a girl named Jenny jumped off a cliff to avoid Indians in the 1700s. Park literature, however, points out that it's just as likely that "Jenny Jump" is an anglicized version of a Lenape name for the mountain. See the book *Weird N.J.* by Mark Sceurman and Mark Moran (Sterling Publishing Company, 2004) for all the lurid legends surrounding the region.

Ghost Lake is famed more for its bass fishing opportunities than for its eeriness. Anglers can fish from small boats or canoes as well as from the shore. In addition to bass, you can also catch crappie, sunfish, and catfish in the shallow lake. Hunting is also permitted in some parts of Jenny Jump State Forest.

Faery Hole, a small cave, is accessible from the Ghost Lake dirt parking lot on Shades of Death Road. Look for a trail that goes up a rocky slope. The cave itself is simple and flat. All of its artifacts, including mammal bones and pottery, were excavated long ago.

Five short hiking trails, as well as the 3.7-mile Mount Lake multiuse trail, wind through the 4,200-acre forest. You can access Orchard, Swamp, Summit, and Spring Trails from the camping area, while 1.3-mile Ghost Lake Trail meets East Road by the group camping area. The 1.5-mile Summit Trail climbs to 1,090 feet and offers panoramic vistas of the surrounding area. Hikers may encounter deer and turkey as well as a wide variety of birds. But keep your eyes on the ground as well. A number of snakes inhabit the forest.

On Saturday evenings between April and October, the United Astronomy Clubs of New Jersey offers public astronomy programs at their Jenny Jump observatory. The club's 16-inch Newtonian telescope is housed in leased state property that used to be a private

The walk up to sites 10 and 11 is a bit steep, but the seclusion is worth the effort.

home. The club chose Jenny Jump for its dark sky—one of the few dark spots left in the most densely populated state in the country.

For younger campers, the Land of Make Believe amusement park is nestled in the foothills of Jenny Jump State Forest. It offers a water park, carnival-style rides, and a small roller coaster. It's not for those seeking an adrenaline rush, as it's aimed at children ages 12 and younger. Rides include a turn-of-the-century carousel, a spinning *T. rex,* and waterslides. There's also a petting zoo and a participatory theater where kids get to dress up and be part of a medieval show.

But the main attraction at Jenny Jump is the wilderness and the campground, not the local carnival. Reserve in advance in the summer—the cool, elevated sites under the trees go quickly.

Jenny Jump State Forest Campground

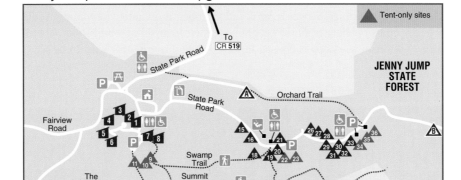

GETTING THERE

From I-80, take Exit 12 for County Road 521 (Hope/Blairstown). Take Hope Blairstown Road south for 1.3 miles; then turn left onto High Street, which quickly becomes Johnsonburg Road/CR 519, and drive about 1 mile. Turn right onto Shiloh Road. After 1.2 miles, turn right onto State Park Road.

GPS COORDINATES: N40° 54.972' W74° 54.887'

Round Valley Recreation Area Campground

Beauty ★★★★ / Privacy ★★★★ / Spaciousness ★★★ / Quiet ★★★★★ / Security ★★★ / Cleanliness ★★★

These wilderness campsites are spread out over 3.5 miles of lakefront and are totally inaccessible by road.

The 85 campsites on the eastern shore of Round Valley Reservoir are among the most rustic developed sites in New Jersey. Officially classified as wilderness campsites, they are completely inaccessible by vehicle. Sites are spread out along 3.5 miles of lakefront, and the closest site to the parking area is a 3-mile hike away on a rugged trail.

Campers must carry in all gear and must carry out all garbage. Firewood may be gathered from the ground but cannot be cut from trees—doing so detracts from the privacy that the surrounding woodlands provide between sites. Remember that New Jersey has an abundance of black bears, and you will have no car in which to lock your food. Bring along a bearproof container, and store it at least 100 feet away from your tent; also, do not put food residue into your campfire. See the Introduction for more information on how to camp safely in bear country.

The farthest campsites are 6 miles from the South Parking Lot, on a gravel path that runs parallel to Cushetunk Trail. In addition to hiking in, campers can also travel to sites by boat or mountain bike.

A pleasant place to sit, rest, and take in the view near the entrance to Round Valley Recreation Area

KEY INFORMATION

ADDRESS: 1220 Lebanon Stanton Road, Lebanon, NJ 08833

OPERATED BY: New Jersey State Park Service

INFORMATION: 908-236-6355, njparksandforests.org/parks/round.html; reservations: camping.nj.gov

OPEN: April 1–October 31

SITES: 77 tent sites, 8 group sites

EACH SITE HAS: Fire ring

WHEELCHAIR ACCESS: None

ASSIGNMENT: First-come, first-served or by reservation (minimum 2 nights)

REGISTRATION: On arrival or online

FACILITIES: Vault toilets, water

PARKING: At South Parking Lot; 3–6 miles to campsites

FEES: New Jersey residents, $20/night; nonresidents, $25/night

RESTRICTIONS:

PETS: Permitted at all sites on leash, 2 pets/site; pet permit and proof of current vaccinations required. See njparksandforests.org/parks/pet_friendly_camping.html for more information.

FIRES: In fire rings only

ALCOHOL: Prohibited

VEHICLES: Not applicable (hike-in sites)

OTHER: Quiet hours 10 p.m.–6 a.m.; 14-day stay limit; all guests must obtain camping permit from park office by 4 p.m. (3 p.m. in October); 6-person/2-tent site limit; sites must be vacated by noon

Campers are the only people permitted to launch boats from the divers and campers boat ramp near the South Parking Lot. Others will have to travel to the public boat launch, which is administrated by the fish and game commission and is located about a mile from the recreation area. Only sailboats, canoes, or motorboats up to 10 horsepower are permitted on the reservoir. Life vests are required for each person on all vessels.

Sites that have good boat access and are close to the reservoir's edge include sites 10, 13, 16, 22, 23, 26, 38, 40, 47, 48, 72, and group site 7. Watch for high winds; when wind speeds hit 20 mph, warning lights flash and boaters must immediately pull into shore. Boating campers then have to wait or hike out of the campground. Do not ignore these warnings: Round Valley is known for strong winds that can be deadly. There are no boat rentals at Round Valley, so getting a kayak or canoe to access your campsite requires some creative planning and forethought.

Arrive early if you want to camp at Round Valley. Because of the long haul to the campground, no one is allowed to check in later than 4 p.m. (3 p.m. in October).

At 180 feet deep, man-made Round Valley Reservoir is New Jersey's deepest and second-largest lake. It's an ideal spot for those learning or practicing their open-water scuba skills. The deepest part of the diving area, a protected cove near the divers and campers boat ramp, is 60 feet deep. Divers enter the water from the beach, and there is an underwater training platform in the cove. Diving groups are required to display the scuba flag while under water and must check in and out at the ranger station. Certification and presentation of safety equipment are required to obtain a permit. Call ahead for details.

Boating and fishing are both allowed from the campsites. Swimming is not, though it is allowed at the day-use area when lifeguards are on duty. Note that the day-use area is near the parking lot, 3 miles from the nearest campsites, so you'd be wise to leave your mask and fins and other swim-related gear in your car. The beach complex contains changing rooms, restrooms, showers, and concessionaires. No grilling is allowed on the beach, but three nearby picnic areas have grills.

Round Valley Recreation Area is one of New Jersey's most challenging mountain biking spots. Bikers and hikers (and the occasional horse) share the rocky Cushetunk Trail for the first 3 miles, until the trail splits. Campers take the left fork down to the shore through 3 miles of carefully spaced campsites. The right fork goes up a ridge and continues for another 3 miles. Most bikers go right, testing their mettle on a challenging aerobic workout. They then return on the campground trail. Mountain biking at Round Valley consists of hard, sustained uphills, technical descents, and many rocks—definitely not for beginners.

Anglers must follow special fishing regulations at Round Valley Reservoir, as it is one of New Jersey's two trophy trout lakes (Merrill Creek Reservoir is the other). Some of the largest trout in the state have been caught at Round Valley. Large bass and bluegill are also found there, and some anglers call Round Valley the "valley of the giants." Fishing is prohibited near the swimming area.

Between fishing, biking, and diving, there's no shortage of things to do at Round Valley. But there *is* a shortage of parking spaces, so get here early on summer weekends.

Round Valley Recreation Area Campground

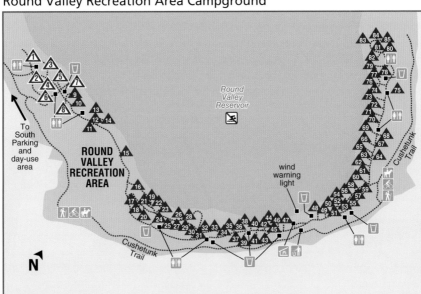

GETTING THERE

From I-78, take Exit 18 for US 22 East (Annandale/Lebanon). Continue onto US 22 East, and drive 1 mile; then turn right onto Round Valley Road. After 1.5 miles, the park entrance will be on your left.

GPS COORDINATES: N40° 37.550' W74° 51.215'

19

Spruce Run Recreation Area Campground

Beauty ★★★★ / Privacy ★★ / Spaciousness ★★★ / Quiet ★★★ / Security ★★★ / Cleanliness ★★★★

Spruce Run Reservoir is renowned for its beach and excellent fishing opportunities.

Spruce Run Recreation Area, with its sandy freshwater beach, caters to Central Jersey's sun and water lovers. Fifteen miles of shoreline surround man-made Spruce Run Reservoir, one of the largest reservoirs in New Jersey. Most of the land around the lake is part of the 1,475-acre Clinton Wildlife Management Area, which is undeveloped and almost exclusively dedicated to wildlife or recreation.

The campground and day-use facilities are located on two peninsulas that jut into the water from the northern side of the lake. The campground lies at the tip of the larger peninsula and consists of three loops set around a large, grassy field. No electrical or water hookups are available, but there is a dump station. The spacious, open sites are used most frequently by multifamily groups who take up multiple sites and don't require privacy barriers. A few sites are shaded, but the real appeal is in the waterfront real estate. Sites along the outer rim of the campground sit directly on the 1,290-acre lake.

Spruce Run's campground may be lacking in shaded areas, but it does not lack conveniences. Both bathhouses contain showers, and the lakeside bath also has a dishwashing station. Additionally, the bathhouse by the swimming beach contains showers as well as changing areas, restrooms, a first aid room, and concessions.

One of the nice open lakeside sites at Spruce Run Recreation Area

KEY INFORMATION

ADDRESS: 68 Van Syckels Road, Clinton, NJ 08809

OPERATED BY: New Jersey State Park Service

CONTACT: 908-638-8572, njparksandforests .org/parks/spruce.html; reservations: camping.nj.gov

OPEN: April 1–October 31

SITES: 67; sites 19, 20, 25, 28, 29, 32, 44, 46, 48, 50, 53, 58, 60, and 63 are tent-only

EACH SITE HAS: Picnic table, grill, lantern posts

WHEELCHAIR ACCESS: Sites 12, 23, 34, 57, and restroom/showers are ADA-accessible

ASSIGNMENT: First-come, first-served or by reservation (minimum 2 nights)

REGISTRATION: On arrival or online

FACILITIES: Water, flush toilets, showers

PARKING: At campsites; 2-vehicle limit

FEES: New Jersey residents, $20/night; nonresidents, $25/night

---

RESTRICTIONS:

PETS: Prohibited

FIRES: In grills only

ALCOHOL: Prohibited

VEHICLES: Up to 50 feet; no RV hookups

OTHER: Quiet hours 10 p.m.–6 a.m.; 14-day stay limit; 6-person/2-tent site limit; check-in at noon

The beach is open for swimming Memorial Day weekend–Labor Day, when lifeguards are on duty. There is a playground as well as open fields for setting up ball games. Grilling is not allowed on the beach, but there are charcoal grills at the picnic areas. Visitors may bring their own grills to the picnic areas but not to the beach.

Swimmers are only allowed to enter the water from the beach, and not from campsites or boats. The reservoir is famed for its favorable sailing winds, and several sailing events occur at the recreation area. Canoeing, kayaking, and motorized boating (maximum 10 horsepower) are popular. Boating is allowed 24 hours a day. A warning light flashes when wind speeds are too fast to cruise, reminding boaters to get to shore immediately.

Spruce Run Reservoir, along with its tributaries, is renowned for its excellent fishing opportunities. Both boat fishing and shoreline fishing are permitted. Thirty species of fish call the region home, with various types of trout, bass, catfish, and crappie stocked, along with northern pike and tiger muskies. A drawdown has diminished aquatic vegetation, which in turn affected the populations of bass and northern pike, but other species are thriving. For anglers wishing to test their skills at Spruce Run, the New Jersey Division of Fish and Wildlife puts out a free digest that includes informative articles as well as rules and regulations. Pick one up at the visitor center.

Cyclists and runners use the park roadways and grounds, but the only major hiking trail at Spruce Run is a 2.6-mile portion of the Highlands Trail. The bistate trail extends for over 150 miles from Riegelsville, Pennsylvania, on the Delaware River to Storm King Mountain along the Hudson River in New York. The trail is open only to pedestrians and offers the opportunities for day and overnight excursions. Camping along the trail, though, is not permitted, so overnighters will need to make use of bed-and-breakfasts or similar accommodations along the way (for information, visit nynjtc.org/book/highlands-trail-guide). While wandering the trail, keep an eye open for birds. Spruce Run is home to dozens of species. A birding checklist, complete with visual profiles, is available at the visitor center.

In addition to being sought after by picnickers, hikers, anglers, swimmers, boaters, and campers, these Hunterdon County hills are popular with deer, rabbits, ducks, turkeys, and small mammals. Public hunting is allowed in parts of the Clinton Wildlife Management Area during specific periods between September and January, while Spruce Run Recreation Area allows only seasonal waterfowl hunting. Waterfowl hunters are not allowed near the day-use or camping areas. Permits must be obtained for all hunting in New Jersey. Check the *New Jersey Hunting & Trapping Digest*, available at the Spruce Run Visitor Center and online, for details, as hunting seasons change yearly.

Consider a day trip to nearby Clinton, where you can stroll past two historic mills built in the 1700s. The Raritan River flows through town, and the mills flank it where it dips into a wide waterfall. The stone mill is currently used as an art museum, and the red mill houses a Hunterdon County history museum, along with community and school programs. Many of Clinton's original buildings burned down in 1891, but the townspeople immediately began to rebuild. Today the historic center is filled with boutiques and specialty shops.

Special events occur regularly on the Spruce Run grounds, so keep your eyes open for walkathons, triathlons, weddings, watershed cleanup days, and sailing events. But the reservoir, with its beach and fishing opportunities, is worth a visit any time.

Spruce Run Recreation Area Campground

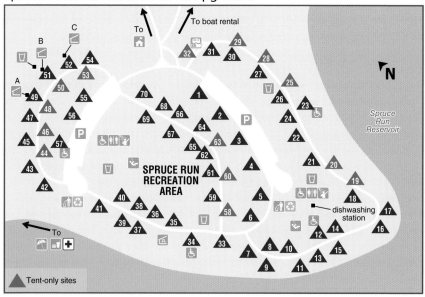

GETTING THERE

From I-78, take Exit 17 for NJ 31 (Clinton/Flemington/Washington). Merge onto NJ 31 North, and drive to the third traffic light; then turn left onto Van Syckels Road, and drive 1.5 miles. The park entrance will be on the left.

GPS COORDINATES: N40° 39.774' W74° 56.325'

20

Stephens State Park Campground

Beauty ★★★★★ / Privacy ★★★★ / Spaciousness ★★★ / Quiet ★★★★★ / Security ★★ / Cleanliness ★★★

Visitors come to commune with nature, to fish, to boat, and to hike ruins of the Morris Canal.

The 40 choice campsites of Stephens State Park lie in an unobtrusive shady valley alongside the Musconetcong River, near the ruins of the Morris Canal. Most are individual clearings set on grass or turf among tall hardwood trees. Sites are level and private, with most visible only from the small loop road and not from adjoining clearings.

Five of Stephens's campsites can accommodate either tents or small trailers. As in many New Jersey state parks, no hookups are available. Only six sites are open; the rest are forested. Many are small, but some can be combined with adjacent sites to form larger units. Use caution when camping on site 5, as it sometimes floods. Avoid sites 1, 2, 28, and 40, as they're next to the road—the campground at Stephens is wooded and feels rural, so avoid this reminder of civilization if at all possible. Site 33 is the most private of all the sites.

There are recently constructed showers at this campground, but visitors don't come to Stephens for the bathhouses—they come to commune with nature, to hike the trails, to fish,

This small island is a perfect place to sit and enjoy the river.

KEY INFORMATION

ADDRESS: 866 Willow Grove St., Hackettstown, NJ 07840

OPERATED BY: New Jersey State Park Service

CONTACT: 908-852-3790, njparksandforests .org/parks/stephens.html; reservations: camping.nj.gov

OPEN: April 1–October 31

SITES: 40; all are tent-only except 1, 4, 5, 22, and 34, which can accommodate either tents or trailers

EACH SITE HAS: Picnic table, fire ring, lantern post

WHEELCHAIR ACCESS: Facilities are partially accessible; contact the park for details

ASSIGNMENT: First-come, first-served or by reservation (minimum 2 nights)

REGISTRATION: On arrival or online

FACILITIES: Water, flush toilets, showers

PARKING: At campsites; 2-vehicle limit

FEES: New Jersey residents, $20/night; nonresidents, $25/night; $5/night pet fee

---

RESTRICTIONS:

PETS: On leash, sites 30–41 only, 2 pets/site; pet permit and proof of current vaccinations required. See njparksandforests.org /parks/pet_friendly_camping.html for more information.

FIRES: In fire rings only

ALCOHOL: Prohibited

VEHICLES: Up to 40 feet; no RV hookups

OTHER: Quiet hours 10 p.m.–6 a.m.; 14-day stay limit; 6-person/2-tent site limit

and to boat. They come for the Morris Canal and Waterloo Village or to visit neighboring Allamuchy Mountain State Park.

In the 19th century, the 102-mile-long Morris Canal was one of two major transportation arteries that brought anthracite coal east to New York City, returning goods west to Pennsylvania. The other canal, the Delaware and Raritan Canal, fared better—nearly the entire length of the D&R is now a New Jersey state park. By contrast, much of the Morris Canal was demolished. Parts of the former waterway form the bed of the Newark City Subway or the Hudson–Bergen Light Rail, and much of the right-of-way has been transformed into roads or utility lines. Some regional governments and citizens groups have recognized the historical value of the "mountain-climbing canal," which has more elevation changes than any other canal in the world. Development has been halted in favor of preservation and greenways.

Lock 5 West sits at Saxton Falls, less than a mile upstream from Stephens State Park. The towpath alongside it is gradually being restored, and the publicly owned Allamuchy Mountain section of the towpath is the centerpiece for the canal trail, which hopefully will one day extend from Hackettstown to Ledgewood.

Other parts of the towpath have been preserved at Waterloo Village, a restored 19th-century Morris Canal town. Waterloo was an inland port that possessed one of the 23 inclined planes that made the Morris Canal a technological marvel. A National Historic Site, it features a gristmill, sawmill, blacksmith shop, church, school, tavern, and inn. But the boom years of the Morris Canal are not the only ones featured. Revolutionary War–era buildings share space with Lenape Indian huts, in addition to structures from the Morris Canal heyday.

Saxton Falls isn't just recommended for history buffs; it's also popular with anglers. On the first day of trout season, the scene has been described as "mayhem," but it's calm on other days. The Musconetcong (or "Musky") waters are stocked annually with brown, rainbow, and brook trout. Rock bass and sunfish are present in addition to trout, and the occasional eel is caught. In Allamuchy Mountain State Park, largemouth bass, sunfish, perch, and pickerel can be found in the lakes and ponds. Parts of Allamuchy Mountain State Park are open for hunting, subject to the rules and regulations of the New Jersey Division of Fish and Wildlife. Half of 805-acre Stephens is designated "no hunting."

Six miles of marked trails crisscross Stephens State Park, including a 2-mile section of the Highlands Trail, which connects the Delaware River in New Jersey with the Hudson River in New York State. Allamuchy Mountain State Park features 15 miles of trails within the Allamuchy Natural Area, as well as an additional 25 miles of unmarked trails in the park's northern section. Trails within both parks are designated as multiuse and can be used by hikers, equestrians, and cyclists, although some trails are rocky. One 3-mile trail is designated a water trail and follows the Musconetcong River from Waterloo Road to the Saxton Falls Dam.

Stephens is well known for its interpretive nature programs. On weekends and holidays, rangers and naturalists present educational workshops on many topics, including ecology, trees, insects, owls, orienteering, bears, camping safety, and the culture of the Lenape Indian Tribe. Programs are popular with older children as well as with adults.

Stephens State Park Campground

GETTING THERE

From I-80, take Exit 19 for County Road 517 (Hackettstown/Andover/Allamuchy). Drive south on CR 517 for 3.3 miles; then turn left onto Bilby Road, and drive 0.9 mile. Turn left onto Willow Grove Street, and drive 0.2 mile. The park entrance will be on your right.

GPS COORDINATES: N40° 52.507' W74° 48.522'

Teetertown Preserve Campground

Beauty ★★★★★ / Privacy ★★★★★ / Spaciousness ★★★★★ / Quiet ★★★★★ / Security ★★★ / Cleanliness ★★★★★

This is a perfect example of private stewardship of a public park.

Local families will love these serene wilderness sites tucked away in this densely wooded haven in Hunterdon County, near the Morris County border. Opened in June of 2003, the five sites of the Mountain Farm section of Teetertown Preserve are spread out along a forest trail. It's a half-mile hike from the parking lot, but campers are rewarded with their own private, tree-lined sanctuaries.

No shortcuts to the sites exist, and campers must carry in all supplies, including water. The inconvenience of the sites is by design, not by accident. The sites are geared toward nature lovers and those seeking a true backcountry experience. Campers hike between 0.5 and 0.75 mile and pass by small mammals, birds, rock outcroppings, and a pond before they get to the sites.

Hikers are rewarded for their efforts when they reach some of the nicest campsites in New Jersey. Sites are spread out across two groups and are isolated from other sites. Paths connect sites within groupings. The sites are distant enough to ensure privacy but close enough to allow multiple sites to be used with a single reservation. Each site has a fireside bench in addition to the standard picnic table and fire ring. Adjustable cooking surfaces sit

Hilltop Site A has a hardened surface, making it wheelchair-accessible.

KEY INFORMATION

ADDRESS: 20 Pleasant Grove Road, Port Murray, NJ 07865

OPERATED BY: Hunterdon County Park System

CONTACT: 908-782-1158, co.hunterdon .nj.us; reservations: call the previous phone number or email parks@co.hunterdon.nj.us

OPEN: Year-round, conditions permitting; weekends only

SITES: 6 tent sites, 4 group sites

EACH SITE HAS: Picnic table, fire ring, bench, firewood

WHEELCHAIR ACCESS: Hilltop Tent Site A and its adjacent portable restroom are wheelchair-accessible

ASSIGNMENT: By reservation only

REGISTRATION: By phone or email

FACILITIES: Portable toilets, water available in parking lot

PARKING: At central lot; hike to sites

FEES: Hunterdon County residents, $10/ night; others, $20/night

---

RESTRICTIONS:

PETS: On leash; must sleep in occupied tent; prohibited in ponds and grasslands

FIRES: Permit required; use firewood supplied

ALCOHOL: Prohibited

VEHICLES: Not applicable (hike-in sites)

OTHER: 6-person/2-tent site limit; collecting downed wood prohibited; camping permitted on weekends only

above the fire rings, and each site accommodates two tents. Two portable toilets are a nod to convenience in this rustic area, as are the mulch tent pads, ground to a fine, powdery base for sleeping comfort.

Hunterdon County's first public camping facility is a perfect example of private stewardship of public parks. The grounds were acquired through the cooperation of multiple public organizations, but the labor was nearly all volunteer. Almost all building materials were recycled from other projects. Materials for the group camping parking lot and the single-lane road that winds through the picnic area, for example, were recycled from remnants of a nearby country road, which was repaved with new materials.

Boy Scout Eagle Service Projects, Mountain Farm Campmaster Corps, Student Conservation Association, students and faculty of the Educational Service Commission at Mountain Farm, park staff, and individual volunteers all worked together to identify and build the camping area, picnic area, and trails. Volunteers cleared the land, dug out hundreds of boulders, framed sections, restored old picnic tables, and graded sites. They surrounded each concrete fireplace base with a 2-foot bed of quarry millings. Volunteers also staff the visitor center on weekends.

Teetertown Preserve, accessed from the camping area on a trail and a steep footpath, is a geologist's paradise. Dense rock called diabase was quarried from the area between 1896 and 1923. Today these rocks, along with a softer type called gneiss, adorn the green ravine. The quiet gorge is bisected by a paved road and bubbling stream. Rock climbing is illegal and strictly prohibited.

When the ravine was a quarry, the rocks were carried out on a purpose-built 1.3-mile-long railroad that went from the ravine to the main Central Railroad line. The small line closed with the quarry, and the last train ran on the Central route in 1976. Today, the main line has been transformed into the Columbia Trail, a 7-mile hiking and biking trail that goes all the way to High Bridge, the weekday terminus of New Jersey Transit's Raritan Valley Line.

Fishing is popular in the small ponds, which have healthy populations of bass and sunfish. Native trout can be found in Hollow Brook. Pond fishing is catch-and-release only.

Sites must be reserved in advance—walk-ins are not accepted—and are open on weekends only, with the earliest check-in allowed on Friday at 5 p.m. Confirm check-in times in advance so that staff or volunteers will be present. Campers must break camp by noon on Sunday but are free to use the trails, ponds, fields, and picnic tables of the preserve until closing time at sunset.

Firewood is included with the fee at Mountain Farm; this is also part of the park's effort to maintain the natural habitat. Small mammals live on the forest floor and use the brush as cover. Don't use the brush and fallen limbs for your fire—use the firewood provided. The usual warnings about bears and ticks apply. Use sensible precautions to make your stay at New Jersey's newest sites an enjoyable one.

Teetertown Preserve Campground

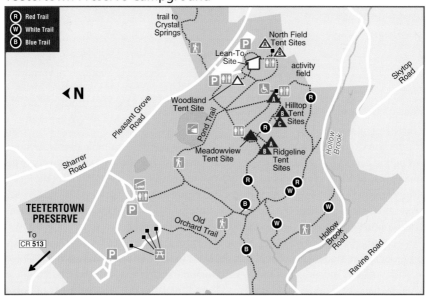

GETTING THERE

From I-78, take Exit 17, and drive north on NJ 31 for 1.7 miles. Turn right onto County Road 513/West Main Street, and drive 1.1 miles. Turn right onto Bridge Street, and then make an almost immediate left onto Main Street (follow the signs for CR 513). After 0.2 mile, turn right onto Church Street, and then make an immediate left onto Fairview Street (still following signs for CR 513). Drive 5.2 miles, during which Fairview Street becomes High Bridge–Califon Road. Turn left onto Sliker Road, and drive 1.6 miles. Turn right onto Pleasant Grove Road, and drive about 1 mile; the entrance to the campground parking and the Crystal Springs section of Teetertown Preserve is on the right.

GPS COORDINATES: N40° 45.393' W74° 51.112'

Triple Brook Camping Resort

Beauty ★★★ / Privacy ★★ / Spaciousness ★★★★ / Quiet ★★★ / Security ★★★★ / Cleanliness ★★★★

Unexpectedly wooded and scenic, Triple Brook offers activities every weekend of its operating season.

Families searching for a compromise between rural seclusion and activities for the younger set should be happy to set up camp at Triple Brook Camping Resort. At first glance, it doesn't seem tent-friendly, since each site can accommodate a small trailer, and all sites have water and electric hookups. No sites are dedicated solely to tent campers, but they are located in spacious wooded clearings. Many sites are hidden from the view of neighbors by lines of trees and foliage. (*Note:* Tent campers may not bring their pets.)

Don't be put off by the sight of dozens of RVs lined up around a sunny field when you first enter the campground. Instead, drive straight down the main road until it ends. To the right is a line of open sites under a line of trees (sites 57–86). These sites are popular with groups or multifamily parties. To the left are several wooded loops. Follow the one-way loop directly to the left as sites become increasingly more private. Finally, as you veer back toward the main road, you'll pass by sites as secluded as any you'll find in New Jersey's lovely public campgrounds. Some sites along Pine Parkway and Fern Lane even sit beside a small creek.

The 250-acre campground is no longer the working farm it once was, but visitors are welcome to visit the resident lambs, rabbits, and ponies near the old farm buildings. Campers can

Some of the sites at Triple Brook are about as streamside as you can get.

ADDRESS: 58 Honey Run Road, Hope, NJ 07825

OPERATED BY: Private

CONTACT: 888-343-2267, triplebrook.com; reservations: call the previous phone number or go to triplebrook.com/reservations

OPEN: April–October

SITES: 220, about 100 of which are appropriate for tents; 8 cabins

EACH SITE HAS: Picnic table, fire ring

WHEELCHAIR ACCESS: Some sites and restrooms; call for more information

ASSIGNMENT: First-come, first-served or by reservation (minimum 2 nights)

REGISTRATION: On arrival or by phone/email

FACILITIES: Water, flush toilets, showers, laundry room

PARKING: At campsites; 1-vehicle limit/ wooded site; additional parking in lot

FEE: $47/night (2 people)

RESTRICTIONS:

PETS: RV guests only; see website for rules

FIRES: In fire rings only

ALCOHOL: Permitted at campsites but prohibited at pools

VEHICLES: No stated length limits

OTHER: Quiet hours 11 p.m.–8 a.m. (lights and music must be turned off); 2-night minimum stay (3-night minimum on holiday weekends); don't feed farm animals

still experience some of the activities typically associated with rural life, including hayrides, horseshoes, and arts-and-crafts activities through the campground's extensive weekend programming. Triple Brook offers activities every weekend of their operating season.

Catch-and-release fishing is allowed in the small pond, which offers an excellent opportunity to introduce young aspiring anglers to the art of fishing. The use of barbed hooks is prohibited. No glass containers are allowed by the lake.

Triple Brook also features a miniature golf course, swimming pool, small adults-only pool, adults-only spa, volleyball net, basketball court, horseshoe pit, and tennis court. A few cabins and rental RVs are available in addition to the many campsites.

Triple Brook is centrally located near many of central Jersey's star attractions. Jenny Jump State Forest (see page 63) is a short drive away, with its hiking trails and Saturday-night public access to the United Astronomy Clubs observatory. The Delaware Water Gap (see pages 26 and 29), with trails, canoeing, and fishing, is only 7 miles away. The Lakota Wolf Preserve at Camp Taylor (see page 20) is nearby, and New York City is an hour's drive to the east. Other local attractions include the Land of Make Believe amusement park, horse and pony

One of Triple Brook's adorable ponies

stables, and the village of Hope. Originally a religious Moravian settlement, Hope is on the New Jersey and National Registers of Historic Places. For those interested in antiquing and flea markets, the area has no shortage of places to indulge your passion.

Anglers can take an interesting day trip 7 miles away to the Pequest Trout Hatchery. The center is open daily, except on holidays, from 10 a.m. to 4 p.m. Visitors watch a video that demonstrates the trout-raising process and then can view the real thing.

Triple Brook, in the foothills of the Kittatinny Mountains, is not the right place for campers looking for a weekend of solitude and stargazing. But for families needing entertainment options along with their natural retreat, it offers a great balance between the outdoors and organized activities.

Triple Brook Camping Resort

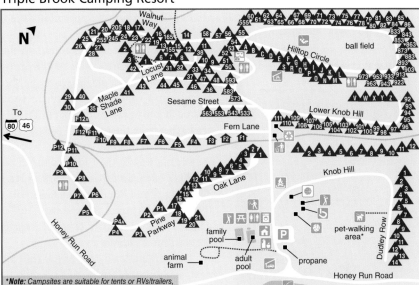

Note: Campsites are suitable for tents or RVs/trailers, but pets are prohibited in tents and cabins.

GETTING THERE

From I-80 West, take Exit 12 for County Road 521 (Hope/Blairstown). Turn left on Hope Blairstown Road, and drive 1.2 miles to the stop sign. Turn right onto High Street/CR 609, and drive 3.1 miles. Turn right onto Nightingale Road, and drive 1.1 miles. Turn right onto Honey Run Road, and drive 0.4 mile. The campground entrance will be on your left.

From I-80 East, take Exit 4B for US 46 East (Portland, PA/Buttzville). Drive 3.4 miles on US 46 East. Turn left onto Knowlton Road/CR 616, and drive 2.7 miles. Turn right onto Nightingale Road, and drive 0.4 mile. Turn left onto Honey Run Road, and drive 0.4 mile. The campground entrance will be on your left.

GPS COORDINATES: N40° 54.719' W75° 01.092'

Voorhees State Park Campground

Beauty ★★★★ / Privacy ★★★★ / Spaciousness ★★★ / Quiet ★★★★ / Security ★★★ / Cleanliness ★★★

The CCC built many of the trails, trees, and structures at Voorhees in the 1930s.

Nestled in the hills north of High Bridge is forested Voorhees State Park, former home to ex-Governor Foster M. Voorhees as well as to the Civilian Conservation Corps (CCC). Currently, the 640-acre park houses recreational sites, natural areas, and the New Jersey Astronomical Association Observatory.

The campground has no hookups, but this doesn't stop small-RV owners from driving up the hill to the grassy sites. Tent campers may initially be dismayed by the sunny, open field and the trailers. Don't be fooled—follow the small road as it disappears into the trees behind a NO RVS sign. The sites beyond are shady, secluded, and green.

Three roads cross a triangle housing two dozen wooded alcoves. Continue to the far loop, on the north side of the field, to find the most private area. Sites 42–48 are small clearings carved out of wild vines and shrubs, set against a wilderness that seems ready to encroach on unaware campers. These sites are farther from the restroom facilities but are ideal for those desiring solitude.

On the way to the campground, a scenic overlook offers an expansive view of Hunterdon County and Round Valley Reservoir. Farther along Hill Acres Road is the Vista Trail, which leads to another overlook that faces Spruce Run Reservoir.

The parking lot by the Vista Trail is also next to the trailhead for the 1.5-mile Cross Park Trail, a pedestrian-only trail that connects the northern and southern parts of Voorhees. Cross Park Trail is part of the 150-mile Highlands Trail, which, when completed, will connect the Delaware River in New Jersey with the Hudson River in New York. Hikers can also try the 5 miles of trails at nearby Hacklebarney State Park.

Voorhees's only other pedestrian-only trail is the 1-mile Parcourse Circuit, a fitness route with 18 exercise stations. The remaining five trails are designated as multiuse, but most are too short for a satisfying bike ride. If you bring your bike, try combining Hill Acres Trail with the Brookside–Tanglewood Loop. Swimming is prohibited in Willoughby Brook

The red color of the pine needles suggests that this tree might not be in the best of health.

KEY INFORMATION

ADDRESS: Observatory Road, Clinton, NJ 08809

OPERATED BY: New Jersey State Park Service

CONTACT: 908-638-8572, njparksandforests .org/parks/voorhees.html; reservations: camping.nj.gov

OPEN: April 1–October 31

SITES: 47 (tent-only except sites 1–4 and 37–40), plus 2 group sites and 3 lean-tos

EACH SITE HAS: Picnic table, fire ring

WHEELCHAIR ACCESS: Site 8

ASSIGNMENT: First-come, first-served or by reservation (minimum 2 nights)

REGISTRATION: On arrival or online

FACILITIES: Currently only portable toilets, dishwashing facility, and potable water; campers may use showers at nearby Spruce Run Recreation Area (see page 70).

PARKING: At campsites

FEES: New Jersey residents, $20/night; nonresidents, $25/night

---

RESTRICTIONS:

PETS: Prohibited

FIRES: In fire rings only

ALCOHOL: Prohibited

VEHICLES: Up to 42 feet; no RV hookups

OTHER: Quiet hours 10 p.m.–6 a.m.; 14-day stay limit; 6-person/2-tent site limit

---

and in Voorhees's tiny ponds. Instead, campers may use the swimming beach at Spruce Run Recreation Area (see page 70).

Anglers can test their skills on the wild trout in Willoughby Brook. Chefs are not so lucky; all fish caught in the stream must be released. Children can fish in two ponds in the park where bass and bluegill are often caught. Between September and January, two-thirds of the park is open to hunting, which is subject to regulation. Check with a ranger.

If you visit Voorhees State Park on a summer weekend, be sure to visit the observatory. The Paul Robinson Observatory at the Buzz Aldrin Astronomical Center (named after the second man on the moon, a Montclair native) opens its doors to the public on summer Saturday nights between 8:30 p.m. and 10:30 p.m. and on Sunday afternoons. Visitors can look through a 26-inch Cassegrain reflector telescope (the largest telescope in New Jersey that offers public access) or through a number of smaller telescopes. Astronomers request that visitors dim their headlights upon entering the center's parking area.

Voorhees State Park is a carry-in/carry-out park, as are many New Jersey public areas. Day

The Paul Robinson Observatory is a short walk from the campground at Voorhees. Here you will find a very informative Star Walk about the natural history of the solar system.

visitors are given trash bags when they enter the park and are asked to take their trash home for disposal; campers can leave their rubbish and recycling in designated bins at the campground. Do not leave trash or food around your campsite or in your tent, and pay attention to warnings of bears. See the Introduction for more information on how to camp safely in bear country.

The CCC built many of the trails, trees, and structures at Voorhees in the 1930s, right after former Governor Voorhees donated his 325-acre farm to New Jersey. The Voorhees camp housed as many as 200 members of Franklin D. Roosevelt's "tree army"—unemployed young men sent to remote areas to work on conservation projects in response to the Great Depression. It was one of the most successful New Deal programs. Over the nine years it existed, the CCC built more than 40,000 bridges, planted 2 billion trees, improved or built thousands of structures and roads, and created 800 state parks across the country.

FDR's "army with shovels" would be amazed today. While still suitably rustic and rural in appearance, Voorhees can no longer be considered remote. A New Jersey Transit train from the nearby picturesque town of High Bridge whisks daily commuters to Manhattan in an hour and a half.

Voorhees State Park Campground

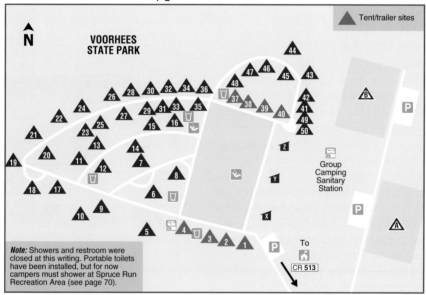

Note: Showers and restroom were closed at this writing. Portable toilets have been installed, but for now campers must shower at Spruce Run Recreation Area (see page 70).

GETTING THERE

From I-78, take Exit 17 for NJ 31 North. Merge onto NJ 31 North, and drive 3.2 miles. Turn right onto Cregar Road. Drive 1.3 miles, and turn left onto Fairview Avenue/CR 513. Drive 0.6 mile; then turn left onto Observatory Road to head to the campground, on the right.

GPS COORDINATES: N40° 40.922' W74° 53.697'

EAST
CENTRAL
NEW JERSEY

Pakim Pond at sunset (see Brendan T. Byrne State Forest Camping Area, page 93)

Allaire State Park Campground

Beauty ★★★ / Privacy ★★ / Spaciousness ★★★ / Quiet ★★★ / Security ★★★ / Cleanliness ★★★

The roar of civilization seems far from the campground, although historic Allaire Village is only a mile away.

In 1822, businessman James P. Allaire headed south from Manhattan to found the Howell Works on an industrial bog iron–processing area that had been active since 1793. His integrated mining, smelting, and forging business thrived for a few decades, with more than 400 people living on company land during the 1830s. The self-contained private community of Howell Works included homes, a church, a school, and service businesses such as a general store, blacksmith shop, carpenter's shop, and a bakery.

By the 1850s, bog furnaces were well on their way to extinction. Howell Works became a ghost town and was later used as a movie studio, a French restaurant, and a Boy Scout camp before volunteers began restoring it in the 1950s. Today Howell Works is called Allaire Village and is an outdoor living-history museum within Allaire State Park.

Today, the only residents of Allaire live in its campground for a maximum of two consecutive weeks. The tranquil campground, more than a mile away from the village and central activity area, consists of four small loops around a central bathhouse and playground.

The 45 campsites can be used for tents or small trailers, but the only concession to motorized camping is the dump station located near the entrance. There are no electrical or water hookups, but there are four yurts and six cabinlike shelters; these contain bunks and locking doors but no running water or electricity. Shelters feature woodstoves for those months when sleeping in a tent in the northeastern winter is unadvisable.

Tent sites are spacious, with varying degrees of privacy. Most are shaded, but there is little undergrowth or shrubbery between sites inside the loops. Try to get a site along the outer loop edges. Sites 23–26 are particularly large and spacious and are worth trying to reserve in advance if possible. All are within comfortable walking distance of the bathhouse and pay phone.

Allaire's campground is open year-round, but Allaire Village keeps seasonal hours. Most of the historic buildings are open Wednesday–Sunday

A mountain biker takes a break along one of the many trails at Allaire State Park.

KEY INFORMATION

ADDRESS: Atlantic Avenue, Howell, NJ 07731

OPERATED BY: New Jersey State Park Service

CONTACT: 732-938-2371, njparksandforests .org/parks/allaire.html; reservations: camping.nj.gov

OPEN: Year-round

SITES: 45 tent/trailer sites, 4 yurts, 6 lean-tos

EACH SITE HAS: Picnic table, fire ring

WHEELCHAIR ACCESS: Restrooms and yurts are accessible

ASSIGNMENT: First-come, first-served or by reservation (minimum 2 nights)

REGISTRATION: On arrival or online

FACILITIES: Water, flush toilets, showers

PARKING: At campsites; 2-vehicle limit

FEES: New Jersey residents, $20/night; nonresidents, $25/night; $5/night pet fee

RESTRICTIONS:

PETS: On leash, sites 1–8 and 13–22 only, 2 pets/site; pet permit and proof of current vaccinations required. See njparksandforests.org/parks/pet_friendly _camping.html for more information.

FIRES: In fire rings only

ALCOHOL: Prohibited

VEHICLES: No RV hookups

OTHER: Quiet hours 10 p.m.–6 a.m.; 14-day stay limit; 6-person/2-tent site limit

during summer but only on weekends in the fall. The general store and bakery open earlier in the season and stay open until December. Some holidays and weekends feature special events, such as hayrides, antique shows, or period-dress re-creations. Visit allaire.org for information on hours and events at the village.

The other man-made attraction within Allaire is the Pine Creek Railroad, New Jersey's only narrow-gauge preservation train. Pine Creek Railroad runs under its own steam on summer weekends and during the December holiday season but is diesel-powered in spring, fall, and on summer weekdays. Celebrities such as Santa Claus and the Easter Bunny have been known to join the crowds for the 10-minute, 1.5-mile whirl around the park during holiday seasons.

The park also features more traditional state park offerings. Allaire's 3,086 acres include hiking, bridle, and biking trails along with opportunities for boating, fishing, and birding. The state-run Spring Meadow Golf Course is adjacent to the park. Cross-country skiing is allowed in winter, and limited deer hunting is allowed seasonally.

Much of the park has been left in its natural state as a habitat for wildlife and plants. Several trails wind through the forest, but when visiting, you are encouraged to stick to official blazed trails to avoid damaging both the environment and yourself (say, by getting bitten by a tick carrying Lyme disease). So always stay on the trail and, in summer, do a full-body tick check after each foray into the woods.

Yellow-, red-, and green-blazed trails are easy trails designated for pedestrians only. The 16.5-mile-long orange-blazed trail is the official multiuse track, although some cyclists have complained that sand on the trail makes it less than appealing.

An easy ride begins right near the park visitor center where cyclists can hop on the path of the old Freehold and Jamesburg Agricultural Railroad line. The purple-blazed trail extends for 2 miles to the park boundary where it joins the Edgar Felix Bicycle Path. That path continues for another 5 miles to the center of the seaside town of Manasquan. It will eventually be part of New Jersey's Capital to the Coast Trail, a projected 55-mile bike path that will link Trenton and the Atlantic Coast via a scenic greenway.

The Manasquan River winds through the park and is stocked seasonally with trout. Anglers have reportedly caught sea-run brown trout as large as four pounds within Allaire, which has three stocking points. Canoeing and kayaking the east-running river is also popular. Several boat rental agencies are nearby.

When James P. Allaire purchased Howell Works, he lobbied hard for better transportation connections between Monmouth County and New York City. He'd be pleased if he were alive today. His former company is not only a destination in and of itself, but it is also conveniently located at the nexus of two major highways, I-195 and the Garden State Parkway. But you wouldn't know it from within the campground. The roar of civilization is far away from the shaded sites.

Allaire State Park Campground

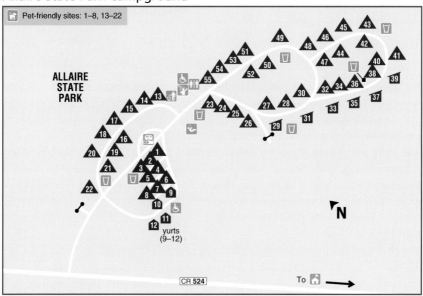

GETTING THERE

From the Garden State Parkway, take Exit 98 for I-195 West. Merge onto I-195 West, and then follow the directions below.

From I-195, take Exit 31B for County Road 547/CR 524. Merge onto Lakewood Farmingdale Road, and almost immediately turn right onto Allaire Road. In 0.4 mile, the campground entrance will be on your left.

GPS COORDINATES: N40° 09.929' W 74° 08.800'

Bass River State Forest:
NORTH SHORE CAMPGROUND

Beauty ★★★★ / Privacy ★★★ / Spaciousness ★★★★ / Quiet ★★★ / Security ★★★ / Cleanliness ★★★

This century-old state forest in New Jersey features wooded campsites near a 67-acre lake.

New Jersey's first state forest has come a long way since it was acquired in 1905. The Civilian Conservation Corps (CCC) altered the landscape significantly in the 1930s, when they planted 4,500 acres of trees. When they dammed two streams and constructed the park's centerpiece, Lake Absegami, a public park was born.

More than 110 years later, the lake is surrounded by 176 campsites, 6 cabins, 6 lean-tos, 9 primitive shelters, and 6 group sites. Eighty-three campsites line the thin loop that comprises the South Shore Campground. A separate loop sits on the farther bank, housing 93 additional sites at the North Shore Campground.

All sites are wooded and shady, with convenient access to modern facilities. Both loops have a central bathhouse that includes laundry and shower facilities in addition to sinks and toilets. The cabins and lean-tos sit on Lake Absegami's north shore.

Hardwood and pine trees grow along the shore of Absegami Lake.

KEY INFORMATION

ADDRESS: 762 Stage Road, Tuckerton, NJ 08087

OPERATED BY: New Jersey State Park Service

CONTACT: 609-296-1114, njparksandforests .org/parks/bass.html; reservations: camping .nj.gov

OPEN: Year-round

SITES: 176, plus 6 cabins, 6 lean-tos, 9 shelters, and 6 group sites

EACH SITE HAS: Picnic table, fire ring

WHEELCHAIR ACCESS: Sites 173 and 175, restrooms, and showers

ASSIGNMENT: First-come, first-served or by reservation (minimum 2 nights)

REGISTRATION: On arrival or online

FACILITIES: Water, flush toilets, showers, laundry room

PARKING: At campsites; 2-vehicle limit

FEES: New Jersey residents, $20/night; nonresidents, $25/night; $5/night pet fee

---

RESTRICTIONS:

PETS: Prohibited at North Shore but welcome at South Shore (sites 1–85)

FIRES: In fire rings only

ALCOHOL: Prohibited

VEHICLES: No RV hookups

OTHER: Quiet hours 10 p.m.–6 a.m.; 14-day stay limit; 6-person, 2-tent limit

Campsites are level and spacious enough that neighbors may be visible, but campers aren't exactly piling tents on top of each other. Insects are savage here, so bring bug spray or be prepared to involuntarily be their dinner. Both campgrounds are at least a half mile from the swimming beach, to which campers enjoy free access. Note that the South Shore Campground sits within earshot of Stage Road, which vehicles use at all hours.

Bass River State Forest is just a 20-minute drive from the seaside resort towns of Long Beach Island. Atlantic City is 25 miles to the southeast, but Bass River, with its swimming, boating, fishing, and trails, is a destination unto itself.

When lifeguards are on duty, swimming is allowed at the designated swimming beach on the eastern side of 67-acre Lake Absegami. Lifeguards usually patrol the swimming beach from 10 a.m. to 6 p.m. between Memorial Day weekend and Labor Day; early in the season, the park staff recommends calling ahead to confirm opening hours. The swimming beach complex includes a modern full-service bath-house, first aid station, refreshment stand, and beach-supplies concession. A playground is nearby, along with picnic facilities and a park-ing lot. Note that the beach gets very busy on summer weekends, and the park will close the gates once the capacity of automobiles in the parking area has been reached (they count cars, not the number of people in them). Although campers are always allowed at the beach, day visitors should plan to get here early and have a Plan B on holiday weekends in the event that they can't get into the beach.

Camp among the sand and pines at Bass River State Forest.

A summer rowboat concession and boat launch are also located near the swimming beach. Canoes and kayaks are available for rent in nearby towns. Gas-powered engines are prohibited on Lake Absegami; powerboats are limited to using electric motors. Occupants of all boats must wear life preservers.

Five self-guided hiking trails are located near the campgrounds; all begin in the parking lot near the swimming beach and vary in length from 1 mile to 3.2 miles. Additionally, a 0.5-mile trail runs from the entrance road through the 28-acre Absegami Natural Area. Here you can view a typical cross section of local pinelands. Oak and pine trees tower over a small white cedar bog. An interpretive center at the South Shore Campground provides information on the local ecosystem.

Other hiking trails are designated by colored blazes. The pink-blazed trail is the longest, at 3.2 miles; it crosses Stage Road and passes the CCC/Forest Fire Service Memorial. (The Bass River area has had at least four major fires: in 1936, five CCC workers died fighting a 58,000-acre fire near Bass River, and in 1977, four volunteer firefighters died fighting a 2,300-acre fire in Bass River State Forest.)

The 50-mile-long Batona Trail terminates near the South Shore Campground, at the inter-

A freshwater pond in the state forest

section of Stage and Coal Roads. This level, easy wilderness trail traverses the Pinelands between Brendan T. Byrne and Bass River State Forests. Horses and mountain bikes are prohibited on Batona Trail—it's strictly for hikers.

Miles of sand and gravel roads winding through the forest are open to hiking, biking, horseback riding, and motorized vehicle use. Snowmobiles may use some of the roads in winter. Many roads are marked and can be found on the park map, available at the forest office. Some roads can be wet and muddy. Seek local information first; use caution and common sense before driving into the wilderness.

Fishing is allowed in Lake Absegami as well as in nearby streams and rivers. Pickerel, sunfish, and catfish have been caught at Bass River, but fish are not plentiful. All visitors age 16 and older must get a license before fishing. Both licenses and bait are available nearby.

During the summer, local nature groups and park personnel present films and interpretive programs; past offerings have included films, slideshows, stargazing evenings, and full-moon hikes. Information is provided on the Pinelands, the Bass River, and the 3,830-acre West Pine Plains Natural Area (aka Pygmy Pines), also found within Bass River State Forest. Check with the park office for current information. Throughout the year, interpretive programing includes the Wednesday Walk in the Woods series. These 5- to 8-mile walks, led by a volunteer naturalist, take place once or twice a month and focus on a seasonal aspect of the park's ecology.

It's been more than 100 years since the state of New Jersey established Bass River State Forest. Today, the park is a model of success in the areas of public recreation, water conservation, wildlife, and forest management.

Bass River State Forest: North Shore Campground

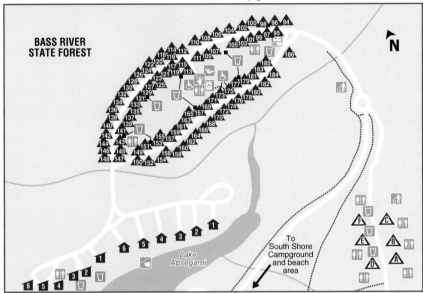

GETTING THERE

Heading southbound on the Garden State Parkway, take Exit 52 for New Gretna. Turn right onto East Greenbush Road, and drive 1.1 miles. Turn right onto Stage Road, and drive 0.8 mile. The park entrance will be on your left.

Heading northbound on the Garden State Parkway, take Exit 50 for US 9 North/New Gretna. Continue onto US 9 North, and drive 1.5 miles. Turn left onto North Maple Avenue, and drive 1.5 miles; then turn right to stay on North Maple Avenue. Drive 0.7 mile; then turn right onto Stage Road. In 1.2 miles, the park entrance will be on your left.

GPS COORDINATES: N39° 37.233' W74° 25.471'

Brendan T. Byrne State Forest Camping Area

Beauty ★★★★ / Privacy ★★★★ / Spaciousness ★★★★ / Quiet ★★★★ / Security ★★★★ / Cleanliness ★★★★

These northernmost Pine Barrens sites are located near old cranberry bogs.

The clean scent of pine permeates the air at Brendan T. Byrne State Forest Camping Area, reminding visitors that they are in the 1.1-million-acre Pinelands National Reserve, a unique protected ecosystem. Eighty-two wooded sites on three flat, sandy loops make up this northernmost Pinelands campground. Like all state campgrounds in New Jersey, this one has no RV hookups, although there is a sanitation dump. Yurts sit permanently on a small loop off of Coopers Road, providing accommodation for campers who do not own tents and for those who need wheelchair-accessible accommodations. Three cabins, located near Pakim Pond, are also available. Cabin tenants share the campground showers in the two modern bathhouses, but the cabins do feature indoor toilets and sinks.

Shrubbery between sites gives the illusion of privacy, but the understory and surrounding forest is less dense than in northern and southwestern Jersey. This is mostly due to environmental differences in spite of the region's history. The forest was clear-cut by Lebanon Glass Works between 1851 and 1867, but you can't tell from today's preponderance of tall trees. The Civilian Conservation Corps replanted the area during the Great Depression.

Lebanon Glass Works employed about 150 men in its heyday, and a small town grew up to support them. The availability of sand and wood for the furnaces provided the ideal situation for the manufacturers of glass for windows and bottles. The glass factory thrived until the forest was depleted. Once the wood ran out, the town was abandoned. The remains of the town can be seen on trails in the form of stone or brick structures and large depressions.

The dam on Pakim Pond

KEY INFORMATION

ADDRESS: Coopers Road, Vincentown, NJ 08088

OPERATED BY: New Jersey State Park Service

CONTACT: 609-726-1191, njparksandforests .org/parks/byrne.html; reservations: camping.nj.gov

OPEN: Year-round

SITES: 82, plus 3 yurts and 3 group sites

EACH SITE HAS: Picnic table, fire ring

WHEELCHAIR ACCESS: Restrooms/showers and yurts are accessible

ASSIGNMENT: First-come, first-served or by reservation (minimum 2 nights)

REGISTRATION: On arrival or online

FACILITIES: Water, flush toilets, showers, laundry room

PARKING: At campsites; 2-vehicle limit

FEES: New Jersey residents, $20/night; nonresidents, $25/night; $5/night pet fee

---

RESTRICTIONS:

PETS: On leash, all sites except 1–13, 2 pets/ site; pet permit and proof of current vaccinations required. See njparksandforests.org /parks/pet_friendly_camping.html for more information.

FIRES: In fire rings only

ALCOHOL: Prohibited

VEHICLES: No RV hookups

OTHER: Quiet hours 10 p.m.–6 a.m.; 14-day stay limit; 6-person/2-tent site limit

The buildings of Whitesbog Village, a turn-of-the-20th-century berry-processing town at the northern end of the park, fared better. While the workers' homes were bulldozed in the early 1970s, the central village area is still standing, and much of it has been restored. Whitesbog was once the center for New Jersey cranberry processing, as well as the first place in the state where blueberries were successfully cultivated. As harvesting technologies became less reliant on human workers, however, the need for a village to house them became less important. Today, New Jersey ranks third in the nation in cranberry production, and some cranberry bogs in the forest are still active. Whitesbog Village is open daily.

More than 30 miles of marked trails crisscross 34,725-acre Brendan T. Byrne State Forest, including 10 miles of the 50-mile Batona Trail. This wilderness hiking trail cuts across Wharton State Forest and Bass River State Forest, in addition to Byrne, allowing hikers to traverse the Pinelands (locally called the Pine Barrens). The pink-blazed path is mostly level, with a few small hills and some wet areas. Hikers may camp only at designated campgrounds. No horses or mountain bikes are permitted on Batona Trail.

Mount Misery Trail, an 8.5-mile loop from Mount Misery to Pakim Pond, does allow mountain bikes, as do the 10.8-mile Bike Trail and 2.7-mile Cranberry Trail. The Bike Trail begins and ends at NJ 70, though riders can pick it up at the Forest Office and make a loop through the forest using a 1.5-mile cutoff trail that precludes having to head out to the highway. Wheelchairs can also be used on the Cranberry Trail, which is paved. Horses are permitted on all sand and gravel roads within the forest. In winter, cross-country skiers use some of the trails. A trails map is available at the office.

Three of the trails—Cranberry, Mount Misery, and Batona—cut across the Cedar Swamp Natural Area, a 735-acre Pine Barrens in miniature. Most of the trees and plants of the Pinelands are represented, including upland pine and oak, lowland pitch pine, Atlantic white cedar, and swamp pink. The area also supports two New Jersey endangered lilies and a similarly endangered rush.

Hikers, campers, and other recreational users are reminded that ticks and biting deer fleas populate the area. Ticks can carry Lyme disease, so take precautions (see Introduction for more information).

Motorized vehicles are allowed on more than 50 miles of unmarked gravel and sand roads. Acceptable vehicles include four-wheel-drive autos, motorcycles, and snowmobiles. It's possible to become bogged down in sand or water on backcountry roads, so motorists should not travel alone and should be prepared. All-terrain vehicles and unlicensed vehicles are prohibited.

Swimming in 5-acre Pakim Pond is not allowed, but visitors may fish and canoe here, as well as in forest streams.

Brendan T. Byrne State Forest was known as Lebanon State Forest until it was renamed in honor of a former governor in 2002. (Byrne was governor of New Jersey during most of the 1970s, a tumultuous time in New Jersey history.) The forest is referred to as Lebanon State Forest in older publications, but even some new references still use the older name. Either way, the campground in this state forest is worth a stop.

Brendan T. Byrne State Forest Camping Area

GETTING THERE

From I-295 North, take Exit 40A, merge onto NJ 38 East, and drive 9.7 miles. Continue straight onto South Pemberton Road, and drive 2.8 miles. Turn right onto Magnolia Road, and drive 6.8 miles. At the traffic circle, take the second exit onto NJ 72 East, and drive 4.1 miles. Turn left (north) onto Glass Works Road; the campground is 0.8 mile straight ahead.

Heading southbound on the New Jersey Turnpike, take Exit 7. Merge onto US 206 South, and drive 11.9 miles. Turn left onto South Pemberton Road, and continue as above to reach the campground.

GPS COORDINATES: N39° 52.334' W74° 31.274'

Camp Gateway, Sandy Hook

Beauty ★★★ / Privacy ★★ / Spaciousness ★★★ / Quiet ★★★ / Security ★★★ / Cleanliness ★★★

With the opening of Camp Gateway, New Jersey now has its own distinctive tent-only campground by the ocean.

With the opening of its campground in 2012, Camp Gateway became the closest tent campground to the New York City metropolitan area. Nestled away near the beach at Horseshoe Cove in Sandy Hook, the campground consists of 20 tent-only campsites. Plan your trip and reserve well in advance, because these sites get booked very early in the season. Each site has a picnic table, a fire ring, a grill, and—most importantly—a shelter under which you can get a little shade and escape the sun, which can be pretty intense along this stretch of the northern New Jersey coast.

First developed in 1972, the 27,000-acre Gateway National Recreation Area consists of three geographic units in New York and New Jersey, each of which has both historic and natural value. In New York, the Jamaica Bay Unit includes the Jamaica Bay Wildlife Refuge, Fort Tilden, and Jacob Riis Park in Queens, as well as two sites in Brooklyn. The Staten Island Unit includes Great Kills Park, Miller Field, and Fort Wadsworth. The Sandy Hook Unit in New Jersey occupies a barrier island with several beaches and salt marshes, the historic site of Fort Hancock, and the Sandy Hook Lighthouse.

Constructed in 1764, the iconic lighthouse is certainly the most visited and photographed site at Sandy Hook. Although it's no longer manned, its light still shines as a guide to boats passing into New York Harbor and is the oldest operating lighthouse in the United States. The Keeper's House, next door to the lighthouse, now also serves as the park office, and you'll need to pick up your camping permit here. Tours of the lighthouse are free and run daily from 1 p.m. until 4:30 p.m.; children must be at least 48 inches tall so that they can climb the stairs to the top.

Given its location at the mouth of New York Harbor, Sandy Hook has played an important defensive role in the history of American

The lighthouse at Sandy Hook and the adjacent museum are worth the visit to learn about the area.

KEY INFORMATION

ADDRESS: 26 Hudson Road, Highlands, NJ 07732

OPERATED BY: National Park Service

CONTACT: 718-354-4606, nps.gov/gate; reservations: 855-607-3075, reserveamerica.com or 877-444-6777, recreation.gov

OPEN: May 1–October 9

SITES: 20

EACH SITE HAS: Picnic table, fire ring, grill, sun shelter

WHEELCHAIR ACCESS: Portable toilet and site A-1 are ADA-accessible

ASSIGNMENT: First-come, first-served or by reservation (recommended)

REGISTRATION: Register at Keeper's House at Sandy Hook Lighthouse (open daily, 9 a.m.–5 p.m.)

FACILITIES: Water, portable toilet

PARKING: In parking lot; 1-vehicle limit

FEE: $30/night, $15/vehicle beach-parking fee in summer

RESTRICTIONS:

PETS: Prohibited

FIRES: In fire rings only

ALCOHOL: Prohibited

VEHICLES: Not applicable (walk-in sites)

OTHER: Check-in at noon, checkout 10 a.m.; 14-day stay-limit; 6-person/2-tent site limit; must walk to sites from parking lot

---

military encounters. During the American Revolution, British Loyalists occupied the land to ensure access of British naval ships to the harbor. The area was strengthened during the War of 1812. In 1857, the U.S. Army Corps of Engineers began constructing the fort at Sandy Hook, which was designed by Robert E. Lee, who was a captain at the time. The original fort was never officially named or completed. During the 1870s, the Sandy Hook area became a proving ground used for ordnance testing, and much of the original fort was destroyed as the proving grounds became more established. In 1890, the construction of a seawall and new fort began. In 1895 it was named Fort Hancock after Major General Winfield Scott Hancock.

The site remained active continually until 1950, when it was determined to be obsolete. It was reactivated and deactivated several times during the early 1950s, eventually becoming a Nike missile base during the Cold War in 1956; the site was permanently decommissioned in 1974 after the Nike defense system was abandoned. Visitors to Sandy Hook can now walk the streets of Fort Hancock's Officers' Row, whose abandoned buildings look out over Raritan Bay, and take in views of the old batteries that line some of the roads at the tip of Sandy Hook. The National Park Service offers tours of the old Nike missile radar site near the campground from time to time.

In addition to the historical sites that one can visit at Sandy Hook, the recreation area has its share of oceanfront, some of which is open to swimming from Memorial Day to Labor Day, but only when lifeguards are present. The bay side of the island provides

Some of the old structures along Officer's Row at Fort Morgan

protected waters where you can take out a kayak and explore some of the coastline from the vantage of the water. Boat rentals are available in Atlantic Highlands on the mainland, as are several very good seafood restaurants. Birders will appreciate the variety of seabirds and waterfowl that can be seen at Sandy Hook.

Cyclists, hikers, and in-line skaters will enjoy the 7-mile Multi-Use Pathway, which runs the length of the recreation area. The National Park Service sponsors a host of natural and historical programs and activities throughout the year. Fishing is also a popular activity at Sandy Hook, and often at night. Campers don't need a night-fishing permit but must show their camping permit if asked.

Camp Gateway, Sandy Hook

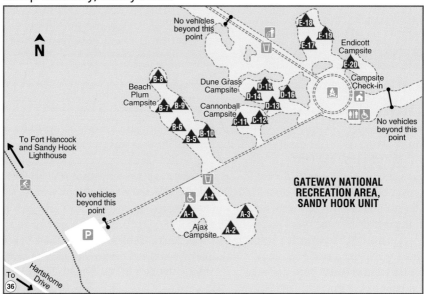

GETTING THERE

From the Garden State Parkway, take Exit 109 for County Road 520/Red Bank/Lincroft. Turn left onto Half Mile Road, and drive 0.5 mile. Turn right onto West Front Street, and drive 0.8 mile. Turn left onto Hubbard Avenue, and drive 0.6 mile. Turn right onto Navesink River Road, and drive 4.9 miles. Turn right onto Locust Avenue, and drive 0.4 mile. Turn right onto Monmouth Avenue, and then almost immediately make a slight left onto Navesink Avenue. Drive 0.9 mile; then turn right onto NJ 36 South, and drive 1.7 miles. Keep right and follow signs for Sandy Hook; then merge onto Hartshorne Drive. Drive north about 4.5 miles, following the road to its end, and look for the lighthouse. The visitor center, where you'll pick up your camping permit, is next to the lighthouse. Then return south on Hartshorne Drive and, in 1.3 miles, turn left into the campground parking lot.

GPS COORDINATES: N40° 26.217' W73° 59.327'

Cheesequake State Park Campground

Beauty ★★★ / Privacy ★★★ / Spaciousness ★★★★ / Quiet ★★★ / Security ★★★ / Cleanliness ★★★★

This is a great base for traveling campers who want to tour New York City.

Cheesequake is the most urban state park in the densest, most urbanized state in the country. A mere 36 miles from Manhattan, its wooded and marsh 1,292 acres play host to swimmers, anglers, hikers, bikers, picnickers, sports enthusiasts, small mammals, deer, and 186 species of birds. The Garden State Parkway, a congested coastal toll highway that can be scenic or aggravating (depending on traffic), runs right through it. The PNC Bank Arts Center, a 17,500-seat amphitheater that features multimillion-dollar live concerts, is just 8 miles away.

But its disadvantages are also advantages: Travelers who want to be near New York happily set up tents here. Concertgoers enjoy Cheesequake for its access to the arts center. And its proximity to the Garden State Parkway makes Cheesequake desirable for budget-conscious campers who want to be near Jersey's northern beaches.

Even without the local attractions, Cheesequake is a destination in its own right. Its ecosystem is diverse, as it lies in the transitional zone between northern and southern New Jersey. Cheesequake features salt and freshwater marshes as well as pine barrens and a northeastern hardwood forest. The marshes are home to a wide variety of birds that are of interest to birders and naturalists.

The campground is located on the southeastern edge of the park, in a relatively unspoiled area. Most of the trails and recreational facilities are located across the Garden State Parkway. The Stump Creek area north of the campground is completely undeveloped.

Some of the beautiful wetlands for which the New Jersey coast is known

KEY INFORMATION

ADDRESS: Campground Road, Laurence Harbor, NJ 08879

OPERATED BY: New Jersey State Park Service

CONTACT: 732-566-2161, njparksandforests .org/parks/cheesequake.html; reservations: camping.nj.gov

OPEN: April 1–October 31

SITES: 53

EACH SITE HAS: Picnic table, fire ring

WHEELCHAIR ACCESS: Restrooms and site 6 are ADA-accessible

ASSIGNMENT: First-come, first-served or by reservation (minimum 2 nights)

REGISTRATION: On arrival or online

FACILITIES: Water, flush toilets, showers

PARKING: At campsites; 2-vehicle limit

FEES: New Jersey residents, $20/night; nonresidents, $25/night; $5/night pet fee

RESTRICTIONS:

PETS: On leash, sites 23–27 and 37–40 only, 2 pets/site; pet permit and proof of current vaccinations required. See njparksandforests .org/parks/pet_friendly_camping.html for more information.

FIRES: In fire rings only

ALCOHOL: Prohibited

VEHICLES: 11-foot height limit; no hookups

OTHER: No cutting of live trees; quiet hours 10 p.m.–6 a.m.; 14-day stay limit; 6-person/2-tent site limit; no refunds due to biting insects

The 53 quiet campsites are impeccably maintained. The forest canopy shades all sites, and the vegetation between sites makes the spacious sites seem even more private. Firewood is sometimes supplied with campsites. Two dead-end spurs house the quietest, most secluded sites; unfortunately, they're also the farthest from the single bathhouse and closest to Laurence Harbor Parkway, with its cars and housing developments. A tall fence and some understory separate the campground from the road. Also worth noting is the group camping area, with five sites scattered about a large field south of the park office. Each has a fire ring and picnic tables. These have become increasingly popular with groups of families getting together for a weekend of camping. Each allows a maximum of 25 people, and there is ample space for several cars.

The park entrance fee comes with a disclaimer: "There will be no entrance fee refund due to the seasonal insect problem." Parts of Cheesequake are located on a salt marsh rife with mosquitoes, biting flies, and midges. The campground itself isn't in the salt marsh, but be prepared to deal with insects nonetheless as you use some of the recreational facilities.

Sandy Hook, a 1,665-acre barrier beach peninsula, is 15 minutes away via Exit 117 of the Garden State Parkway. Part of the Gateway National Recreation Area, it has a fort, historical exhibits, fishing, hiking, and the oldest operating lighthouse in the country. Swimming and ocean sports are popular at Sandy Hook. Its camping area has recently been developed for public use, although it fills quickly (see previous profile).

Those with a fear of sharks and an overactive imagination may prefer to swim in 6-acre Hooks Creek Lake at Cheesequake. Forty-foot-wide tidal Matawan Creek—right where it meets the Garden State Parkway at milepost 119.4—was the unlikely site of three of the five shark attacks in 1916 later made famous in *Jaws*. Fortunately, no sharks have been seen in Matawan in decades, and Matawan Creek does not connect with landlocked Hooks Creek Lake.

Anglers catch trout, largemouth bass, catfish, and sunfish in the lake. Cheesequake is also renowned for its crabbing, which can be done from the crabbing bridge. Access is from the lake parking lot.

Four of Cheesequake's five trails are for hiking only, while the remaining 3.5-mile single-track trail is also open to cyclists. Trails are classified as easy to moderate and have some inclines. The longest hiking trail is the Green Trail, a 3.5-mile loop that passes by examples of the various ecosystems that make up Cheesequake State Park. First, you'll walk by a salt marsh before going through a hardwood forest. You'll pass under pitch pines before continuing on to a freshwater swamp and a white cedar swamp. Finally, the trail passes 150-year-old white pines before ending back at the parking area. Kayak touring is another recreational option available to park visitors. The park office has brochures with information on how to make reservations as well as the cost.

The Lenape Indian Tribe originally inhabited the Raritan Bay area. They called it "land which has been declared," or *chis-kahki.* New Jerseyans call it "Cheesequake," which rhymes with "cheesecake." (Be advised that inquiring about the availability of cheesecake at Cheesequake will only get you a glare, just as one gets from a native of New Jersey after delivering the tired old line "You're from Jersey? What exit?") But you will find shaded campsites, plenty of wildlife, and many recreational opportunities in Cheesequake State Park.

Cheesequake State Park Campground

GETTING THERE

From the Garden State Parkway, take Exit 120 for Matawan/Laurence. Turn right on Matawan Road, and drive to the first light. Turn right onto Cliffwood Road, and drive 0.3 mile. Turn right on Gordon Road, and drive 0.7 mile to the park entrance.

GPS COORDINATES: N40° 26.479' W74° 15.294'

Riverwood Park Campground

Beauty ★★★ / Privacy ★★★★ / Spaciousness ★★★ / Quiet ★★★ / Security ★★ / Cleanliness ★★

Canoeing and fishing are popular at these free, wooded riverside sites.

It's free to camp with a permit at Toms River Township's Riverwood Park, but you have to pay in sweat. Only one of the five sites is accessible from a motor vehicle, and even then the potable water and toilets are a half mile away. The other sites are hike-in or canoe-in only.

Campsites stretch out along 2 miles of the eastern shoreline of the North Branch of the Toms River. Amenities vary by site—some have brick fireplaces, trash cans, or benches, but the Toms River Township Department of Recreation guarantees only the presence of a picnic table.

In spite of efforts to keep the park clean, litter tends to show up along the shoreline and near picnic tables. The park is still pleasant and wooded, though, with sites sitting far apart in private clearings among thick underbrush. The two sites at the northern end of the park are almost never used. Another nearby site, located off Medjay Lane and known as the Kiwanis Campsite (site 3 on the map on page 104), is used frequently as it's just 120 steps from a secondary parking area. Medjay is two streets north of the main park entrance—follow it to its end, and then turn right onto a dirt road to reach the Kiwanis Campsite as well as the two other seldom-used sites (4 and 5 on our map). Canoes can easily be pulled out of the river here, allowing canoeists an easy and legal night of camping, provided that you have a permit.

Riverwood Park is a long, thin strip of green that stretches along about 2 miles of riverfront and is no more than a half mile wide at its thickest point. Nevertheless, Toms River

The North Branch of Toms River offers campers at Riverwood Park opportunities for fishing.

KEY INFORMATION

ADDRESS: Riverwood Park, Riverwood Drive, Toms River, NJ 08755

OPERATED BY: Toms River Township Department of Recreation

CONTACT: 732-341-1000, ext. 8415, tomsrivertownship.com

OPEN: Year-round

SITES: 5

EACH SITE HAS: Picnic table, grill

WHEELCHAIR ACCESS: None at campsites (park playground is accessible)

ASSIGNMENT: Obtain permits at the Toms River Township Department of Recreation, 1810 Warren Point Road, Monday–Friday, 9 a.m.–4 p.m.

REGISTRATION: Permit must be obtained in advance and in person

FACILITIES: Flush toilets

PARKING: At central lot—hike to sites

FEE: None

RESTRICTIONS:

PETS: On leash

FIRES: Permitted in grills only, using only charcoal for fuel; must be extinguished completely before leaving site

ALCOHOL: Prohibited

VEHICLES: Must display permit on dashboard

OTHER: Discuss stay limits with the recreation supervisor when you obtain your camping permit

Township has managed to fit in 2.5 miles of forest trails, three picnic areas, soccer fields, and a playground for children with disabilities. Even with all the amenities, the park still feels rural and wooded.

Fishing is popular in the Toms River along Riverwood Park. Trout are stocked several times a season. Some sites are right on the bank, close enough that you could fish in your pajamas without even getting out of bed in the morning. Canoeing is also popular but somewhat challenging because the river is shallow and winds sharply at several points. Canoeing south from Riverwood takes canoeists near Surf & Stream Campground (see page 124) and through Winding River Park.

Toms River Township also oversees Winding River Park, a 500-acre property of which only 40 acres are developed. Canoeists follow the river alongside the park for 6 miles. No camping is allowed at Winding River Park, but visitors can easily reach it from Riverwood or Surf & Stream. Winding River features 8 miles of hiking trails, 3 miles of bikeway, picnic areas, softball and soccer fields, equestrian trails, and an ice/roller skating rink. To drive to Winding River Park from Riverwood Park, turn right onto Whitesville Road/County Road 527. After 2 miles, turn left onto Head Road/CR 571 and then right onto Oak Ridge Parkway to reach Winding River.

Those interested in less-natural pastimes can drive either 15 minutes to Six Flags Great Adventure theme park or 10 miles in the other direction to Seaside Heights, an old-style Jersey Shore beach-and-boardwalk area that features carnival games and recreation (and was made world-famous as the setting of MTV's *Jersey Shore*). South of Seaside Heights is Island Beach State Park, a sandy 3,000-acre undeveloped barrier beach known for its saltwater fishing and ocean swimming.

Riverwood is also a good base for a trip 10 miles south to Double Trouble State Park, a 7,300-acre forest in the New Jersey Pinelands with 12 miles of hiking trails and 10 miles of Cedar Creek, which is popular with canoeists and kayakers. Double Trouble is best known for its historic village, a onetime company town for the cranberry-processing industry.

Fourteen buildings from the late 1800s still stand in the village, including a general store, schoolhouse, cottages, and sawmill. Cranberries are still harvested in the state park on lands leased from New Jersey.

Few people know that camping is allowed in Riverwood Park. For those willing to rough it, the campsites are ideal for the outdoors enthusiast on a budget.

Riverwood Park Campground

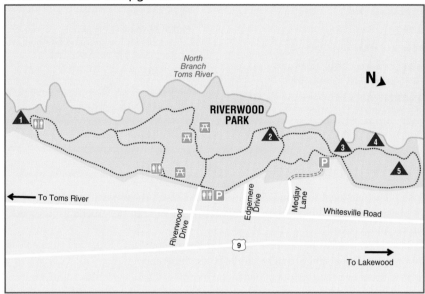

GETTING THERE

Heading northbound on the Garden State Parkway, take Exit 83 for US 9 North/Lakewood. Merge onto US 9 North, and drive 0.6 mile. Turn left onto Indian Head Road/County Road 571, and drive 1.3 miles. Turn right onto Whitesville Road/CR 527, and drive 1.3 miles. Turn left onto Riverwood Drive, and park at the end of the road in the lot on the right.

Heading southbound on the Garden State Parkway, take Exit 89B for Lakehurst/Brick. Merge onto NJ 70 West, and drive 3.9 miles. Turn left onto Whitesville Road/CR 527, and drive 1.4 miles. Turn left onto Riverwood Drive into the park.

You must obtain your camping permit in advance at the main office of the Toms River Township Department of Recreation, about 7 miles from the park at 1810 Warren Point Road, off Fischer Boulevard by the bay in Toms River. From Exit 89A of the Garden State Parkway, drive to Shorrock Street, which is just ahead of you coming off the ramp if you're driving southbound or to the right down NJ 70 East if you're driving northbound. Drive 2.3 miles on Shorrock Street; then turn right to merge onto County Road 549 South, and drive 2.3 miles. Use the right lane to take the ramp to Fisher Boulevard/CR 549 Spur, and drive about 1 mile. Turn left onto Merrimac Drive; Warren Point Road is at the end of Merrimac. The office is open weekdays, 9 a.m.–4 p.m.

GPS COORDINATES: N40° 01.043' W74° 14.095'

Timberline Lake Camping Resort

Beauty ★★★ / Privacy ★★★ / Spaciousness ★★★ / Quiet ★★★★ / Security ★★★★ / Cleanliness ★★★★

Campers can bring their dogs without giving up the seclusion and rustic atmosphere of a tent environment.

Although you will encounter no shortage of RVs at Timberline Lake, the campground is ideally located in the New Jersey Pinelands. The waterfront is beautiful, the proprietors are very friendly, and the tent camping isn't bad either. This is a great place to visit with kids as well as dogs.

Fifteen tent sites with no hookups are located in the woods surrounding three sides of a large recreation field. These sites are wooded, secure, and isolated from the denser RV area. Most sites are open to the other tent sites and to the field, but the woods provide a buffer between campers and the activity section of the campground. A trail connects the tenting area to the activity area, and a short gravel road leads to the office and bathhouse. The tent area itself is considered primitive, with portable toilets and no water faucets. Water must be carried in from the office area. A large additional tent site, referred to as the Pit, is located farther back in the woods from the other tent sites. It is suitable for up to 12 adults and is a favorite when several families choose to camp together.

Reservations are necessary only on holiday weekends. Nine lakefront sites are also available to tent campers, as are three other sites among the loops. They have electric and water hookups, so expect to have RVs as neighbors if you opt for a site with a water view.

The lakeside beach is guarded and open to swimmers during the day on weekends. The swimming pool is open daily during summer months. Campers can rent canoes on weekends, and recreational equipment is available at the office; in exchange for a deposit, campers can borrow bats, baseballs, gloves, volleyballs, basketballs, footballs, horseshoes, and soccer

A stretch of the scenic shore of Timberline Lake

KEY INFORMATION

ADDRESS: 365 Route 679, New Gretna, NJ 08224

OPERATED BY: Private

CONTACT: 609-296-7900, timberlinelake.com/reservations.html

OPEN: May 1–mid-October

SITES: 185 (28 tent sites)

EACH SITE HAS: Picnic table, fire ring

WHEELCHAIR ACCESS: None

ASSIGNMENT: First-come, first-served or by reservation (minimum 2 nights)

REGISTRATION: On arrival at office

FACILITIES: Portable toilets; office and RV area have water, flush toilets, showers, laundry room, store; dog beach

PARKING: At campsites; 2-vehicle limit

FEES: $40/night for tent sites with no hookups; $45/night for sites with water and electric ($55/night + cable TV); $5/night sewer-hookup fee

---

RESTRICTIONS:

PETS: Must be leashed and picked up after

FIRES: In fire rings only; no woodcutting

ALCOHOL: Permitted

VEHICLES: Up to 35 feet; 5-mile-per-hour speed limit

OTHER: Check-in 2 p.m., checkout 1 p.m.; 4-person site limit; no maximum stay limit; 2-night minimum stay, 3 nights on holiday weekends; quiet hours 11 p.m.–8 a.m.

balls. (Be warned that the ball field is also the tent campers' front yard, so expect to have some company during the afternoons.) Table tennis is available in the store game room. Fishing is popular in the 30-acre lake.

Kids will appreciate the campground's organized activities. In addition to sporting events, activities are scheduled for every weekend during the season, including arts and crafts, game nights, the occasional ice cream social, Holidayfest (aka "Christmas in July"), and beach games. Adult activities include bingo and horseshoe tournaments, and fishing derbies. The remote tenting area makes it easy for tent campers to avoid the organized fun and enjoy a more primitive experience.

Timberline Lake Camping Resort sits squarely in the middle of the Pinelands, the unique ecological region that covers 1.1 million acres of southern Jersey. Visitors can enjoy other activities at nearby Bass River State Forest (see page 89), where park personnel offer interpretive programs and films. Past programs have included stargazing and full moon hikes through local Pinelands trails. Bass River also has an excellent swimming beach, though it can get crowded on warm summer weekends. Additionally, Bass River's hiking trails wind through the forest's 27,000 acres and are open to visitors. Vehicle entrance fees are charged.

The 50-mile-long Batona Trail ends near the campground in Bass River State Forest near the intersection of Stage and Coal Roads. Hiking this level, easy trail is a great way to get to know the plants and animals of the Pinelands.

For beach lovers, Long Beach Island, a half-hour drive away, is one of the best-known barrier islands along the Jersey Shore. Beach badges ($7 per day) must be purchased during the summer; see lbtbp.com/beach-badges for more information. The northern tip of the island features Barnegat Lighthouse State Park; its namesake 172-foot-tall lighthouse is open throughout the year and affords panoramic views of the region. You can reach all of the Long Beach Island towns from NJ 72, a causeway that intersects both US 9 and the Garden State Parkway.

A half-hour drive in the other direction will take you south to the casinos and beaches of Atlantic City. Even if you're not a gambler, it's worth visiting for the lights and atmosphere of the busy boardwalk (the world's first).

If the crowds of the casinos, the shore, and the bingo games back at camp are too much for you, take some time out at the Edwin B. Forsythe National Wildlife Refuge. Its 40,000 acres include tidal salt meadows and marshes, preserved for use by migratory shorebirds, woodland trees and plants, and upland species. There are few hiking paths because the refuge is dedicated to wildlife, not to humans. View the refuge from your car as you drive the 8-mile auto trail—stop to read the brochure at viewpoints.

Timberline Lake Camping Resort is ideally situated for access to the wildlife refuge, Pinelands, and shore. Its best feature is that it allows primitive tent camping for both people and dogs, but developed facilities are never far away.

Timberline Lake Camping Resort

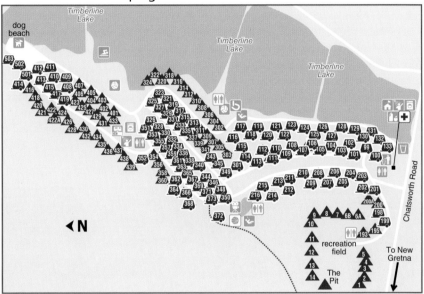

GETTING THERE

Heading southbound on the Garden State Parkway, take Exit 52 for New Gretna. Turn right onto East Greenbush Road, and drive 1.1 miles. Turn left onto Stage Road, and drive 0.4 mile; then keep left to continue onto Leektown Road. Drive 1.1 miles; then make a slight right onto Chatsworth Road/County Road 679, and drive 0.9 mile. The campground entrance will be on your left.

Heading northbound on the Garden State Parkway, take Exit 50 for US 9 North/New Gretna. Continue onto US 9 North, and drive 1.5 miles. Turn left onto North Maple Avenue, and drive 1.5 miles; then North Maple will curve and become Chatsworth Road. In 2.2 miles, the campground entrance will be on your left.

GPS COORDINATES: N39° 37.986' W74° 28.734'

Turkey Swamp Park Campground

Beauty ★★★★ / Privacy ★★★ / Spaciousness ★★★ / Quiet ★★★ / Security ★★★ / Cleanliness ★★★★

Its proximity to nature, theme parks, and the beach should keep everyone in the family happy, even the dog.

Despite its unusual name, this gem of a county park is not a swamp overrun with gobbling turkeys. The turkey in question was once the name of Adelphia, a nearby town. The park and surrounding Turkey Swamp Wildlife Management Area sit on sandy land just above the water table. Groundwater sometimes appears on the surface as small bogs.

Turkey Swamp's campsites are among the region's best: 64 wooded sites lie under a canopy of trees at the northern edge of the Pinelands, a protected unique ecosystem covering 1.1 million acres of land that includes swamps, farms, and forests. Although the overall campground is a compact crisscrossed loop, sites are spacious enough to accommodate large trailers. Green undergrowth, pitch pines, and tall oak trees between sites assure privacy. The bathhouse has hot showers, flush toilets, and laundry facilities. Unfortunately, just one bathhouse serves all 64 sites.

From the campground entrance, it's a short walk to the boathouse on the banks of the central 17-acre lake. The lake was man-made but is now sustained by natural springs that feed the lake. Visitors can rent paddleboats, rowboats, and canoes by the half hour; you must wear a life vest. Fishing for bass, catfish, and bluegill is popular from boats and from

The 17-acre lake at Turkey Swamp Park attracts anglers in search of crappie and catfish.

KEY INFORMATION

ADDRESS: 200 Georgia Road, Freehold, NJ 07728

OPERATED BY: Monmouth County Park System

CONTACT: 732-462-7286, tinyurl.com /turkeyswamp (click "Reservation Request Form" for a printable mail-in form)

OPEN: April 1–November 15

SITES: 64, plus 2 cabins

EACH SITE HAS: Picnic table, fire ring, lantern post

WHEELCHAIR ACCESS: Sites A-10, C-2, D-5, and D-11; restrooms

ASSIGNMENT: 12 sites are first-come, first-served; 52 sites can be reserved (minimum 2 nights)

REGISTRATION: On arrival, by phone, or by mail

FACILITIES: Water, flush toilets, showers, laundry room, vending machines

PARKING: At campsites (2-vehicle limit); overflow parking at entrance

FEES: Monmouth County residents, $30/ night; nonresidents, $34/night

---

RESTRICTIONS:

PETS: Must be leashed, attended, and picked up after

FIRES: In fire rings, permitted 7 a.m.– 11 p.m. only

ALCOHOL: Prohibited

VEHICLES: No length limits

OTHER: 3-day minimum stay on holiday weekends; firewood for purchase at park; quiet hours 10 p.m.–8 a.m.

---

the shore. Swimming in the lake is prohibited, but campers may use the swimming pool at the Nomoco Activity Area on a limited basis when programs are not being conducted. Ice skating on the lake is permitted when the water freezes in winter, although the campground is closed December–March.

Turkey Swamp also makes a great base camp for canoeing or kayaking the Manasquan River. Boats rented in the park cannot be removed from the lake, but you'll find commercial rental outfitters nearby.

There are 8 miles of level trails in this 1,180-acre park. The mile-long fitness trail, with its 20 exercise stations, provides the only challenging option. Puddles of water occasionally bubble up through the trails. Trails are designated as multiuse, although mountain bikers often scoff at the easy trails. Turkey Swamp's thorny trails will eventually be part of the statewide Capital to the Coast Trail, which, when complete, will reach from the Atlantic Ocean to Trenton, roughly paralleling I-195.

The adjacent state-managed Turkey Swamp Wildlife Management Area has an archery range that is open to the public and run jointly by the Monmouth County Park System and the New Jersey Division of Fish & Wildlife. Note that the WMA is open to deer hunting during varying autumn and winter weeks, so exercise caution during deer season.

In addition to being a recreational destination, Turkey Swamp makes a good base camp for family holidays. It's near Monmouth Battlefield State Park, the site of one of the largest battles of the Revolutionary War. Featuring restored fences, lanes, and a farmhouse, the park is also the site of two natural water sources dubbed the Molly Pitcher Springs. According to legend, Mary Ludwig Hays was the heroine of the Battle of Monmouth—she was nicknamed "Molly Pitcher" because she was said to have carried spring water to thirsty soldiers on a day with 100-degree heat (she also reportedly took her husband's place in a gunnery crew after he was injured in battle). Arrive around June 28 to see the annual battle reenactment, in which none other than General George Washington commands the Continental Army. He and his forces spent more time in New Jersey than in any other state, in part because of its key location between New York and Philadelphia.

For those looking for other types of fun, the Atlantic Ocean and the Jersey Shore are a short drive to the east, while Six Flags Great Adventure theme park is an equally short drive to the west. Nearby Freehold is home to a horse raceway and the Old Tennent Presbyterian Church built in 1751, but it's most notable as the hometown of Jersey rock icon Bruce Springsteen. Walking tours visit two of his former homes.

Those wishing to visit New York City on a day trip can take New Jersey Transit's North Jersey Coast Line from Spring Lake or Belmar. Alternatively, commuter buses leave from Freehold. Inquire at the campground office for details.

Turkey Swamp Campground is unique among public campgrounds with its combination of natural forest, friendliness to dogs, and modern amenities. Its proximity to nature, theme parks, and the beach should keep everyone in the family happy, Fido included.

Turkey Swamp Park Campground

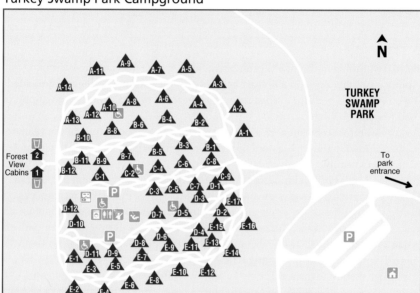

GETTING THERE

From I-195, take Exit 22 for Jackson Mills/Georgia. Turn north onto Jackson Mills Road, and drive about 2.5 miles. Turn left onto Georgia Road, and drive a little over a mile. Turn left to enter Turkey Swamp Park; the campground is about 0.4 mile farther.

GPS COORDINATES: N40° 11.799' W74° 18.174'

THE JERSEY SHORE

Golden sand and big surf on the Jersey Shore

Adventure Bound Camping Resort

Beauty ★★ / Privacy ★★ / Spaciousness ★★★ / Quiet ★★ / Security ★★★★ / Cleanliness ★★★

Adventure Bound has the only tent sites on Cape May.

The Cape May Peninsula, 16 miles long and 8 miles wide, has more than a dozen camp-grounds; many more line US 9 north of the peninsula. Nearly all of these campgrounds densely pack in RVs, and almost none are tent-friendly. Most encourage seasonal camping. Some don't even *allow* tent camping. Adventure Bound Camping Resort is included here not because it has the most pristine, rustic, wilderness sites in the Garden State—rather, it's included here because it has a tent section and is therefore a beacon of light among the glut of southern coastal RV parks.

The RV section of Adventure Bound looks similar to those of neighboring campgrounds, but continue driving past the 11 small hookup lanes to the very end: a small dedicated tent loop sits on a northern spur apart from the other sites. There is no underbrush between sites, but there are trees and shade above the tents. Tent campers aren't shoved in among the RVs here; they have their own real estate and are given the respect they miss at many RV parks.

Adventure Bound has the usual amenities found in private campgrounds, such as a pool, a store, a playground, and a few game courts. But campsites and comfort take precedence over organized activities. A small area solely for dog walking lies at the southwestern end of this pet-friendly campground.

The camping resort is located in Cape May Court House, about 5 miles from the Wild-woods (North Wildwood, Wildwood, and Wildwood Crest) on New Jersey's southernmost barrier island. Beach access is free along the 5 miles of coast—a rarity on the Jersey Shore (Atlantic City's beach also has no admission charge).

Two anglers enjoy surf-fishing on the Jersey Shore.

KEY INFORMATION

ADDRESS: 240 W. Shellbay Ave.,
Cape May Court House, NJ 08210

OPERATED BY: Private

CONTACT: 609-465-4440, abcamping.com
/abcapemay (click "Book Now" for online
reservations)

OPEN: March 31–first weekend in October

SITES: 15 tent-only sites and 34 deluxe cabins
in upper section, with additional tent space

EACH SITE HAS: Picnic table, fire ring

WHEELCHAIR ACCESS: Restrooms are
ADA-accessible

ASSIGNMENT: First-come, first-served or
by reservation

REGISTRATION: On arrival, by phone,
or online

FACILITIES: Water, flush toilets, showers,
laundry room, store

PARKING: At campsites; 1-vehicle limit

FEES: $32–$49/night, depending
on season; $50 pet fee (maximum 2 pets)

RESTRICTIONS:

PETS: Must be leashed and
picked up after

FIRES: Buy firewood at camp store or
bring your own from Cape May
County only

ALCOHOL: At campsites only

VEHICLES: No length limits in tent area

OTHER: Quiet hours 11 p.m.–8 a.m.; check-
in 3 p.m., checkout 11 a.m.; no maximum
stay limit; 2-night minimum stay, 3 nights
on holiday weekends

A preservation group and the Greater Wildwoods Tourism Authority have noted that the Wildwoods' claim to fame is its "large collection of mid-century doo-wop architecture." In layman's terms, this means the Wildwoods had a boom during the 1950s. Hotels and clubs were built, and entertainers visited. Some nicknamed Wildwood "Little Las Vegas." Chubby Checker debuted "The Twist" here, and the first national broadcast of *American Bandstand* was aired from Wildwood.

That moment passed, however, and Wildwood became a resort area past its prime. The beachfront property was ignored long enough

A group of tent-camping sites at
Adventure Bound Camping Resort

so that when the area became desirable again, enough time had passed that the "doo-wop architecture" was preserved instead of destroyed, thanks to the efforts of the preservation group and local citizens. Pick up a map at the Doo-Wop Preservation League headquarters at Pine and Pacific Avenues, or join one of their trolley tours. You can see the boomerang roofs, faux Chinese temples, tiki-style shops, wacky neon signs, and kidney-shaped pools that were once state-of-the-art in Eisenhower's America. The largest concentration of these cool-turned-tacky-turned-retro-kitsch buildings is in the borough of Wildwood Crest. Visit the Preservation League's website at doowopusa.org for more information.

Wildwood has a 2-mile boardwalk with piers full of amusement rides, but it's not known strictly for its man-made attractions. Besides the free beach, which is getting bigger every year due to the southern movement of the sand, there are excellent opportunities for crabbing, whale-watching, and dolphin-watching.

A 10-minute ride south down the Garden State Parkway or US 9 takes campers from the 1950s to the 1850s. Cape May is best known not for its lovely beaches or migratory birds, but for its collection of beautiful Victorian-era buildings and historic lighthouse. But architecture isn't the only attraction—the peninsula is a major feeding and resting place for migratory birds. Cape May Point State Park and Cape May Migratory Bird Refuge comprise a variety of habitats that nature lovers and birds alike enjoy.

Bird-watchers don't even have to drive the 10 miles from Adventure Bound Camping Resort to Cape May to get a look at the tens of thousands of birds that stop over on the Cape May Peninsula. Instead, they can drive a few miles north to Stone Harbor Bird Sanctuary, a 21-acre municipal heron sanctuary given landmark status by the National Park Service.

Stone Harbor is also home to the Wetlands Institute, a 34-acre salt marsh. Exhibits include hands-on aquariums and live-turtle exhibits. If you can tear the kids away from the Wildwood boardwalk, there are children and family interpretive programs at the Wetlands Institute during the summer.

Adventure Bound Camping Resort may not have bushy privacy barriers between sites or miles of hiking trails. What it does have is proximity to dozens of seashore attractions—both natural and man-made.

Adventure Bound Camping Resort

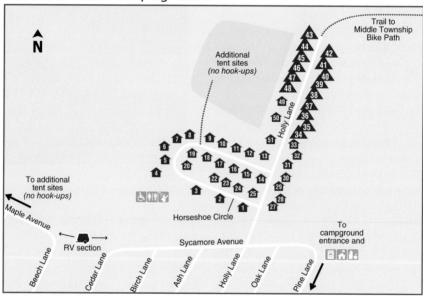

GETTING THERE

From the Garden State Parkway, take Exit 9 for US 9/Shell Bay Avenue. Drive west on Shell Bay Avenue for 0.8 mile The campground entrance will be on your right.

GPS COORDINATES: N39° 04.322' W74° 50.630'

Cedar Creek Campground

Beauty ★★ / Privacy ★★ / Spaciousness ★★★ / Quiet ★★★ / Security ★★★★ / Cleanliness ★★★

Most visitors come for the canoeing, but there are 29 shaded tent sites at Cedar Creek.

Cedar Creek Campground has tent sites, RV sites, cabins, and trailer rentals. It's near beaches, boardwalks, forests, and man-made attractions. But most visitors stay overnight at Cedar Creek not because of its location or amenities, but for the canoeing. Cedar Creek doesn't have the only canoe and kayak livery in the area, but it does have an enviable combination of canoe rentals, beach access, and tent campsites.

The 29 tent sites sit along the southern and western ends of the park, under hardwood trees; they are well shaded and well separated from the RV sites. The tent sites closest to Cedar Creek are 1, 3, 7, 9, 11, 13, 14, and 15. All of the tent sites are near the canoe take-out at Cedar Creek. Some sites are surrounded by understory nearby, while most are open to other sites.

Canoe and kayak trips are offered in three lengths: 6, 12, or 17 miles. Reservations during busy summer weekends are a must and are recommended at other times as well (the canoe livery is closed during winter). Note that while you can drink alcohol at your campsite, you can't drink on the water because the trips pass through New Jersey state parklands, where alcohol consumption is prohibited. You may bring your own canoe, which the staff will transport for a fee.

The 6-mile trip provides a nice, meandering hour-long journey along Cedar Creek, but the longer trips begin in Double Trouble State Park and take a minimum of 3 hours to

The Ocean City boardwalk with its shops and amusement park

KEY INFORMATION

ADDRESS: 1052 Atlantic City Blvd. (US 9), Bayville, NJ 08721

OPERATED BY: Private

CONTACT: 732-269-1413 or 908-783-9884; cedarcreekcampground.com

OPEN: Year-round

SITES: 29 tent sites (192 total), plus 10 cabins and 3 group areas

EACH SITE HAS: Picnic table, fire ring

WHEELCHAIR ACCESS: Partial (contact the campground for more information)

ASSIGNMENT: First-come, first-served or by reservation

REGISTRATION: On arrival or by phone

FACILITIES: Water, flush toilets, showers, laundry room, store

PARKING: At campsites (1-vehicle limit) or in overflow lots (daily fee applies)

FEES: $49/night for 2 people, summer, no water/electricity ($44.50 spring/fall); $10/additional person age 16 and above, $6 age 15 and below; $5/day parking fee. See website for additional rates and fees.

RESTRICTIONS:

PETS: Must be leashed, attended, and cleaned up after; prohibited in pool area and cabins; bring proof of vaccination

FIRES: In fire rings only

ALCOHOL: At campsites only

VEHICLES: Up to 60 feet (RV sites)

OTHER: Check-in 2 p.m., checkout at noon; no stay limit; quiet hours 11 p.m.–7 a.m.

---

complete. Cedar Creek's staff encourages paddlers to take their time and enjoy the trip, but all boats must be returned to the canoe livery by 6 p.m.

Double Trouble State Park is a 7,000-acre typical Pinelands forest, complete with a historic village and cranberry bogs. Cedar Creek is sometimes narrow, but its waters flow quickly and can be an excellent run for inexperienced canoeists. Keep your eyes open, and in addition to cranberry bogs and Pinelands plants, you might see deer, beavers, otters, and birds. The park, which also has multiuse trails, fishing, and cedar swamps, is a designated stop on the 300-mile auto route called the New Jersey Coastal Heritage Trail Route.

The Barnegat Branch Trail, a rail-trail that, when completed, will extend 15.6 miles from Barnegat north to Toms River, passes along the west side of the campground.

If you prefer salt water and sailing to canoeing under the pines, cross US 9 and drive a half mile east to Cedar Creek Marina. Barnegat Bay Sailing School and Sailboat Charters offers both sailing lessons and sailboat rentals. Afternoon or sunset sail cruises are available, letting the crew do the work while you enjoy the ocean views. Visit sailingnj.com for more information.

For those with energy left after a day of canoeing, the boardwalk thrills of Seaside Heights are only 15 miles away. Leave the peaceful forest behind and head to the mile-long boardwalk for some electronically powered fun at the arcades, carnival rides, miniature golf, fast-food stands, and antique carousel of this shore resort.

Just south of Seaside Heights, but more suited to a daylight visit, is Island Beach State Park. The 3,000 acres of 10-mile-long Island Beach State Park have been deliberately undeveloped and feature one of the longest remaining stretches of barrier beach along the northern Atlantic Coast. One mile of the park is open to swimmers during the summer, with bathhouses and parking—concessions to modern life in this natural environment. Scuba diving, saltwater fishing, and surfing are also allowed at Island Beach. Additionally, the park features a 5-mile bike path, hiking trails, horseback riding trails, and a bird observation blind.

Immediately south of Island Beach, at the northern tip of Long Beach Island, is Barnegat Lighthouse State Park. The lighthouse is no longer in service and has been a state park since the 1950s; both the lighthouse and its interpretive center were renovated in 2003. Climb the 217 lighthouse steps for a panoramic view of the ocean and surrounding beaches, or take a short walk through the park on the Maritime Forest Trail, perfect for viewing the environment once found all along the coast.

Beaches closer to Cedar Creek Campground include those at Berkeley Island County Park and William J. Dudley Park. The latter, located just south of the campground, has barbecue areas and a roller-hockey rink, along with a swimming area. Twenty-five-acre Berkeley Island County Park, 2 miles west of Cedar Creek, has a fishing and crabbing pier in addition to a beach. Both parks are in protected Barnegat Bay, not directly on the Atlantic Ocean.

Cedar Creek Campground may not be ideal for someone searching for a deserted forest campsite, but for families or groups looking for a wide variety of activities, it's a great choice.

Cedar Creek Campground

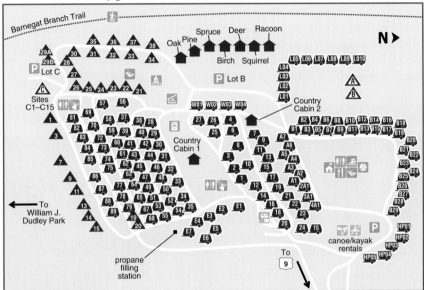

GETTING THERE

From the Garden State Parkway, take Exit 77 (Berkeley). Exiting southbound, take a left at the end of the ramp and then another left at the first intersection, onto Pinewald Keswick Road, which becomes Forest Hills Parkway after about 0.6 mile. Then follow the directions below.

Exiting northbound, turn right onto Forest Hills Parkway, and drive 1.9 miles. Turn right onto Serpentine Drive, and drive 0.3 mile. Turn right to stay on Serpentine Drive, and drive another 0.6 mile. Turn right onto US 9 South, and drive 0.7 mile. The campground will be on your right.

GPS COORDINATES: N39° 52.470' W74° 10.097'

Frontier Campground

Beauty ★★★ / Privacy ★★★ / Spaciousness ★★★ / Quiet ★★★ / Security ★★★★ / Cleanliness ★★★★

Pleasant, wooded sites near the shore are available to all, not just tent campers.

Frontier Campground, which has no dedicated tenting area, merits a mention for its pleasing all-purpose sites and agreeable camping philosophy. The campground brochure includes six paragraphs that declare that Frontier's management—three brothers who have run the campground for many years—understand that people camp for various reasons. Some people camp to play bingo or participate in square dances, but Frontier's declared purpose is to offer a peaceful, private, natural setting for families who wish to relax.

RV and tent campers both get the same treatment, which is quite considerate. Most people associate tent camping with privacy and shady, natural settings. RV campers will be happy to know that they will not be stuck out in a sunny parking lot at Frontier. Instead, they're given trees and private clearings along with their canvas-covered friends.

This doesn't mean Frontier is as rustic or secluded as a state park—those seeking a forest with miles of hiking trails or a park that is a destination unto itself should head west to Belleplain State Forest (see page 136). But for those seeking pleasant, wooded sites with access to the beach and recreation options for the kids, Frontier is your best local option.

Historic Steelmantown Cemetery in Belleplain State Forest

ADDRESS: 84 Tyler Road, Ocean View, NJ 08230

OPERATED BY: Private

CONTACT: 609-390-3649, frontiercampground.com; reservations: 800-277-4109 (click "Rates & Reservations" at the website)

OPEN: Mid-April–mid-October

SITES: 192; 10 sites (8, 16, 18, 20, 22, 24, 28, 44, 64, and 68) have no hookups and are suitable for tents

EACH SITE HAS: Picnic table, fire ring

WHEELCHAIR ACCESS: None

ASSIGNMENT: First-come, first-served or by reservation (3-day minimum stay on holidays)

REGISTRATION: On arrival, by phone, or online

FACILITIES: Water, flush toilets, showers, laundry room, store

PARKING: At campsites

FEES: $45–$75 for sites with no hookups, depending on day of week and season; $5/night pet fee

---

RESTRICTIONS:

PETS: Must be leashed, attended, and picked up after; no pit bulls, Rottweilers, Dobermans, or other aggressive dog breeds

FIRES: In fire rings only

ALCOHOL: Prohibited

VEHICLES: Up to 40 feet

OTHER: Quiet hours 11 p.m.–7 a.m.; no stay limit; Sunday checkout by 5 p.m.

Many sites on the 50 acres have privacy barriers, such as hedges and undergrowth. Hardwoods tower over most sites, and each is spacious and clean. The central bathhouse receives frequent cleanings. Sites easily are on par with municipal and county park sites in New Jersey.

You won't find a pool at Frontier, but visitors can go fishing and crabbing right by the entrance. For novice campers, the campground has "treehouses" (cabins built on stilts), which come equipped with utensils and basic furniture. For the kids, there's a game room. For the sports-minded, there are ball courts and a playing field.

The famous Jersey Shore is a quick 10-minute drive away. Head northeast to go to Ocean City, with its 2.5-mile boardwalk and amusement pier. Go southeast to reach Sea Isle City, but note that there's no boardwalk here—it was destroyed by a storm in 1962 and replaced by a 1.5-mile blacktop promenade.

Between Ocean City and Sea Isle City is Corson's Inlet State Park, a 350-acre protected coastline area devoted to migratory birds, marine life, and waterfowl. Visitors can view undeveloped beach and waterfront, particularly in the 98-acre Strathmere Natural Area. The park has a free boat ramp, three hiking trails, fishing, crabbing, and interpretive tours; guided beach walks are scheduled during summer months. Swimming is not allowed at Corson's Inlet, but sunbathing and bird-watching are not only allowed but also very popular.

Ten minutes of driving south along Ocean Drive will take you to the Wetlands Institute in Stone Harbor. It's a 34-acre environmental education facility dedicated to the preservation of 6,000 acres of coastal ecosystem. Interpretive programs and hands-on exhibits for children and adults are offered at the center daily. The Wetlands Institute and Corson's Inlet State Park are both points of interest on the 300-mile New Jersey Coastal Heritage Trail Route, an auto route that follows the coast from the Delaware Bridge to Perth Amboy. Slightly farther afield from Frontier are the casinos of Atlantic City to the north and the Victorian homes of Cape May to the south. Drive straight up Ocean Drive from Ocean City to enjoy a scenic coastal ride to Atlantic City.

Below Wetlands Institute in North Wildwood is the Hereford Inlet Lighthouse. Built in 1874 and listed on state and national historic registers, it's still active and looks more like a Victorian home than a working lighthouse. Tours are available.

Hiking enthusiasts should head to 20,000-acre Belleplain State Forest. More than 40 miles of trails traverse the park. Fourteen of those trails are open to motor vehicles, and 16 miles of trails are designated multiuse. Nature Trails 1 and 2 along with the 1-mile Eagle Fitness Trail are for pedestrians only. The fitness trail has 10 exercise stations, while the nature trails include self-guided routes past habitats and plant species. Belleplain's Lake Nummy has a bathhouse and swim area for relaxation after a long day of hiking.

Another option for hiking considerably closer to Frontier Campground is the Cedar Swamp Trail, off nearby Tyler Road. Although the loop is only a mile long, the trail passes through cedar forest and open meadows and provides excellent opportunities for bird-watching. *Note:* Be careful about ticks along this grassy path.

Frontier Campground may not separate tents from RVs, but it doesn't have to. All sites are equal here, each being of a high standard normally not seen at RV sites. The location is near the shore, where most campgrounds pack RVs in so densely you would mistake camping for urban living. Peaceful Frontier feels rural without sacrificing convenience.

Frontier Campground

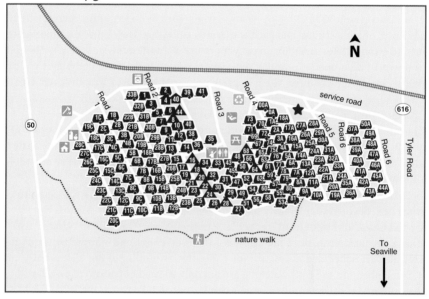

GETTING THERE

From the Garden State Parkway, take Exit 25 for US 9 South/Ocean City. Turn northwest onto Roosevelt Boulevard, and drive 3.4 miles. Turn left onto Tyler Road/County Road 616, and drive 1.4 miles. The campground will be on your right.

GPS COORDINATES: N39° 14.526' W74° 42.794'

Ocean View Resort Campground

Beauty ★★ / Privacy ★★ / Spaciousness ★★★ / Quiet ★★★ / Security ★★★★★ / Cleanliness ★★★★★

If you want to mix a little golf with your camping experience, this is the place to stay.

Camping at Ocean View Resort Campground is not exactly a wilderness experience. In fact, camping here is kind of the antithesis of a wilderness experience. With more than a thousand sites, it's a very large campground, almost a small town. Many of the sites are seasonal rentals, so you'll encounter lots of large RVs parked in semipermanent arrangements. As you drive the roads through the campground, it's easy to get disoriented—the map that you receive upon registering is necessary for figuring out where you're going.

As its name indicates, Ocean View is more of a camping resort than a campground. Although these aspects of campground life might be unappealing to those more interested in a wilderness-type experience, there are many good reasons to camp here, especially if you're camping with kids or are looking for a place where convenience and community are more important than solitude.

The first thing you'll notice when you visit Ocean View Resort is a big emphasis on security. A gate secures the campground, and campers and visitors must use a pass card to open and close it—that's a plus along this stretch of the New Jersey coast, where security can be of some concern. When you enter the office to register for your site and pick up your pass card, you'll also discover that the campground has a large and well-stocked camp store. If you need full groceries, local supermarkets are located about 5 minutes north and south of

A few folks out enjoying the beach on the first warm weekend of the year

KEY INFORMATION

ADDRESS: 2555 Shore Road (US 9), Ocean View, NJ 08230

OPERATED BY: Private

CONTACT: 609-624-1675, ovresort.com /reservations.php

OPEN: Last week of April–first week of October

SITES: 1,173; see below for suggested sites

EACH SITE HAS: Picnic table, fire ring, electric and water hookups

WHEELCHAIR ACCESS: Restrooms, showers

ASSIGNMENT: First-come, first-served or by reservation

REGISTRATION: At main office on arrival, by phone, or online

FACILITIES: Showers, flush toilets, laundry room, store

PARKING: At campsites; 2-vehicle limit

FEES: $42–$98/night, depending on location and season (assumes 4 people)

RESTRICTIONS:

PETS: Must be leashed, attended, and cleaned up after; proof of current vaccinations required

FIRES: In fire rings only

ALCOHOL: At campsites only

VEHICLES: No stated length limits; largest sites can accommodate big-rig RVs

OTHER: No stay limit; campers must have cars on-site in case of emergency

the campground. But for general camping supplies, snacks, drinks, sunscreen, and the like, you'll probably be able to find it at the camp store.

Perhaps the most significant thing you'll notice is how friendly and helpful the staff of the campground is. You'll be greeted with a smile, and whatever questions you have will be answered in similar form. The friendliness isn't surprising—Ocean View has been family owned and operated for more than 50 years.

Once inside the campground, you'll have plenty to do. Kids will love the Buccaneer Bay Splash Pad, a small pirate-themed pool and water-play area. Nearby is Trails End Lake, surrounded by a white sand beach; here you'll find beach volleyball nets, a shuffleboard court, a playground, a snack bar, and plenty of room to swim. The campground also has biking trails, a pool, miniature golf, a game room—the list goes on. In addition to these amenities, Ocean

Ocean View Resort has a shuffleboard court in addition to its playgrounds and beach.

View also creates an impressive schedule of activities for their summer season. Mostly oriented toward the younger campers, the activities include dances, magic shows, candy bingo, a carnival, and Halloween in August.

Although the campground has no designated tent areas, several areas are more suited to tenting than others, largely because of their proximity to the restrooms, which is less of an issue for RV campers. Ask the staff to help you secure a site along Fir Trail, Elm Trail, Redwood Trail, or Walnut Trail. For those who don't mind walking a couple of minutes to the restrooms, sites E14–E27 are quite nice. Like all of the sites in the park, these are clean, spacious, and wooded. Plus, they're located on a road that runs along the boundary of the park, so there are no sites across from them, which affords slightly more privacy than you might get elsewhere.

For those campers who just can't find enough to keep themselves occupied around the campground, Sea Isle City and the ocean beaches are just 3 miles away. Sea Isle City is an especially nice town that offers easy access to the beach as well as a promenade along which you can stroll and take in the sites. It's considerably less hectic than some of the more popular areas nearby such as Ocean City and Atlantic City. North of Sea Isle City, you'll find Corson's Inlet State Park, with its stretch of undeveloped shore, along with hiking trails and crabbing and fishing spots. The 98-acre Strathmere Natural Area within the park is a protected stretch of oceanfront that serves as a nesting site for the endangered piping plover. You can see a wide variety of other seabirds and waterfowl here, and the species vary seasonally.

Ocean View Resort also manages an award-winning 18-hole golf course that's right next to the campground. So if you want to mix a little golf with your camping experience, this is the place to stay.

Ocean View Resort Campground

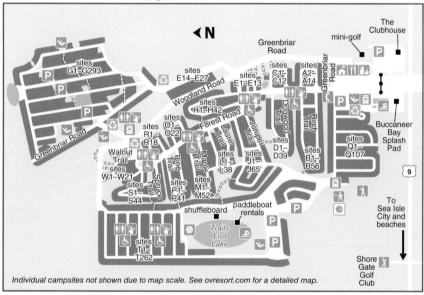

Individual campsites not shown due to map scale. See ovresort.com for a detailed map.

GETTING THERE

Heading northbound on the Garden State Parkway, use the left lane to take Exit 20 for US 9/NJ 50/Upper Township. Merge onto NJ 50 North, and turn left at the first light onto US 9 South. In 2.4 miles, the campground will be on your right.

Heading southbound on the Garden State Parkway, take Exit 17 for Sea Isle City, and turn left onto Sea Isle Boulevard. At the next light, turn right onto US 9 North, and drive 0.3 mile. The campground will be on your left.

GPS COORDINATES: N39° 10.781' W74° 43.767'

Surf & Stream Campground

Beauty ★★★ / Privacy ★★★ / Spaciousness ★★★★ / Quiet ★★★ / Security ★★★★ / Cleanliness ★★★

This private campground has a wooded island devoted solely to walk-in tent camping.

From the outside, Surf & Stream Campground looks like another in a long line of generic RV parks that are located near the shore. Dozens of trailers are packed into a large loop that circles a busy recreation area.

Look a little closer, though, and you'll start to notice a bit more character. Many of Surf & Stream's clients are longtime repeat seasonal customers—not what you'd expect from a campground located close to some of the region's top attractions.

But the most unexpected perk of Surf & Stream is not its quirky cast of characters or its amenities: it's a small, wooded island devoted solely to walk-in tent camping.

Tenters must park their cars nearby and carry their gear across a narrow wooden footbridge. There are no specific sites, but rather a number of clearings on the island. Campers can pick an open area to be near other campers or make their way to a private area on the island's tip. Plenty of picnic tables and grills are available, so drag them over to your space in the woods and designate it as a site for the night.

A stream separates the island tent-camping area on the left from the main campground.

KEY INFORMATION

ADDRESS: 1801 Ridgeway Road, Toms River, NJ 08757

OPERATED BY: Private

CONTACT: 732-349-8919, surfnstream.com /reservations

OPEN: Year-round

SITES: Open "tent island" with 30-tent limit; 202 sites and 3 cabins in main campground

EACH SITE HAS: Picnic table, grill

WHEELCHAIR ACCESS: None

ASSIGNMENT: First-come, first-served or by reservation (minimum 2 nights)

REGISTRATION: At office on arrival, by phone, or online

FACILITIES: Water, flush toilets, showers, laundry room, store

PARKING: At central parking area

FEES: $40–$50/night depending on season; rates include free TV and Wi-Fi

---

RESTRICTIONS:

PETS: Prohibited on tent island

FIRES: In fire rings only

ALCOHOL: At campsites only

VEHICLES: None on tent island

OTHER: Check-in 3 p.m., checkout at noon; 15-day stay limit; must be age 21 or older to register

Modern restrooms are a short walk away, back over the bridge. Water spigots are located on either end of the island. The central recreation area has a miniature golf course, basketball court, swimming pool, volleyball court, and horseshoe pit. The main building includes a store, recreation hall, snack bar, laundry room, and adult lounge. You can fish from the dock or riverbank; catfish, pickerel, and bass have been caught in the river, a branch of the Toms.

Theme park aficionados should note that Six Flags Great Adventure is 15 miles away; next door to the theme park is a 45-acre water park and the world's largest drive-through animal preserve outside of national parks in Africa. For those who prefer deer to rhino, the campground is also located near Pinelands National Reserve.

Just south of Surf & Stream, hikers and bikers can take advantage of the Barnegat Branch Trail, a rail-trail that follows the path of the old Barnegat section of the New Jersey Central Railroad. When completed, the trail will extend for approximately 16 miles between Barnegat and Toms River. Currently the longest section of trail extends for 7 miles between Barnegat and Forked River. Numerous access points and parking lots are located just west of NJ 9. The trail surface is finely crushed stone that is suitable for both bikers and hikers.

Many campers who visit Surf & Stream come here for the easy access to the sea. The Atlantic Ocean and Seaside Heights are just 10 miles away. Seaside Heights, together with its less famous neighbor Seaside Park, is a major beach and recreation destination, its boardwalk and pier crowded with thrill rides, arcades, snack bars, and carnival games. Casino Pier, at the northern end, is renowned for its lovingly restored turn-of-the-century carousel. Some of the attractions have seen better days—the boardwalk is, after all, more than 60 years old, but the frenetic pace of the boardwalk at night continues to attract fun seekers from all over New Jersey. Both towns offer beach access, but you must pay fees on weekends and designated days of the week. Parking is difficult, and visitors must use high-priced lots.

To avoid the crowds and hubbub of the boardwalk, head south down to Island Beach State Park. Its 9.5 miles of dunes and white sandy beaches stand in stark contrast to the commercialism and frenzied pace of Seaside Heights. Its 3,000 mostly undeveloped acres give visitors an idea of how the shore used to be. One mile of the beach, in the center of the park, is designated for swimming. Lifeguards patrol the area during the summer. Parking, a bathhouse, and a snack bar are nearby.

There is a natural area on either end of the beach. Access to the 659-acre Northern Natural Area is restricted. The 1,237-acre Southern Natural Area, together with its northern neighbor, houses a wide variety of wildlife, including New Jersey's largest osprey colony. There are bird-observation blinds, and in summer visitors may watch wildlife from naturalist-guided canoe and kayak tours. Eight trails wind through the park. Scuba diving, fishing, sailing, and surfing are allowed. Check with the visitor center for regulations and locations.

Surf & Stream's tenting island is a gem among private campgrounds, especially those nearest the shore.

Surf & Stream Campground

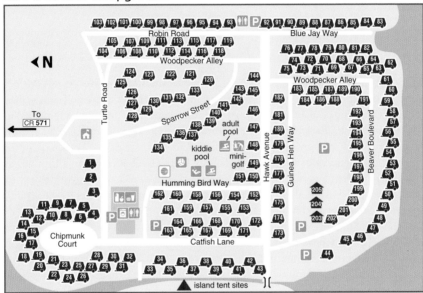

GETTING THERE

Headng northbound on the Garden State Parkway, take Exit 83 for US 9 North/Lakewood. Merge onto US 9 North, and drive 0.6 mile. Turn left onto Indian Head Road/County Road 571, and drive 1.7 miles. The campground entrance will be on your left.

Heading southbound on the Garden State Parkway, take Exit 89B (Lakehurst/Brick). Merge onto NJ 70 West, and drive 3.9 miles. Turn left onto Whitesville Road/CR 527, and drive 2.7 miles. Turn right onto Ridgeway Road/CR 571 West, and drive 0.4 mile. The campground entrance will be on your left.

GPS COORDINATES: N40° 00.227' W74° 14.168'

SOUTHERN NEW JERSEY

A peninsula of trees on the Wading River (see Wharton State Forest campground profiles)

Atlantic County Park:
ESTELL MANOR CAMPGROUND AND CAMP ACAGISCA

Beauty ★★★★ / Privacy ★★★★ / Spaciousness ★★★★ / Quiet ★★★★★ / Security ★★ / Cleanliness ★★

If you want to get away from it all while not disappearing into the bush, these two locations are for you.

If you're looking for convenience, comfort, and small luxuries such as hot showers and well-marked roads, the camping at Estell Manor and Camp Acagisca won't suit your tastes. If, however, you want to get away from it all without heading very far afield, these two locations are worth trying out. While Lake Lenape (see next profile) is the signature campground for the Atlantic County park system, the camping at both Estell Manor and Camp Acagisca is considerably more low-key. You'll have plenty of room to roam, and the possibility of having neighbors of any sort other than the resident wildlife is pretty slim.

The sites at both locations are technically group sites, but since organized groups don't use them every weekend, they're often available for groups as small as a family. Camping at either location requires that you register at the boathouse/reservations office at Lake Lenape; the office closes at 5 p.m. during spring and fall; closing time is at 9 p.m. throughout summer. The single site at Estell Manor is located about 10 minutes south of Mays Landing near the end of easy-to-miss Artesian Well Road, so be sure to get directions at the office when you register. The two sites at Camp Acagisca are located about 10 minutes north of Lake Lenape. Its access road and two sites are easy to find.

The Great Egg Harbor River meanders past Camp Acagisca.

KEY INFORMATION

ADDRESSES: Estell Manor Campground, 109 Artesian Well Road, Mays Landing, NJ 08330; Camp Acagisca, 6755 Weymouth Road, Mays Landing, NJ 08330

OPERATED BY: Atlantic County Parks & Recreation

CONTACT: 609-625-8219, atlantic-county .org/parks

OPEN: April 1–November 1

SITES: 1 at Estell Manor, 2 at Camp Acagisca (all are group sites)

EACH SITE HAS: Picnic table, fire ring

WHEELCHAIR ACCESS: None

ASSIGNMENT: In person at the Lake Lenape Reservation Office, 6303 Old Harding Highway, Mays Landing, NJ 08330

REGISTRATION: In person at the Lake Lenape Reservation Office

FACILITIES: Portable toilet

PARKING: At campsites; 2-vehicle limit

FEE: $25/night; pay in person by check or money order at the Lake Lenape Reservation Office

---

RESTRICTIONS:

PETS: Prohibited

FIRES: Permit required

ALCOHOL: Prohibited

VEHICLES: No RVs, but pop-up campers are allowed

OTHER: No wood collecting; 14-day stay limit; must be at least age 21 years to register

The campsite at Estell Manor is utterly off the beaten path but is still accessible to those on an overnight trip. Estell Manor used to be the location of a campground with about 10 sites, but that was closed to protect nesting birds. Now the group site is the only option for camping in the area. The site is set off in the woods, about 100 feet south of Artesian Well Road. A portable toilet is located near the road across from the campsite. The site is secure by default—only those aware of its existence would think to look for it—but it is not within a guarded region or fence. The area is popular with boaters because a ramp into the South River is located right next door. (Boaters must abide by state boating regulations.)

The nearby Swamp Trail Boardwalk, a 6-foot-wide thoroughfare, winds through wetlands and wildlife habitats. It passes deserted building remains from when the Bethlehem Loading Company maintained rail tracks in the area. The company was one of four munitions factories that were opened in New Jersey during World War I; today, little evidence of that time remains.

The boardwalk provides access to nature without damaging the plants underneath the walkway; it also keeps hikers away from ticks and mud. Bicycles are not allowed on the boardwalk. Several more-traditional trails, which allow cyclists as well as hikers, meander through the 1,700-acre forest as well. Many of the 15 miles of trails, including the boardwalk, eventually lead to the developed section of Estell Manor, which includes a nature center and a loop road.

The Warren E. Fox Nature Center is the headquarters of the developed section of Estell Manor and is also headquarters for environmental education in Atlantic County. Lectures and meetings are held in its auditorium. Small exhibits detail the area's wildlife activities and explain which trees live within the park. Most popular are the live indigenous animals and carnivorous plants kept in the nature center. Visitors can examine frogs, lizards, turtles, and snails up close.

Camp Acagisca is off Weymouth Road, a few miles north of Lake Lenape. Although the name of the area may sound like a native Lenape word, its origins are slightly less colorful—it's actually an acronym for "**A**tlantic **C**ounty **A**rea **Gi**rl **Sc**out **Ca**mp." Two group sites are located here: at the intersection where a road forks left, continue straight to reach the first site, just ahead on the right. It has a picnic pavilion and a portable toilet. Across from the camping area is a lodge that may be rented for events. The second campsite is a quarter mile down the left turn mentioned above, toward the Great Egg Harbor River on the right side of the road. It's considerably smaller than the other site, with room for a couple of tents. Like the first site, it has a small picnic pavilion and a portable toilet. It would be the more suitable of the two sites for a small group.

Not far beyond the second site, the road ends at a small cul-de-sac, from which there is access to the river. Boaters will have to carry their boats up or down a steep hill to reach the launch; they will also need to purchase a permit at the Lake Lenape Reservations Office.

Eight miles northeast of Lake Lenape and four miles north of Camp Acagisca is 11-acre Weymouth Park. This is a popular take-out spot for canoeists and is also the site of the ruins of Weymouth Forge, which produced iron for about 60 years during the 1800s. At its height, the tract contained the furnace, 20 houses for workers, a forge, gristmill, church, sawmill, store, barn, blacksmith shop, wheelwright, and owner's mansion. The forge was destroyed in 1862, but its usefulness had already ceased when Pennsylvania's coal-powered forges took over.

Some of the forge property was purchased with money from county funds, as was Atlantic County Park at Lake Lenape. The county's dedication to preserving outdoors space is obvious from the excellent upkeep at Lake Lenape, Camp Acagisca, and Estell Manor, as is its dedication to tent camping, apparent in the camping areas found in Atlantic County.

Atlantic County Park: Estell Manor Campground

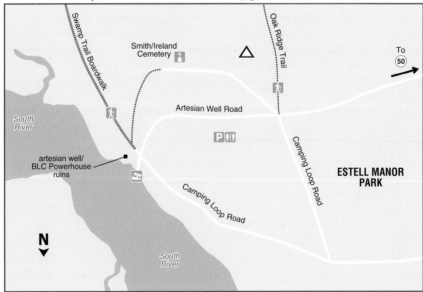

Atlantic County Park: Camp Acagisca

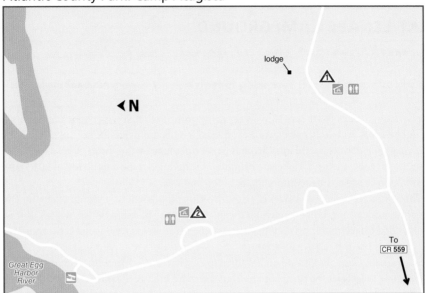

GETTING THERE

You must first register at the Lake Lenape Reservation Office. To get there from the Atlantic City Expressway, take Exit 28 for NJ 54 South. Drive 1–1.4 miles (depending on whether you took the southbound or northbound exit), and then turn left onto NJ 73 South/Mays Landing Road. In 2.2 miles, turn left onto US 322 East/Black Horse Pike. Drive 4.6 miles, and bear right onto County Road 559 South/Weymouth Road. Drive 4.9 miles, and turn left to continue on CR 559/Old Harding Highway. In 0.2 mile, turn left at the entrance for Lake Lenape Park. In another 0.2 mile, turn right; the Lake Lenape Boathouse/Reservations Office will be just ahead on your right. Parking is available on both sides of the road just before you reach the boathouse.

Estell Manor: From the reservations office, backtrack to the park entrance road and turn left; in 0.2 mile, turn left onto CR 559. Drive 0.2 mile; then turn right onto Mill Street. At the intersection with US 40, Mill Street becomes NJ 50 South. Continue on NJ 50 South for 2.5 miles; then turn left at the brown ATLANTIC COUNTY PARK SYSTEM sign onto Artesian Well Road. The campsite is 0.25 miles ahead, on the right.

Camp Acagisca: From the reservations office, backtrack to the park entrance road and turn left. In 0.2 mile, turn right onto CR 559; then take the first right to continue on CR 559 North/Weymouth Road. In 2.8 miles, the entrance to Camp Acagisca will be on the right.

GPS COORDINATES:
ESTELL MANOR: N39° 24.924' W74° 44.023'
CAMP ACAGISCA: N39° 29.348' W74° 45.946'

Atlantic County Park:
LAKE LENAPE CAMPGROUND

Beauty ★★★ / Privacy ★★ / Spaciousness ★★★★ / Quiet ★★★ / Security ★★ / Cleanliness ★★

This lakeside campground is open solely to tenters—RV owners need not apply.

Lake Lenape is one of those rare New Jersey campgrounds that are open to tent campers only. But unlike most tent-only campgrounds, these 18 sites are drive-in, not hike-in. Campers enter via a long driveway and loop around to set up house by the shore. A new loop with an additional 11 tent sites and 6 lakeside cabins was scheduled to be completed in 2018 but was not yet open at press time; contact the park for updates.

Campsites are spacious and level, with towering woods offering plenty of shade. There's almost no understory, however, which means no privacy barriers between sites. But while campers don't have much privacy from each other, the access road is not a thoroughfare—only campers use the dead-end drive.

Several campsites are located on Lake Lenape itself; sites 7–13 are particularly scenic. Several portable toilets dot the camping area, but the more high-tech shower and flush toilets are near the park entrance at the boathouse. The boathouse is also home to the Atlantic County Rowing Association, a public nonprofit group that promotes rowing in Atlantic County.

Kayakers enjoy a spring day on Lake Lenape in Atlantic County Park.

KEY INFORMATION

ADDRESS: 6303 Old Harding Highway, Mays Landing, NJ 08234

OPERATED BY: Atlantic County Parks & Recreation

CONTACT: 609-625-8219, atlantic-county .org/parks

OPEN: April 1–November 1

SITES: 18 (11 additional sites and 6 cabins scheduled for completion in 2018)

EACH SITE HAS: Picnic table, fire ring, trash can

WHEELCHAIR ACCESS: Boathouse at day-use area

ASSIGNMENT: In person at the Lake Lenape Reservation Office, 6303 Old Harding Highway, Mays Landing, NJ 08330

REGISTRATION: In person at the Lake Lenape Reservation Office

FACILITIES: Portable toilets, water; flush toilets and showers at boathouse

PARKING: At campsites; 2-vehicle limit

FEE: $25/night; pay in person by check or money order at the Lake Lenape Reservation Office

---

RESTRICTIONS:

PETS: Prohibited

FIRES: Permit required; use firewood provided

ALCOHOL: Prohibited

VEHICLES: No RVs, but pop-up campers are allowed

OTHER: Must be at least age 21 to register; 14-day stay limit; check-in before 5 p.m.; no swimming from sites

---

Campers must book in person at the Lake Lenape Reservation Office in the boathouse; reserve ahead on weekends and also if you expect to arrive late. Permits are not issued after the office closes at 9 p.m. in summer or at 5 p.m. at other times of the camping season. The Lake Lenape Reservation Office also issues permits for the sites at Estell Manor and Camp Acagisca (see previous profile).

The 1,921-acre Lake Lenape Park is the largest park in the Atlantic County system. Most of it has been intentionally left wild. It is one of 13 parks acquired through New Jersey State Green Acres funds and a local tax. (County citizens voted the tax into existence in 1990, expressly for the purpose of acquiring open space, recreational land, and historic sites.)

Ten miles of trails wind through Lake Lenape's forests. Guided hikes begin at the boathouse on weekends during summer months. Call ahead for the schedule. Naturalists advise hikers to take standard precautions against ticks: tuck the cuffs of your pants into your socks, and use insect repellent. Keep your eyes on the sky as well as the trail, as bald eagles are often seen at Lake Lenape in colder months.

The 344-acre lake is home to several species of fish, including bluegill, chain pickerel, yellow perch, crappie, largemouth bass, and sunfish. Fishing is allowed.

Boating is allowed on the lake from the launch near the reservation office. Boaters are asked to check in before launching. The ramp is open 365 days a year, from 7:30 a.m. until 30 minutes after sunset. Motorized and nonmotorized craft are allowed, but a host of rules applies—see atlantic-county.org/parks/lake-lenape-boating.asp for details.

Kayak, canoe, and small-vessel owners may also travel the scenic Great Egg Harbor River. Boaters must purchase permits for $5 at Lake Lenape Boathouse; leave one permit in your car, which can be left near the boat launch, 250 yards north of campsite 18, and display the other permit in your pick-up vehicle. Boats can also be launched from Camp Acagisca.

Canoes can be rented near the park. Parts of Great Egg Harbor River can be difficult and wild, so research routes in advance.

The Lake Lenape gazebo can be rented for parties, weddings, and other events; it's on the lake next to the playground. Parents must be present when children use the playground.

Atlantic County Park: Lake Lenape Campground (Loop A)

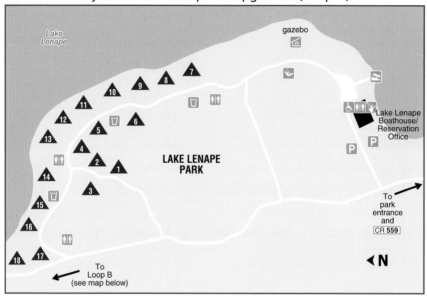

Atlantic County Park: Lake Lenape Campground (Loop B)

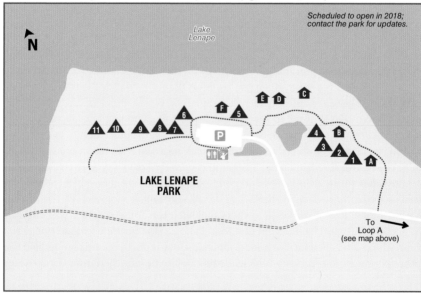

GETTING THERE

From the Atlantic City Expressway, take Exit 28 for NJ 54 South. Drive 1–1.4 miles (depending on whether you took the northbound or southbound exit), and then turn left onto NJ 73 South/Mays Landing Road. In 2.2 miles, turn left onto US 322 East/Black Horse Pike. Drive 4.6 miles, and bear right onto County Road 559 South/Weymouth Road. Drive 4.9 miles, and turn left to continue on CR 559/Old Harding Highway. In 0.2 mile, turn left at the entrance for Lake Lenape Park. In another 0.2 mile, turn right; the Lake Lenape Boathouse/Reservations Office will be just ahead on your right. Parking is available on both sides of the road just before you reach the boathouse. After you register, continue north along the lake on the access road; the campsites are just a short distance ahead.

GPS COORDINATES: N39° 27.427' W74° 44.343'

Several sites at Lake Lenape Campground sit right above the lake.

Belleplain State Forest:
MEISLE FIELD AND CCC CAMP

Beauty ★★★★ / Privacy ★★★ / Spaciousness ★★★★ / Quiet ★★★ / Security ★★★ / Cleanliness ★★★

This is the closest tenters can get to Cape May without sacrificing their wilderness experience.

Unassuming and modest compared with their private cousins that pervade the nearby Cape May Peninsula, the campgrounds of Belleplain State Forest offer a respite from the Jersey Shore's dense RV lifestyle. Belleplain, with its 20,000 acres, is not the southernmost of New Jersey's state parks, but it does contain the three southernmost public campgrounds. It's the closest tent campers can get to Cape May without sacrificing their wilderness experience for more-organized, close-knit fun. Belleplain is located within the Pinelands National Reserve, a unique ecosystem also known as the Pine Barrens.

Belleplain's centerpiece, 26-acre Lake Nummy, was the Meisle family's cranberry bog before 1933, when the Civilian Conservation Corps (CCC) Reforestation Relief Act transformed it. Three separate camps were set up, and the CCC got to work digging and constructing. Lake Nummy was then called Meisle Lake and was later renamed after a Lenni Lenape Indian chief.

Meisle Field and CCC Camp are two adjacent campgrounds located at the southern end of Lake Nummy. Unlike their counterpart on the north shore of the lake, both of these campgrounds are pet-friendly. They are both large loops bisected by roads that create smaller loops. Meisle Field features 14 lean-tos and 5 yurts in addition to 49 basic sites. Trailers and tenters are welcome in Meisle Field, but tent campers will want to head to the

Spring has sprung at Belleplain State Forest.

KEY INFORMATION

ADDRESS: 1 Henkinsifkin Road, Woodbine, NJ 08270

OPERATED BY: New Jersey State Park Service

CONTACT: 609-861-2404, njparksandforests .org/parks/belle.html; reservations: camping.nj.gov

OPEN: Year-round

SITES: 85, plus 14 lean-tos and 5 yurts

EACH SITE HAS: Picnic table, fire ring

WHEELCHAIR ACCESS: All sites are ADA-accessible

ASSIGNMENT: First-come, first-served or by reservation (minimum 2 nights)

REGISTRATION: On arrival or online

FACILITIES: Water, flush toilets, showers, laundry room

PARKING: At campsites; 2-vehicle limit

FEES: New Jersey residents, $20/night; nonresidents, $25/night; $5/night pet fee

RESTRICTIONS:

PETS: On leash, all sites (except group sites, lean-tos, and cabins), 2 pets/site; pet permit and proof of current vaccinations required. See njparksandforests.org/parks /pet_friendly_camping.html for more information.

FIRES: In fire rings only

ALCOHOL: Prohibited

VEHICLES: No RV hookups

OTHER: Quiet hours 10 p.m.–6 a.m.; 14-day stay limit; 6-person/2-tent site limit

back of Meisle Field or to CCC Camp for more privacy. Owners of larger RVs will also want to go to the CCC Camp, as several large, open sites are located along its three roads. Both Meisle Field and CCC Camp have modern bathhouses with flush toilets, hot showers, and laundry facilities.

Eagle Fitness Trail, accessed from a dirt track located between Meisle Field and CCC Camp, is a mile-long self-guided fitness loop that features 10 exercise stations. After warming up, hikers can tackle a long trail such as the 7.16-mile East Creek Trail, or they can just head to Lake Nummy and do a little fishing.

Fishing is also allowed at East Creek Pond, Holly Lake, and Cedar Lake. Pickerel, perch, catfish, and sunfish have been caught in Lake Nummy, while East Creek Pond is also home to largemouth bass. The floating dock on Lake Nummy, near the CCC-built Interpretive Center (once park headquarters), is used for launching small boats and canoes. There is also a boat ramp on the western shore of East Creek Pond. Gas-powered boats are prohibited in Belleplain State Forest. Visitors may rent canoes and paddleboats from the floating dock and the swimming area. The bathhouse and white-sand beach are described in the profile for Belleplain's North Shore Campground (see next profile).

Belleplain State Forest is a great base from which to explore the Victorian seaside resort city of Cape May. It's a 30-mile drive from the campground to the town, but it makes for a pleasant day trip. Cape May, 2.3 square miles in size, is a living-history landmark replete with restored Victorian homes. Once you've strolled the streets and marveled at the architecture, head over to Cape May Point State Park. Its 235 acres are for day use only—no camping allowed.

Cape May Lighthouse is a good place to start your tour of the park. For $8, visitors can climb the 199 steps for a panoramic view of the surrounding peninsula. Back down on earth during low tide, you can see a World War II bunker that was built when the area was a military base. Cape May Point also has a 153-acre natural area, and 4 miles of trails wind through the park so visitors can view regional flora and fauna. But most nature lovers come to Cape May to see one thing: birds.

Cape May lies along a major migratory-bird route. The New Jersey Audubon Society maintains the Cape May Bird Observatory, which serves as an information hub and resource center for birders; it also hosts birding workshops and walks throughout the year. Lists of recently spotted rare birds can be found on the sightings page of its website, tinyurl.com /njsightings. The society also hosts the annual World Series of Birding. For 24 hours on a May weekend, teams of birders rush around the state spotting and identifying birds. They must return to Cape May at the end of the day to cross the finish line. Participants have a lot of fun, but the main purpose is fundraising: sponsors donate money, and 100% of funds raised go to the participants' choice of environmental funds.

Belleplain State Forest may not be the most convenient campground to Cape May—more than a dozen campgrounds are located on the Cape May Peninsula itself—but most of those sites are RV-oriented, with no privacy or space between sites. They're geared toward shore access, not toward wilderness and nature. At Belleplain State Forest, campers get the best of the lot: natural beauty, seclusion, shore access, and proximity to the Cape May Peninsula.

Belleplain State Forest: Meisle Field and CCC Camp

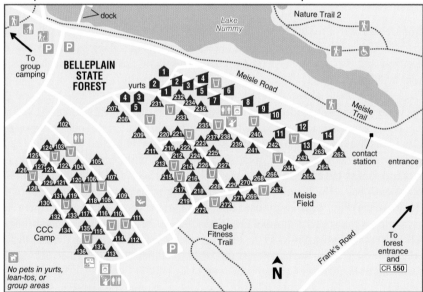

GETTING THERE

Heading northbound on the Garden State Parkway, take Exit 10 (Stone Harbor). Turn left onto Stone Harbor Boulevard, which almost immediately becomes Court House South Dennis Road, and drive 6.1 miles; then turn right onto NJ 47 North, and drive 2 miles. Turn right onto Tyler Road, and drive 2.9 miles. Merge onto Washington Avenue, and then almost immediately turn left onto Webster Street/County Road 550, and drive 1.4 miles.

The park entrance will be on your left. Drive 0.6 mile, and turn left; in another 0.5 mile, make another left into the campground.

Heading southbound on the Garden State Parkway, take Exit 17 (Sea Isle City). Turn left onto Sea Isle Boulevard, and then take the first right onto US 9 North. Drive 0.6 mile; then turn left onto Woodbine Ocean View Road/CR 550. Continue on CR 550 for 6.2 miles. In Woodbine, turn left on Washington Avenue, and drive 0.4 mile (this keeps you on CR 550). Turn right onto Webster Street (which again keeps you on CR 550), and drive 1.4 miles. The park entrance will be on your left. Drive 0.6 mile, and turn left; in another 0.5 mile, make another left into the campground.

GPS COORDINATES: N39° 14.745' W74° 51.432'

A kayaker enjoys a paddle on Lake Nummy.

Belleplain State Forest:
NORTH SHORE CAMPGROUND

Beauty ★★★★ / Privacy ★★★★ / Spaciousness ★★★★ / Quiet ★★★★ / Security ★★★ / Cleanliness ★★★★

With tranquil campsites and easy access to the Cape May Peninsula, Belleplain offers the best of both worlds.

North Shore Campground, like the other two Belleplain State Forest campgrounds (see previous profile), is secluded, pleasant, and located in a shady forest. Unlike the other two, however, North Shore Campground does not allow pets. Understory provides privacy between sites, although nearly all sites can be seen from the mazelike road that loops through these 82 sites. As in most New Jersey state parks, site sizes vary from small areas that comfortably house two tents to large clearings that can handle a 40-foot RV. No hookups are available.

The sites along the eastern edge of the campground border Lake Nummy. Shrubs and bushes surround most of them, but sites 25–27 are open and can provide space for a small group or large family.

A campsite among the dogwoods

Booking ahead might get you a coveted lakeside site because the staff does attempt to satisfy requests, but plenty of scenic non-lakeside spots are available on summer weekdays. Reserve ahead on holidays and weekends.

Belleplain's North Shore Campground is located near 26-acre Lake Nummy's white sandy beach and swim area. The bathhouse, beach, and snack bar are open Memorial Day weekend–Labor Day. For those who prefer to swim in the sea, the Atlantic Ocean is only 10 miles away.

The 20,000-acre Belleplain State Forest sprawls across both Cape May and Cumberland County. The park has more than 40 miles of trails; some are dedicated solely to hikers, while others are multiuse. Fourteen trails offer access to motorized vehicles, but ATVs are prohibited throughout the park. Note that several of these motorized trails are backcountry routes and are not passable by regular cars. Some pass through large pools of water or along steep grades. Trucks, snowmobiles, and motorcycles are commonly used on the trails.

Along with the Eagle Fitness Trail, two trails are dedicated solely to pedestrians. Nature Trail 1 and Nature Trail 2 wind around the northern shore of Lake Nummy and through the nearby forest; 32 stations highlight plants and habitats. Pick up a

KEY INFORMATION

ADDRESS: 1 Henkinsifkin Road, Woodbine, NJ 08270

OPERATED BY: New Jersey State Park Service

CONTACT: 609-861-2404, njparksandforests .org/parks/belle.html; reservations: camping.nj.gov

OPEN: Year-round

SITES: 82

EACH SITE HAS: Picnic table, fire ring

WHEELCHAIR ACCESS: All sites are ADA-accessible

ASSIGNMENT: First-come, first-served or by reservation (minimum 2 nights)

REGISTRATION: On arrival or online

FACILITIES: Water, flush toilets, showers, laundry room

PARKING: At campsites; 2-vehicle limit

FEES: New Jersey residents, $20/night; nonresidents, $25/night; $5/night pet fee

RESTRICTIONS:

PETS: Prohibited here but allowed at Meisle Field and CCC Camp (see previous profile)

FIRES: In fire rings only

ALCOHOL: Prohibited

VEHICLES: No RV hookups

OTHER: Quiet hours 10 p.m.–6 a.m.; 14-day stay limit; 6-person/2-tent site limit

booklet at the forest office to follow the self-guided route. Hikers should remember that the forest is home to ticks and deer lice. Wear repellent, long sleeves, trousers, and socks.

The remaining 16 miles of trails are open to hikers, cyclists, horses, and cross-country skiers. Cyclists and hikers must yield to horses. Trails are marked with signs that indicate their designations. All users, regardless of their chosen method for traversing the trails, will enjoy the shade of tall cedar, pine, holly, and laurel trees.

Belleplain State Forest is also a main stop on another sort of trail. It's an information site for the Delsea Region of the New Jersey Coastal Heritage Trail Route, a 300-mile-long auto tour.

The New Jersey Coastal Heritage Trail Route begins where many people first enter New Jersey, near the Delaware Memorial Bridge at the southwestern tip of the state. The route hugs the coast all the way to Cape May in the east, then follows the Jersey Shore north to Raritan Bay, ending just before the New York City metropolitan area begins. It's a cooperative project involving the National Park Service and New Jersey. The route was established in 1988 and features the five categorical themes of maritime history, coastal habitats, wildlife migration, relaxation and inspiration, and historic settlements.

Pick up a brochure for the Delsea Region at the forest office, and you can drive from the Delaware Memorial Bridge to Cape May Court House, stopping at designated sites en route. Highlights include wildlife management areas, wetlands, and the Greenwich Tea Burning Monument. In 1774, young men dressed as American Indians and burned East India tea. This was after the famous Boston Tea Party but prior to the start of the Revolutionary War.

Another notable feature of the Delsea Region is the annual horseshoe crab spawning at Heislerville Wildlife Management Area. Horseshoe crabs lay eggs on the beach in May, which in turn attracts thousands of migratory shorebirds. Horseshoe crabs and migratory birds can also be observed at East Point Lighthouse; in early fall, you can observe migrating monarch butterflies there as well.

Bald eagles can often be seen at Stow Creek Viewing Area and have also been observed at Heislerville Wildlife Management Area. Other points of interest include post–Civil War

Fort Mott and Hancock House Historic Site. The latter was the site of a Revolutionary War massacre in which a British force killed 30 sleeping colonial militiamen.

Belleplain State Forest offers the best of both worlds to campers and nature lovers, with its tranquil woodland campsites and easy access to the attractions of the Cape May Peninsula. Couples, families, and solo campers will all enjoy the recreational offerings of the park.

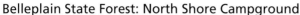

Belleplain State Forest: North Shore Campground

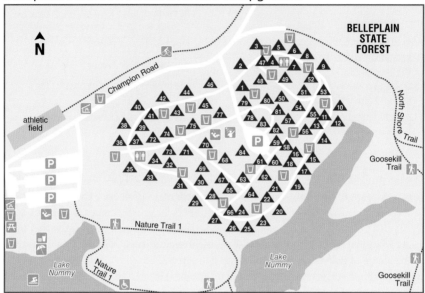

GETTING THERE

Heading northbound on the Garden State Parkway, take Exit 10 (Stone Harbor). Turn left onto Stone Harbor Boulevard, which almost immediately becomes Court House South Dennis Road, and drive 6.1 miles; then turn right onto NJ 47 North, and drive 2 miles. Turn right onto Tyler Road, and drive 2.9 miles. Merge onto Washington Avenue, and then almost immediately turn left onto Webster Street/County Road 550, and drive 1.4 miles. The park entrance will be on your left. Drive 0.6 mile, and turn left; in another 0.6 mile, turn right at the intersection just past the west end of Lake Nummy. In 0.2 mile, make another right; the campground entrance is 0.3 mile ahead, on your right.

Heading southbound on the Garden State Parkway, take Exit 17 (Sea Isle City). Turn left onto Sea Isle Boulevard, and then take the first right onto US 9 North. Drive 0.6 mile; then turn left onto Woodbine Ocean View Road/CR 550. Continue on CR 550 for 6.2 miles. In Woodbine, turn left on Washington Avenue, and drive 0.4 mile (this keeps you on CR 550). Turn right onto Webster Street (which again keeps you on CR 550), and drive 1.4 miles. The park entrance will be on your left. Drive 0.6 mile, and turn left; in another 0.6 mile, turn right at the intersection just past the west end of Lake Nummy. In 0.2 mile, make another right; the campground entrance is 0.3 mile ahead, on your right.

GPS COORDINATES: N39° 14.928' W74° 51.189'

Parvin State Park:
JAGGERS POINT CAMPING AREA

Beauty ★★★★ / Privacy ★★★ / Spaciousness ★★★★ / Quiet ★★★★ / Security ★★★★ /
Cleanliness ★★★★

One of the nicest campgrounds in the region, Parvin State Park is well worth a detour.

Humbly located in southwestern Jersey, near no major tourist attractions and no main highways, Jaggers Point Campground at Parvin State Park is a destination unto itself. You're not likely to stumble across it while going about your daily business in the Garden State.

But Parvin State Park is well worth a detour—its campground is one of the nicest in the region. Six small loops are home to 54 sites, giving campers a choice between secluded wooded sites and larger open sites. Tall hardwood trees shade all of them.

Sites 10, 11, and 13 are highly prized because of their lakeside location; book ahead or go midweek to score the waterfront real estate. The camp playground is located next to site 10, so campers lucky enough to stay there may encounter a few young trespassers. There are no trailer hookups, but RVs are welcome on the larger, open sites. Groups camp separately on a designated island. Additionally, 18 cabins are available for rent April 1–October 31.

The Civilian Conservation Corps (CCC) built the cabins and campground, along with Parvin Lake's beach complex and parking lot, between 1933 and 1941. The CCC, created and deployed as part of FDR's New Deal, built the infrastructure for several of New Jersey's state parks. At Parvin Camp, they dug out and dammed Thundergust Lake, the smaller 14-acre sister to 108-acre Parvin Lake. In 1943, the site was used as a summer camp for the children of displaced Japanese Americans; a year later, it became a detention camp for German POWs. In 1952, it briefly housed refugees from the Kalmyk Republic, a Soviet state that had been dissolved by Josef Stalin during World War II; most of its citizens were deported due to suspected collaboration with Germany, and many languished for years after the war in refugee camps in western Europe before finding new homes elsewhere. The refugees housed

Kayakers negotiate a bit of wind on Parvin Lake.

KEY INFORMATION

ADDRESS: 701 Almond Road, Elmer, NJ 08318

OPERATED BY: New Jersey State Park Service

CONTACT: 856-358-8616, njparksandforests .org/parks/parvin.html; reservations: camping.nj.gov

OPEN: Year-round

SITES: 54

EACH SITE HAS: Picnic table, fire ring, lantern hooks

WHEELCHAIR ACCESS: All sites and facilities are ADA-accessible

ASSIGNMENT: First-come, first-served or by reservation (minimum 2 nights)

REGISTRATION: On arrival or online

FACILITIES: Water, flush toilets, showers, laundry room

PARKING: At campsites; 2-vehicle limit

FEES: New Jersey residents, $20/night; nonresidents, $25/night; $5/night pet fee

---

RESTRICTIONS:

PETS: On leash, sites 44–55 only, 2 pets/site; pet permit and proof of current vaccinations required. See njparksandforests.org /parks/pet_friendly_camping.html for more information.

FIRES: In fire rings only

ALCOHOL: Prohibited

VEHICLES: No RV hookups

OTHER: Quiet hours 10 p.m.–6 a.m.; 14-day stay limit; 6-person/2-tent site limit

at Parvin Camp went on to settle in central New Jersey and Philadelphia, after which time the park returned to its intended purpose of providing nature access and recreation to the public.

Parvin Lake has a boat ramp reserved exclusively for campers. Cabins have their own boat ramps as well, but the public boat launch is at Fisherman's Landing on the east side of the lake, off Parvin Mill Road. Visitors can rent canoes and kayaks at nearby Al and Sam's Canoe, Boat and Kayak (856-692-8440, alandsams.com). Electrical powered boats are also allowed on both lakes, but only canoeists and people-powered boats area allowed on Muddy Run between Parvin Lake and the town of Centerton.

Fishing is popular on both lakes and on Muddy Run. Pickerel, catfish, yellow perch, and sunfish live in Parvin State Park's waters, along with trophy bass. Hunting is prohibited.

Swimming is allowed at the lifeguard-protected beach at Parvin Grove, by the park office. A free parking lot is located across County Road 540, but a fee is charged to enter the beach area. Concessionaires offer snacks and beach supplies, and there are picnic areas, playgrounds, and a bathhouse beside the beach.

Parvin has designated 465 of its 1,309 acres as the Parvin Natural Area, which is permanently protected as undeveloped woodlands. You may spot 172 species of birds here, along with deer, mice, river otters, frogs, salamanders, toads, turtles, and snakes; the state-endangered barred owl and swamp pink live here as well. More than half of Parvin's 15 miles of trails wind through the natural area, under pitch pines and through cedar swamps. Take precautions against ticks, which are common in South Jersey and particularly prevalent in the natural area. Cover up with long sleeves, pants, socks, and hiking boots, and apply repellent regularly while in the area.

Sooner or later, most campers must head to Vineland for supplies; it's the nearest town and home to restaurants, gas stations, and supermarkets. But Vineland has other claims to semi-fame. It's the original home of Welch's Grape Juice and mason jars. In addition, a 30-foot-tall concrete replica of the Statue of Liberty resides in a private backyard sculpture garden built by local resident George Arbuckel during the Great Depression. The statue is visible from Main Street.

Another Vineland eccentric, George Daynor, created an 18-spired castle out of junk and old cars during the Depression. (A former gold miner, Daynor lost his money in the Crash of 1929.) His Palace of Depression stood as an income-generating landmark for many years but fell into disrepair before it was finally torn down in 1969. The Palace of Depression Restoration Association began rebuilding the palace in 2000, using old photos and newsreel footage as a guide; the project continues to this day. When in Vineland, drive down Mill Road near Landis Avenue to have a look at the group's progress.

Another attraction potentially worth checking out is the Cowtown Rodeo, 22 miles northwest of Parvin State Park on US 40 past Sharptown. Though rodeos and New Jersey might seem an unusual pairing, this rodeo has been taking place on Saturday nights since 1929.

Southwestern New Jersey and Parvin State Park are unique in the state. The crowds teeming along the shore and in the north are absent here, and a hike through Parvin Natural Area will most likely be a solitary, enjoyable affair.

Parvin State Park: Jaggers Point Camping Area

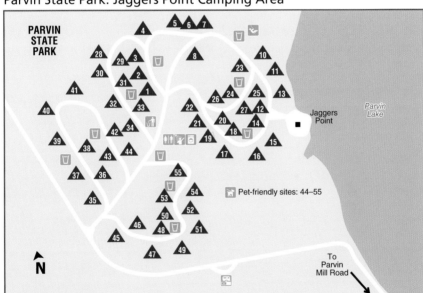

GETTING THERE

From I-295 South, keep right at Exit 26 to stay on I-295 toward NJ 42 South and Atlantic City. Then follow signs for an exit on the left for NJ 42 South, and merge onto it. Drive 1.3 miles; then take Exit 13 for NJ 55 South. Drive 25 miles; then take Exit 35B (Brotmanville). Merge onto Garden Road, and drive 2 miles. Make a slight left onto Parvin Mill Road, and drive 2.3 miles. The signed park entrance will be on your right; the campground is about 0.5 mile farther on the right.

GPS COORDINATES: N39° 30.454' W75° 08.264'

Philadelphia South/Clarksboro KOA Campground

Beauty ★★ / Privacy ★★ / Spaciousness ★★ / Quiet ★★ / Security ★★★★ / Cleanliness ★★★

The nine shady tent sites at this KOA are great for Philadelphia-bound travelers on a budget.

The closest campground to the City of Brotherly Love, Philadelphia South/Clarksboro KOA Campground earns a mention here for its small, shady tenting groves. It's primarily geared toward RV owners and at first glance appears tent-unfriendly. But for the car traveler wishing to visit Philadelphia on a budget or for the urban refugee seeking a quick night away from the city, KOA is a great choice because it's just 15 miles from the city. It's also a friendly place to pitch your tent if you want to visit Valley Forge or the New Jersey State Aquarium, or if you simply need a place to stop for the night on your way in or out of New Jersey.

The crowded, sunny RV sites may appear unwelcoming to rustic tent campers, but there are two small areas dedicated to tenting. Seven of the tent sites (48–54) are positioned across from a central pond and isolated from RVs; the other two, just above this section, are "glamping" ("glamour camping") tents outfitted with beds and wooden decks. All nine campsites are

Many of the tent sites at this KOA campground back up to its pond.

KEY INFORMATION

ADDRESS: 117 Timberlane Road, Clarksboro, NJ 08020

OPERATED BY: Private

CONTACT: 856-423-6677, koa.com /campgrounds/philadelphia-south

OPEN: Year-round

SITES: 109 (9 tent sites), plus 9 cabins

EACH SITE HAS: Picnic table, fire ring

WHEELCHAIR ACCESS: None

ASSIGNMENT: First-come, first-served or by reservation

REGISTRATION: On arrival or online

FACILITIES: Water, flush toilets, showers, laundry room, store

PARKING: At lots

FEE: Tent sites start at $47/night (no hookups)

RESTRICTIONS:

PETS: On leash

FIRES: In fire rings, subject to restrictions

ALCOHOL: At campsites only

VEHICLES: Up to 73 feet

OTHER: Quiet hours 11 p.m.–7 a.m.; no stay limit; no smoking allowed in restrooms or laundry

spacious, wooded, and perfect for those seeking a pleasant campground in close proximity to Philadelphia versus an idyllic outdoors experience. Nine cabins are available for rent as well.

The campground's 20 acres include such amenities as a playground, a recreation room with games, horseshoes, shuffleboard, a pool, a store, and pond fishing. The restrooms are clean and well maintained. Each tent site has a fire ring, and firewood is sold at the store.

The location, near the oil refineries along the Delaware River and an industrial park, is admittedly not a place that springs to mind for outdoor pursuits. But just 5 miles southwest of the campground is Gloucester County's Greenwich Lake Park. The 40-acre lake is a renowned trout-fishing spot. Boating is allowed, and there are picnic facilities and a playground.

A 10-mile drive in the opposite direction takes you to 300-acre Washington Lake Park in Sewell. The park has nearly 5 miles of multiuse trails, soccer fields, ball fields, an amphitheater, a gazebo, a skateboard/in-line skating park, and a roller hockey rink. The main lake is off-limits to fishing, but there is a separate, smaller fishing lake. Free summer concerts and movies are sometimes presented in the amphitheater.

Seven miles to the northwest of the campground, on the Delaware River, is Red Bank Battlefield Park. Although the name may imply otherwise, the Battle of Red Bank was not fought on the Atlantic coast in the town of Red Bank: this Revolutionary War battle was fought at Fort Mercer, to the north of the 400-acre Red Bank Plantation, now the site of the park. Whitall House, the 1748 Georgian mansion that is the park's centerpiece, was used as a hospital after the battle. The house is open for tours, and the grounds, complete with walkways and natural landscaping, are open for walks.

Again, though, most campers don't come here to experience the outdoors—rather, they come for the access to Philadelphia, home of the Liberty Bell and Independence Hall. They come to wander the narrow streets in the older parts of town, take a side trip to Valley Forge, and to experience a slice of American history.

Back on the Jersey side, don't miss the New Jersey State Aquarium in Camden. The aquarium features a 40-foot walk-through shark tunnel and a simulated West African river complete with hippopotamuses. The battleship *New Jersey*, now a museum, is permanently anchored nearby.

The Philadelphia South KOA is also the closest campground to the start of the New Jersey Coastal Heritage Trail. Not many people drive the entire 300 miles of this vehicular trail in one trip, but if you want to be a thru-driver, start at the Delaware Memorial Bridge, stopping en route at Fort Mott State Park in Pennsville. It houses the Welcome Center for the Heritage Trail's Delsea Region, which is the first (or last, from the other direction) information center along the route. Fort Mott was built right after the Civil War. Troops were stationed there for many years, but it became obsolete with the advent of modern defenses. Today, it's a 104-acre free-admission park with an easy nature trail and picnic facilities.

Most campers ignore the southeastern part of New Jersey due to its lack of campgrounds, but there's no shortage of activities and outdoor opportunities if you know where to look. Stop for a few nights and give this often-neglected part of the state a try.

Philadelphia South/Clarksboro KOA Campground

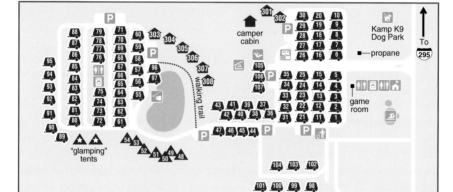

GETTING THERE

Heading southbound on I-295, take Exit 18 and follow the signs for Paulsboro/County Road 667. Turn right onto South Delaware Street/CR 667, and drive 1.1 miles. Turn right onto Friendship Road, and drive 0.3 mile. Turn right onto Timberlane Road, and drive just 0.1 mile. The campground will be on your left.

Heading northbound on I-295, take Exit 18 for Paulsboro/Mt. Royal/ Clarksboro. While still on the exit ramp, take the first right directly onto Timberlane Road. Drive 0.8 mile. The campground will be on your right.

GPS COORDINATES: N39° 48.505' W75° 14.221'

Wharton State Forest:
ATSION FAMILY CAMPGROUND

Beauty ★★★ / Privacy ★★★ / Spaciousness ★★★ / Quiet ★★★ / Security ★★★ / Cleanliness ★★★

Campers today enjoy the scenic clearings at Atsion and throughout Wharton, thanks to the foresight of Philadelphia financier Joseph Wharton.

New Jersey's largest state forest has nine camping areas, with the capacity to hold more than 1,000 campers, but only 50 sites have access to flush toilets and hot showers. These sites are at Atsion Family Campground, the only fully developed campground in Wharton State Forest.

Atsion may not be as remote or secluded as Wharton's primitive wilderness areas, but the sites are nonetheless beautifully wooded and private. The campground is easily reached by car. It has four paved loops suitable for small trailers as well as tents, although there are no hookups. Sites along the inner loops are close to the lake and farther from Atsion Road. Nine furnished cabins also sit along Atsion Road and look out over Atsion Lake.

Cedars and pine trees line the shores of Atsion Lake.

A bonus of staying at Atsion is that access to nearby Atsion Recreation Area is included in the nightly fee; remember to carry your camping permit for free access. Campers at Wharton's wilderness sites (see the following seven profiles in this chapter) pay just $3 per person per night to camp, but parking at the recreation area then costs $5 per car on weekdays and $10 on weekends. Campers who walk in pay a $2 day-use fee, and cars bearing current New Jersey State Park annual passes park for free. Once the parking lot has reached full capacity (300 vehicles), vehicles are asked to wait, regardless of permits.

Atsion Recreation Area sits directly across from the campground, on the southern side of Atsion Lake. It's a long walk around the lake, so drive or ride a bicycle. There is a guarded swimming beach, open during the summer (Memorial Day weekend–Labor Day) from 10 a.m. to 6 p.m. It's popular with groups, so go early to avoid the crowds. The bathhouse is in a full-service complex that includes men's and women's changing rooms with showers and flushing toilets, a concessionaire, and a first aid station.

The recreation area also has two playgrounds, a playing field, and picnic facilities.

KEY INFORMATION

ADDRESS: 905–971 Atsion Road, Shamong, NJ 08088

OPERATED BY: New Jersey State Park Service

CONTACT: 609-268-0444 (Atsion Office) or 609-561-0024 (Batsto Office), njparksandforests.org/parks/wharton.html; reservations: camping.nj.gov

OPEN: Year-round

SITES: 50

EACH SITE HAS: Picnic table, fire ring

WHEELCHAIR ACCESS: Restrooms and showers are ADA-accessible

ASSIGNMENT: First-come, first-served or by reservation (minimum 2 nights)

REGISTRATION: Obtain permit at Batsto Office (31 Batsto Road, Hammonton, NJ 08037) or Atsion Office (744 US 206, Shamong, NJ 08088)

FACILITIES: Water, flush toilets, showers

PARKING: At campsites; 2-vehicle limit

FEES: New Jersey residents, $20/night; nonresidents, $25/night; $5/night pet fee

---

RESTRICTIONS:

PETS: On leash, sites 26–34 only, 2 pets/site; pet permit and proof of current vaccinations required. See njparksandforests.org/parks/pet_friendly_camping.html for more information.

FIRES: In fire rings only

ALCOHOL: Prohibited

VEHICLES: Up to 22 feet; no RV hookups

OTHER: Quiet hours 10 p.m.–6 a.m.; 14-day stay limit; 6-person/2-tent site limit; check-in at noon

Only charcoal fires are permitted in the grills provided. A short nature trail loops around behind the playing field, and you'll find restrooms on either end of the parking lot. Fishing is allowed from the dock and on the lake. Visitors are given trash bags upon entering the recreation area, as Wharton State Forest is a carry-in/carry-out area. Alcohol is not allowed at the campsites, picnic areas, or beach, as in all New Jersey state parks.

A public boat launch is located at the western end of the beach in the recreation area; it's ADA-accessible and open 8 a.m.–4 p.m., Memorial Day–Labor Day. There is no boat rental concession, but canoes can be rented from several locations. The closest is Pinelands Adventures (609-268-0189, pinelandsadventures.org), at 1005 Atsion Road near the campground. Only electric and unpowered boats are allowed on Atsion Lake; engines must be less than 10 horsepower. The other nearby boat launch is the Mullica River canoe put-in, across US 206 from Atsion Lake.

Today, Wharton State Forest sprawls over three counties and encompasses 115,000 wooded acres that reach almost from the Atlantic Ocean to 40 miles shy of Philadelphia. Deer, turkeys, beavers, foxes, bald eagles, river otters, and a huge variety of birds live in the forest. Trails and rivers are popular with hikers, bikers, equestrians, boaters, birders, and other outdoors enthusiasts.

Surprisingly, Wharton State Forest, once inhabited by the Lenni Lenape tribe, was an industrial area from 1766 to 1867. Naturally occurring bog ore was mined from the swamps during the American Revolution and the War of 1812. Bog ore is formed when organic acids from vegetation combine with clay that is rich with iron; Wharton's many streams and rivers created the ideal processing environment for bog ore, which was turned into bog iron and used for munitions. Later, Wharton was the site of both glassmaking and papermaking operations, as were other parts of the Pinelands.

When Philadelphia financier Joseph Wharton (namesake of the famed business school at the University of Pennsylvania) purchased thousands of acres in southern Jersey in 1876, he planned to sell the clean groundwater to Philadelphia; New Jersey's government passed a law banning him from doing so, however. Wharton still loved the Pinelands, though, and continued to acquire more property in the area throughout his life. New Jersey bought the land in the 1950s for access to the same water that Wharton had astutely valued. His accidental preservation and later foresight led to the protection of the heart of the Pine Barrens. Campers can enjoy the scenic clearings at Atsion and throughout the state forest today thanks to Wharton's purchase.

Wharton State Forest: Atsion Family Campground

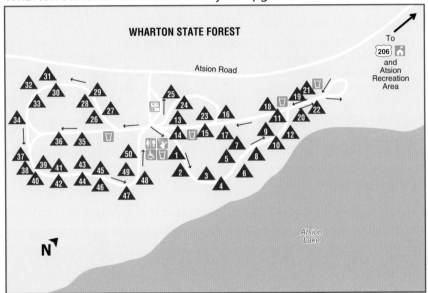

GETTING THERE

From I-295, take Exit 34A for Marlton. Merge onto NJ 70 East/Marlton Pike East, and drive 4.4 miles. Use the exit ramp on the right toward Radnor Boulevard. Turn right onto Radnor, and drive 0.6 mile. Turn left onto East Main Street, and drive 4.7 miles, during which East Main Street becomes Tuckerton Road. Turn right onto Atsion Road, and drive 8.6 miles. The campground entrance will be on your right. The closest park office for registration is the Atsion Office, about a mile farther east on Atsion Road—turn left onto US 206, and the office will be on your right.

GPS COORDINATES: N39° 44.755′ W 74° 44.637′

Wharton State Forest:
Batona Campground

Beauty ★★★★ / Privacy ★★★ / Spaciousness ★★★★ / Quiet ★★★★★ / Security ★★ / Cleanliness ★★★

Quiet, simple Batona Campground sits directly astride the famous Batona Trail.

Far from the beaten path sits distant Batona Campground, directly across the road from Carranza Memorial. No sites are demarcated on the ground alongside the unimproved sand road, and fire pits made by past campers are the only indication that campers have stopped here for the night. Two outhouses, a water pump, and a sign are the only developed features here under the pitch pines.

Campers will encounter little auto traffic in the campground, but they may meet a hiker or two. Batona Campground sits in the sand alongside the legendary Batona Trail, a 50-mile, mostly flat hiking path that traverses Pinelands National Reserve. The Batona (an acronym for **Ba**ck **to Na**ture) Trail passes through parts of Brendan T. Byrne State Forest and Bass River State Forest as it winds its way across the Pinelands, but more than half of it is located within Wharton State Forest. The trail runs the length of the camping area, meandering right down the middle. Campers should avoid setting up tents squarely on the trail.

For those interested in a shorter Batona Trail hike, the section between Carranza Memorial and Apple Pie Hill is a popular alternative to walking the entire 50 miles. Apple

Lower Forge Campground (see page 171) is only 1.2 miles north of this crossroads.

KEY INFORMATION

ADDRESS: Tabernacle, NJ 08088

OPERATED BY: New Jersey State Park Service

CONTACT: 609-268-0444 (Atsion Office) or 609-561-0024 (Batsto Office), njparksandforests.org/parks/wharton.html; reservations: camping.nj.gov

OPEN: Year-round

SITES: 12, plus 1 group site

EACH SITE HAS: Picnic table, fire ring

WHEELCHAIR ACCESS: None

ASSIGNMENT: First-come, first-served or by reservation (minimum 2 nights)

REGISTRATION: Obtain permit at Batsto Office (31 Batsto Road, Hammonton, NJ 08037) or Atsion Office (744 US 206, Shamong, NJ 08088)

FACILITIES: Water, vault toilets

PARKING: At campsites; 2-vehicle limit

FEES: New Jersey residents, $3/night; nonresidents, $5/night; $5/night pet fee

RESTRICTIONS:

PETS: On leash, all sites, 2 pets/site; pet permit and proof of current vaccinations required. See njparksandforests.org/parks/pet_friendly_camping.html for more information.

FIRES: In fire rings only

ALCOHOL: Prohibited

VEHICLES: No RV hookups

OTHER: Quiet hours 10 p.m.–6 a.m.; 14-day stay limit; 6-person/2-tent site limit; check-in at noon

Pie Hill is 3.5 miles north of the camping area, on the Batona Trail just outside the Wharton State Forest border. The hill, at 205 feet, is the highest point in the Pine Barrens. The top is graced by a 60-foot-tall tower that serves as a fire lookout for the 1.1-million-acre reserve. For many years, public access to the tower was unlimited, and many hundreds of hikers made the trek up the stairs to enjoy the expansive view. But due to a persistent problem with vandalism that threatened the tower's intended function, a fence was erected around the lookout in 2016, and access is now prohibited except by appointment, when a fire spotter is on duty. Although it doesn't quite have the view that the tower did, the top of Apple Pie Hill is still worthwhile.

The walk back to the Carranza Memorial takes you through cedar swamps and under tall hardwoods. The memorial is a stone obelisk dedicated to Emilio Carranza Rodríguez, a 23-year-old Mexican pilot; sometimes referred to as the Lindbergh of Mexico, Carranza was on the homeward-bound section of a Mexico City–New York City goodwill journey when he crashed here during a thunderstorm in 1928 (the obelisk was paid for by donations from Mexican schoolchildren). The 3.5-mile Carranza Memorial Loop is a popular hike that goes southeast from the monument; it combines local dirt roads with a section of the Batona Trail.

The Batona Trail is strictly for hikers. Cyclists and horseback riders are prohibited from wandering along the pink-blazed path, although horses are allowed in Batona Campground in designated areas. Dozens of sand and dirt roads crisscross Wharton State Forest, most open to multiple uses. When the Batona Trail merges with dirt roads, those sections are multiuse.

Skit Branch, a narrow creek, sits beyond a line of trees at the northern end of Batona Campground. Sit on the shore in the evenings and listen for frog calls.

The Pinelands Preservation Alliance (pinelandsalliance.org) offers a large variety of interpretive hikes, paddles, and presentations on the Pinelands region in and around Wharton State Forest, some in conjunction with Pinelands Adventures (pinelandsadventures.org). The best way to learn about what's available is by visiting the websites and calendars for both organizations. Some programs require registration, so be sure to check well in advance of your trip.

If you're hiking to your site at Batona, remember that you must obtain a camping permit in advance at either the Atsion or Batsto Wharton State Forest office. This is best done by vehicle, as both offices are miles away from the camping area. The road from US 206 to the Carranza Memorial is paved, but the 0.2-mile driveway into the campground is dirt. Bear in mind that the road becomes much sandier past the camping area and should not be attempted by novices in sedans, particularly while it is raining.

Sites at Batona Campground are isolated and beautiful. There is shade and the sound of crickets and wind rustling the pines overhead. If you are a hiker who enjoys inexpensive, quiet, and lovely sites, and you don't require a place to shower, Batona Campground is the ideal camping area for you.

Wharton State Forest: Batona Campground

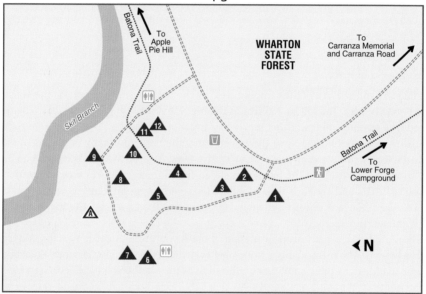

GETTING THERE

You must first register at either the state forest's Atsion Office or Batsto Office; the Atsion Office is more convenient to the campground from points south. To get there from the Atlantic City Expressway, take Exit 28 for NJ 54 North, and head north on NJ 54/Bellevue Avenue, which becomes US 206. About 10.5 miles from the exit, the Atsion Office will be on your right, just after the intersection with Atsion Road/Quaker Bridge Road.

After you register, continue north on US 206 and, in 3.4 miles, turn right onto Forked Neck Road. In 2.8 miles, turn right onto Tuckerton Road; 0.7 mile farther, bear right to continue on Tuckerton. In 2.3 miles, continue straight at the fork onto Carranza Road, and drive 1.4 miles. The Carranza Memorial will be on your right; the dirt road on the left across from the memorial leads 0.2 mile to the campground.

GPS COORDINATES: N39° 46.856' W74° 37.912'

Wharton State Forest:
BODINE FIELD CAMPGROUND

Beauty ★★★ / Privacy ★★★ / Spaciousness ★★★★ / Quiet ★★★★ / Security ★★ / Cleanliness ★★★

This is Pinelands wilderness camping for those who like to rough it.

Wharton State Forest's easternmost camping area is also its largest. Bodine Field Campground, officially capable of holding up to 250 people, is ideal for large groups. Wharton staff also recommends it for use by equestrian groups. The sandy ground is level and wide open. The area is sunny, with only some shade. Sites are roughly designated in this wilderness camping by signs that identify parking spaces and by fire rings left by past campers.

When no large groups are present, Bodine Field is great for family or small-group camping. It's a sunny, inexpensive riverside area with good access by both unimproved-road and canoe routes. Be cautious when bringing in your car, as the sandy roads can get swampy after a rain, and a few large bumps may remain after the roads dry out. High-clearance vehicles should have no problem.

Like other wilderness camping areas in Wharton State Forest, Bodine Field is popular with canoeists. Beaver Branch Canoe Landing lies just beyond the camp and is the endpoint on several daily Wading River canoe routes from as nearby as Evans Bridge (2 hours) and as far away as Speedwell (8 hours). Those who have planned ahead and obtained advance permits from Batsto Visitor Center can stop 20 minutes before Beaver Branch at Bodine Field and set up camp; if possible, leave a vehicle with camping gear at Bodine Field so you can avoid carrying it in your canoe. Several canoe liveries serve the area for those who need to rent canoes or who need shuttles. The nearest ones include BelHaven Paddlesports in Green Bank (609-965-2628, belhavenpaddlesports .com); Mick's Canoe Rental in Chatsworth (609-726-1380, mickscanoerental.com); Pinelands Adventures in Shamong (609-268-0189, pinelandsadventures.org); and Wading Pines Camping Resort, near Godfrey Bridge Campground (609-726-1313, wadingpines.com).

Cyclists also have plenty of opportunities for fun in the area surrounding Bodine Field. The popular 17-mile paved cycling loop from Harrisville Lake to Evans Bridge begins right above Bodine Field at Harrisville Lake on

The Wading River flows right by Bodine Field Campground.

KEY INFORMATION

ADDRESS: Bodine Field Road, Chatsworth, NJ 08019

OPERATED BY: New Jersey State Park Service

CONTACT: 609-268-0444 (Atsion Office) or 609-561-0024 (Batsto Office), njparksandforests.org/parks/wharton.html; reservations: camping.nj.gov

OPEN: Year-round

SITES: 22, plus 8 group sites

EACH SITE HAS: Picnic table, fire ring

WHEELCHAIR ACCESS: None

ASSIGNMENT: First-come, first-served or by reservation (minimum 2 nights)

REGISTRATION: Obtain permit at Batsto Office (31 Batsto Road, Hammonton, NJ 08037) or Atsion Office (744 US 206, Shamong, NJ 08088)

FACILITIES: Water, vault toilets

PARKING: At campsites (2-vehicle limit) and designated lots

FEES: New Jersey residents, $3/night; nonresidents, $5/night; $5/night pet fee

---

RESTRICTIONS:

PETS: Prohibited

FIRES: In fire rings only

ALCOHOL: Prohibited

VEHICLES: Up to 22 feet; no RV hookups

OTHER: Quiet hours 10 p.m.–6 a.m.; 14-day stay limit; 6-person/2-tent site limit; check-in at noon

County Road 679. Head southeast to CR 653, and then go right, following CR 542 to Green Bank. There is a picnic area at Green Bank. Follow CR 563 north to CR 679, which takes you back to your starting point by Harrisville Lake and the Harrisville Ruins. You'll pass through Bass River State Forest as well as Wharton. Some of the roads feature bicycle lanes.

The Pine Barrens River Ramble bike route also passes Harrisville Lake on its 42.6-mile loop. A map is available at as a free download from tinyurl.com/river-ramble, a subsection of the Pinelands Alliance website. The route passes through forests, historical areas, blueberry fields, and cranberry bogs. Standard bicycles are restricted to paved roads, but mountain bikes have the run of the hundreds of sand roads through the Pine Barrens.

The Harrisville Ruins are all that remains of a once-thriving paper mill town. The decaying stone buildings, some of which had 3-foot-thick walls, were active in the 1800s. Like many of the nearby industries, the paper industry made use of the surrounding natural resources. Salt marsh grass from the Jersey Shore was brought in and processed using the vast reserves of Pine Barrens water. Canals and millraces crisscrossed the area. Before it was a paper mill town, Harrisville was an iron-processing facility that made iron into strips and was the site of a gristmill and two sawmills as early as 1750. Joseph Wharton, who eventually acquired most of what is now Wharton State Forest, purchased the property around 1896. The town, by then uninhabited, was devastated by fire in 1914.

Once you're done marveling at man-made objects being reclaimed by the forest, take a ride over to the 1,927-acre Oswego River Natural Area for a look at a forest that has been deliberately preserved by mankind. This region, along with the Batsto Natural Area north of Batsto Village, comprises a variety of Pinelands habitats: you'll spot pitch pines, white cedars, southern swamps, and floodplains. You may also hear the endangered Pine Barrens tree frog during breeding season (May–June). Just an inch and a half long and green, this little frog is difficult to spot. But its nasal honking, often referred to as a "kwonk," is unmistakable.

Swimming is prohibited outside Atsion Recreation Area in Wharton State Forest. Tubing, however, is permitted, so feel free to launch a tube alongside Bodine Field. There is a small beach at Atsion Recreation Area, but the guarded swimming area at Lake Absegami in Bass River State Forest is closer to Bodine Field.

The Wading River, which meets the Oswego River just above Bodine Field, is the most popular paddling river in the Pinelands. Easy to paddle, it passes by cranberries and under pitch pines. And at the end of the west branch sits Bodine Field, an open wilderness camp where you can beach your canoe and sleep under the stars.

Wharton State Forest: Bodine Field Campground

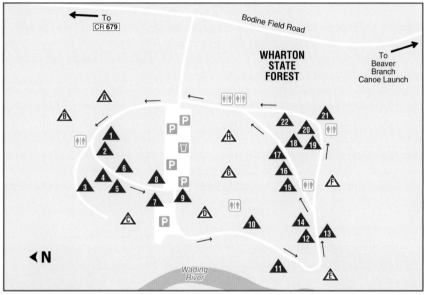

GETTING THERE

You must first register at either the state forest's Atsion Office or Batsto Office; the Batsto Office is more convenient to the campground from points east. Heading southbound on the Garden State Parkway, take Exit 52 for New Gretna. Turn right onto East Greenbush Road, and drive 1.1 miles. Turn left onto Stage Road, and drive 0.4 mile; then keep left to continue onto Leektown Road/County Road 653, and drive 2.7 miles. Just before the bridge over the Wading River, bear right to continue on CR 542. In 8.8 miles, turn right onto Batsto Road and, 0.3 mile farther, turn left to reach the park office. Or, heading northbound on the Garden State Parkway, take Exit 50 for US 9 North/New Gretna. Continue onto US 9 North and, in 0.9 mile, turn left onto CR 542. In 11.7 miles, turn right onto Batsto Road and then left to reach the park office.

After you register, backtrack to CR 542 and turn left, heading east. In 4.3 miles, turn left onto CR 563 and, 5.3 miles farther, make a sharp right onto Chatsworth Road. Drive 1.7 miles; then turn right at the brown BODINE FIELD sign, and immediately make a left at the fork in the sand road. In 0.6 mile, turn right to reach the campground.

GPS COORDINATES: N39° 39.252' W74° 31.373'

Wharton State Forest:
BUTTONWOOD HILL CAMPGROUND

Beauty ★★★ / Privacy ★★★ / Spaciousness ★★ / Quiet ★★★ / Security ★★ / Cleanliness ★★★

Tiny Buttonwood Hill offers inexpensive primitive camping with good road access and proximity to Batsto Village.

The tiny Buttonwood Hill wilderness-camping area is so nondescript that you may accidentally drive right past it, even if you're looking for it and planning to spend the night there. The camp is little more than a clearing among a secluded grove of trees, and the only signs that you're passing a campground and not a grassy field are a few picnic tables and a nearby outhouse. A sign marks the drive off County Road 542, and small trailers can fit onto the dirt road that leads to the camping area.

Thirty people can officially fit into Buttonwood, but on weekdays there's a good chance that your party will be the only one in sight. The area is essentially a half circle alongside an unimproved road that becomes increasingly unimproved as it winds deeper into the forest. Flush toilets and water are located across CR 542 at the Crowley Landing public boat launch. No fees are charged for day use at Crowley Landing, which sits on the Mullica River and features picnic tables and grills in addition to modern restrooms; if you plan to launch a boat here, however, you'll need to pay a fee at the Batsto Office. Motorized boats can be launched

Four of the five sites at Buttonwood Hill Campground

KEY INFORMATION

ADDRESS: Burnt Schoolhouse Road, Egg Harbor City, NJ 08215

OPERATED BY: New Jersey State Park Service

CONTACT: 609-268-0444 (Atsion Office) or 609-561-0024 (Batsto Office), njparksandforests.org/parks/wharton.html; reservations: camping.nj.gov

OPEN: Year-round

SITES: 5

EACH SITE HAS: Picnic table, fire ring

WHEELCHAIR ACCESS: None

ASSIGNMENT: First-come, first-served or by reservation (minimum 2 nights)

REGISTRATION: Obtain permit at Batsto Office (31 Batsto Road, Hammonton, NJ 08037) or Atsion Office (744 US 206, Shamong, NJ 08088)

FACILITIES: Water nearby, vault toilets

PARKING: At campsites; 2-vehicle limit

FEES: New Jersey residents, $3/night; nonresidents, $5/night; $5/night pet fee

---

RESTRICTIONS:

PETS: On leash, all sites, 2 pets/site; pet permit and proof of current vaccinations required. See njparksandforests.org/parks /pet_friendly_camping.html for more information.

FIRES: In fire rings only

ALCOHOL: Prohibited

VEHICLES: No RV hookups

OTHER: Quiet hours 10 p.m.–6 a.m.; 14-day stay limit; 6-person/2-tent site limit; check-in at noon

---

here, so don't expect pristine forest conditions. Crowley Landing is within walking distance of Buttonwood Hill, but consider driving so you can easily return with your supply of water.

Crowley Landing stands on the site of what may once have been Crowleytown. During the 1850s and 1860s, a glassworks and small town sat on the site. And as with so many industrial sites from that era in the Pine Barrens, Crowleytown faded away and disappeared.

Nearby Batsto Village fared better against the assault of time. For a hundred years, industry thrived at Batsto. First, before the American Revolution, Charles Read of Burlington established an iron furnace that was used to process bog ore dug out of the swampy Pineland grounds. John Cox bought Batsto Iron Works from Read and operated it during the war, providing munitions, artillery fittings, and iron fastenings to the Continental Army. Bog ore occurs naturally when decaying vegetation seeps down to iron-rich clay.

From 1784 to 1876, William Richards and his descendants operated Batsto. First it continued as an iron-production facility, manufacturing water pipes and firebacks (cast-iron plates lining the brick wall of fireplaces). Once the iron industry declined, Batsto was a window-glass production plant for a decade. After the economic failure of the glassmaking operation, Philadelphia financier Joseph Wharton purchased Batsto as part of his plan to pump some of the 17 trillion gallons of fresh water that lay beneath the Pine Barrens to Philadelphia. New Jersey's government later blocked his scheme.

During Batsto Village's industrial heyday, hundreds of people lived and worked there before it fell into disrepair. Fortunately, the village was later restored, and today visitors can wander through its 33 historic buildings, including a gristmill, an icehouse, a wheelwright's shop, a general store, workers' homes, and a post office that is one of the four oldest currently operating in the United States. It was never assigned a zip code, and all stamps are canceled by hand.

When Joseph Wharton took over Batsto Village, he added new buildings and enlarged the existing mansion in the Italianate style of the era. Except when closed for renovations, 14 rooms of the mansion are open to the public. Seasonal 45-minute guided tours of the mansion and the village are offered for a small fee during busy summer weekends; self-guided village tours are available at other times.

Between the village sawmill and the workers' homes on the banks of Batsto Lake is the Annie M. Carter Interpretive Center. The focus of the center's displays is on the ecology of the Pinelands and the impact of humans on the area. Activities include slide and video programs, live animal displays, nature hikes, and discussions. The interpretive center has eight canoes available for guided nature trips on Batsto Lake. Several hiking trails between 1 and 3.8 miles in length begin at Batsto and loop through the woods and by Batsto Lake.

Buttonwood Hill is also the closest camping area to Hammonton, the self-proclaimed "Blueberry Capital of the World." New Jersey is responsible for about 20% of all blueberries grown in the United States. Both cranberries and blueberries grow in the Pinelands, and Hammonton has embraced its role as a blueberry production town, celebrating this crop once a year on a Sunday in June at the Red, White, and Blueberry Festival.

Campers interested in less-public displays of blueberry appreciation can wander the trails near Buttonwood Hill. Blueberries grow wild in the Pinelands forests and can sometimes be found along the sand trails that wind through the forest near the camping area. Remember, however, not to indiscriminately eat berries and such in the forest.

Buttonwood Hill doesn't have the amenities of Atsion or the remote, wild feel of the canoe-in sites or Batona Campground. But it offers a great combination of privacy, easy road access, economical camping, and proximity to some of the top natural and historical sites in Pinelands National Reserve.

Wharton State Forest: Buttonwood Hill Campground

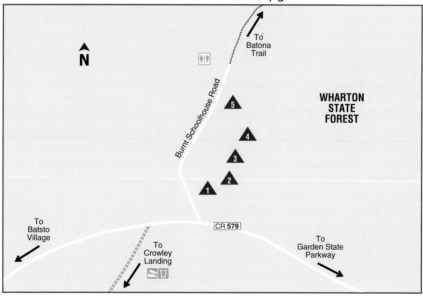

GETTING THERE

You must first register at either the state forest's Atsion Office or Batsto Office; the Batsto Office is more convenient to the campground from points east. Heading southbound on the Garden State Parkway, take Exit 52 for New Gretna. Turn right onto East Greenbush Road, and drive 1.1 miles. Turn left onto Stage Road, and drive 0.4 mile; then keep left to continue onto Leektown Road/County Road 653, and drive 2.7 miles. Just before the bridge over the Wading River, bear right to continue on CR 542. In 8.8 miles, turn right onto Batsto Road and, 0.3 mile farther, turn left to reach the park office. Or, heading northbound on the Garden State Parkway, take Exit 50 for US 9 North/New Gretna. Continue onto US 9 North and, in 0.9 mile, turn left onto CR 542. In 11.7 miles, turn right onto Batsto Road and then left to reach the park office.

After you register, backtrack to CR 542 and turn left, heading east. In 2 miles, turn left onto Burnt Schoolhouse Road. The campground entrance will be on your right.

GPS COORDINATES: N39° 37.718' W74° 37.064'

Spring flowers in Batsto Village

Wharton State Forest:
GODFREY BRIDGE CAMPGROUND

Beauty ★★★★★ / Privacy ★★★★ / Spaciousness ★★★★ / Quiet ★★★★ / Security ★★★ / Cleanliness ★★★

The secluded forest sites are appealing, but Godfrey Bridge is also easily accessed by a paved road.

Wharton State Forest's second most-developed campground has little in common with its first (Atsion, page 149) aside from the trees and picnic tables. Atsion is a family campground with a bathhouse and trailer sanitary station. Godfrey Bridge Campground, in contrast, is a collection of 34 wilderness campgrounds, each with a fire ring and picnic table . . . and not much else. The restroom facilities are rustic. But for many campers, forgoing the modern conveniences available at Atsion is worth the trade-off for what you get at Godfrey Bridge: peace, quiet, and solitude. Many of the sites are extremely private, with years of undergrowth keeping neighbors out of sight.

Godfrey Bridge is appealing if you're looking for a secluded forest site, but it also has the advantage of being easily accessed by paved road. Although Godfrey Bridge Road gets a fair amount of traffic from campers and the occasional canoe-livery shuttle, the campground is far enough away that the occasional din of cars and canoeists isn't an issue. The 35 sites in the main camping area get virtually no traffic. Campers who are worried about being miles from the showers at Atsion Recreation Area or Bass River need not worry; the pay-per-shower facility at Wading Pines Camping Resort is only a short ways east on Godfrey Bridge Road.

The Wading River flows past the Godfrey Bridge picnic area.

KEY INFORMATION

ADDRESS: 85 Godfrey Bridge Campground Road, Chatsworth, NJ 08019

OPERATED BY: New Jersey State Park Service

CONTACT: 609-268-0444 (Atsion Office) or 609-561-0024 (Batsto Office), njparksandforests.org/parks/wharton.html; reservations: camping.nj.gov

OPEN: Year-round

SITES: 34

EACH SITE HAS: Picnic table, fire ring

WHEELCHAIR ACCESS: None

ASSIGNMENT: First-come, first-served or by reservation (minimum 2 nights)

REGISTRATION: Obtain permit at Batsto Office (31 Batsto Road, Hammonton, NJ 08037) or Atsion Office (744 US 206, Shamong, NJ 08088)

FACILITIES: Water, vault toilets

PARKING: At campsites; 2-vehicle limit

FEES: New Jersey residents, $3/night; nonresidents, $5/night; $5/night pet fee

RESTRICTIONS:

PETS: On leash, all sites, 2 pets/site; pet permit and proof of current vaccinations required. See njparksandforests.org/parks /pet_friendly_camping.html for more information.

FIRES: In fire rings only

ALCOHOL: Prohibited

VEHICLES: Up to 21 feet; no RV hookups

OTHER: Quiet hours 10 p.m.–6 a.m.; 14-day stay limit; 6-person/2-tent site limit; check-in at noon

Wading Pines, a private camping resort, caters mostly to RV and cabin campers. A small convenience store at the Wading Pines is open to all who drop in.

Godfrey Bridge and all of the Wharton State Forest camping areas are best known for their access to Pinelands rivers. Noncampers may not use the ramps for putting canoes into or out of the Wading River at Godfrey Bridge, as with the other riverside camps in the forest. Campers are permitted to use the ramps, although this is helpful only to those who travel with their own canoes or kayaks. Those renting boats must use the access points designated by the local canoe outfitters.

The Wading River between Speedwell and Beaver Bridge is one of the easiest, most scenic, and popular canoe routes in New Jersey, and there is no shortage of outfitters ready to supply canoes and transportation. The closest canoe livery to Godfrey Bridge, in addition to the one at Wading Pines Camping Resort (609-726-1313, wadingpines.com), is Mick's Canoe Rental (609-726-1380, mickscanoerental.com), on CR 563 in Chatsworth. Remember that you must plan ahead to camp, because Godfrey Bridge and the other Wharton campgrounds require that you first secure a permit from either the state forest's Atsion or Batsto Office. Popular overnight trips include Oswego Lake or Hawkin Bridge to Bodine Field and Speedwell to Bodine Field.

Plenty of other outdoor recreational activities are available as well. The undeveloped swamps, forests, and floodplains of 1,927-acre Oswego River Natural Area sit directly across CR 563 from Godfrey Bridge Road. The paved roads of the Pinelands National Reserve make great cycling routes, while the unmarked sand paths that wind through Wharton State Forest are open to mountain bikers and hikers. All-terrain vehicles are prohibited in Wharton State Forest, but there are plenty of motor tracks for four-wheel-drive vehicles and motorcycles to use.

Swimming is not permitted in Wading River, but there are guarded swimming areas at Atsion Recreation Area on US 206 and at Lake Absegami in Bass River State Forest. Manmade structures are also present in Wharton State Forest; take a tour of Batsto to view the Pinelands industrial past.

Godfrey Bridge may not have the recreational facilities of Atsion, but its wilderness atmosphere and private setting more than make up for its lack of developed amenities. To some campers, this may even be a strength, making organized but simple Godfrey Bridge the most desirable of the Wharton State Forest campgrounds.

Wharton State Forest: Godfrey Bridge Campground

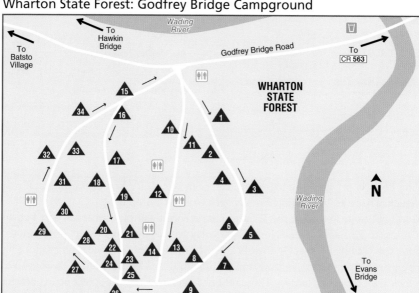

GETTING THERE

You must first register at either the state forest's Atsion Office or Batsto Office; the Batsto Office is more convenient to the campground from points east. Heading southbound on the Garden State Parkway, take Exit 52 for New Gretna. Turn right onto East Greenbush Road, and drive 1.1 miles. Turn left onto Stage Road, and drive 0.4 mile; then keep left to continue onto Leektown Road/County Road 653, and drive 2.7 miles. Just before the bridge over the Wading River, bear right to continue on CR 542. In 8.8 miles, turn right onto Batsto Road and, 0.3 mile farther, turn left to reach the park office. Or, heading northbound on the Garden State Parkway, take Exit 50 for US 9 North/New Gretna. Continue onto US 9 North and, in 0.9 mile, turn left onto CR 542. In 11.7 miles, turn right onto Batsto Road and then left to reach the park office.

After you register, backtrack to Batsto Road, turn left (north), and drive 6.6 miles to reach the campground, which will be on your right. Along the route, Batsto Road becomes Washington Turnpike and then Godfrey Bridge Road.

GPS COORDINATES: N39° 41.406' W74° 32.813'

Wharton State Forest:
GOSHEN POND CAMPGROUND

Beauty ★★★★ / Privacy ★★★ / Spaciousness ★★★★ / Quiet ★★★★ / Security ★★★ / Cleanliness ★★★

The Jersey Devil may live in the nearby woods, but beavers are more common at this primitive camping area.

The physical distance between Atsion Family Campground (see page 149) and Goshen Pond Campground is only a mile, but the differences between the two campgrounds are enormous. Goshen's amenities are few, its only nod to development being a water pump and a few outhouses. The campground, whose sites are walk-in except for two, consists of open sites among the trees, which offer a wonderful view of the night sky. Enjoy the isolation under the stars of New Jersey's Pinelands National Reserve.

Goshen Pond sits by the Upper Mullica River, along a popular canoe route. It's popular with groups and with horse campers because of its spaciousness and openness. There are outhouses and water pumps on-site but no showers or flushing toilets. Swimming in the Mullica River is prohibited. Campers need not worry, however, about being dirty after a long canoe trip. The bathhouse and beach at Atsion Recreation Area are just a few miles down the road on Atsion Lake. Access fees to the recreation area are $2 for walk-ins and more for cars: parking is $5 on weekdays and $10 on weekends but is free for cars bearing a current New Jersey State Parks pass. The bathing area is open only during the summer,

Goshen Pond is one of the more popular campgrounds in Wharton State Forest.

KEY INFORMATION

ADDRESS: Goshen Pond Camping Area Road, Shamong, NJ 08088

OPERATED BY: New Jersey State Park Service

CONTACT: 609-268-0444 (Atsion Office) or 609-561-0024 (Batsto Office), njparksandforests.org/parks/wharton.html; reservations: camping.nj.gov

OPEN: Year-round

SITES: 16 (14 are walk-in), plus 3 group sites

EACH SITE HAS: Picnic table, fire ring

WHEELCHAIR ACCESS: None

ASSIGNMENT: First-come, first-served or by reservation (minimum 2 nights)

REGISTRATION: Obtain permit at Batsto Office (31 Batsto Road, Hammonton, NJ 08037) or Atsion Office (744 US 206, Shamong, NJ 08088)

FACILITIES: Water, vault toilets

PARKING: At campsites (14 and 15; 2-vehicle limit) or designated lots (for walk-in sites)

FEES: New Jersey residents, $3/night; nonresidents, $5/night; $5/night pet fee

RESTRICTIONS:

PETS: On leash, all sites, 2 pets/site; pet permit and proof of current vaccinations required. See njparksandforests.org/parks/pet_friendly_camping.html for more information.

FIRES: In fire rings only

ALCOHOL: Prohibited

VEHICLES: No RV hookups

OTHER: Quiet hours 10 p.m.–6 a.m.; 14-day stay limit; 6-person/2-tent site limit; check-in at noon

when lifeguards are present. Those looking to work up a sweat before showering can hike the 1-mile trail that loops around the southern bank of Atsion Lake. The recreation area also features picnic facilities, playgrounds, and an activity field.

The closest canoe rental is Pinelands Adventures (609-268-0189, pinelandsadventures .org) on Atsion Road. There are many other rental agencies in the Pinelands, most of which offer parking and transportation. A list of outfitters that provide livery and rentals is available at both the Atsion and Batsto Offices. From Goshen Pond, try canoeing 2 hours east to the take-out at Atsion Lake. Drive in using a vehicle with four-wheel-drive, if you can, as the dirt-and-sand roads that lead to Goshen Pond can get treacherous after a rain.

Pets are permitted, with proper documentation, at Goshen Pond Campground. After you read tales of the most famous Pine Barrens resident—the legendary (*perhaps* fictional) Jersey Devil, who is rumored to lurk about the woods near Goshen Pond—you may be glad that you have Rover in tow. This creature has existed in local folklore for hundreds of years.

Legend has it that in 1735 or thereabouts, a local woman named Mrs. Leeds discovered that she was pregnant for the 13th time. Mrs. Leeds was not rich, and she had an unhappy marriage. She was less than thrilled with the news of her pregnancy and cursed the child with the statement "Let it be the devil!" In retrospect, she regretted this remark, as giving birth to a child with horns, claws, and wings must have been more of a change than she was hoping for.

In some tales, the winged monstrosity turned on its mother and others nearby. In another, it flew up the chimney and out into the forest. In all accounts, the Jersey Devil has been credited with mischief such as raiding chicken coops and slaughtering farm animals. But mostly the creature is known for scaring people with its appearance and its piercing howl, along with its heavy breathing and the hoof prints it leaves behind. When canoeing or hiking, keep an eye peeled for a 6- to 10-foot-tall, two-legged, bat-winged reptilian deer with the head of a horse. A clear photo of it might pay for all your Pinelands canoeing trips for the rest of your life.

Regardless of whether you find it or not, your search for the Jersey Devil is more likely to turn up Jersey Devil T-shirts, coffee mugs, or even a professional hockey team than an actual devil. Local entrepreneurs seem to have made their own deals with the devil and present his likeness in a variety of moneymaking schemes. Odds are the only large creatures you will encounter at Goshen Pond are animals or other people. So don't let the Jersey Devil scare you away from Wharton State Forest and the Pinelands.

The Pinelands, referred to locally as the Pine Barrens, cover one-fifth of the state of New Jersey. Wharton State Forest is the largest state forest within not just the Pinelands but the entire state. Goshen Pond is one of nine public sites within the park, and of those, it presents the best combination of primitive camping near developed recreational activities.

Wharton State Forest: Goshen Pond Campground

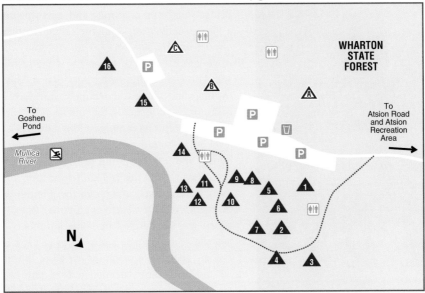

GETTING THERE

From I-295, take Exit 34A for Marlton. Merge onto NJ 70 East/Marlton Pike East, and drive 4.4 miles. Use the exit ramp on the right toward Radnor Boulevard. Turn right onto Radnor, and drive 0.6 mile. Turn left onto East Main Street, and drive 4.7 miles, during which East Main Street becomes Tuckerton Road. Turn right onto Atsion Road, and drive about 7.8 miles to the signed Goshen Pond Campground access road—if you reach Atsion Family Campground, you've gone too far. Turn right and follow the sandy road to the campground. The office for registration is about 1.5 miles farther east on Atsion Road—turn left onto US 206, and the office will be on your right.

GPS COORDINATES: N39° 44.681' W74° 45.644'

Wharton State Forest:
HAWKIN BRIDGE CAMPGROUND

Beauty ★★★ / Privacy ★★★ / Spaciousness ★★★★ / Quiet ★★★★ / Security ★★★ / Cleanliness ★★★★

This is a campground where you definitely won't have cars zooming by your site in the middle of the night.

The Wading River below Hawkin Bridge

The most remote of the Wharton State Forest camping areas that are accessible by car, the Hawkin Bridge Campground is about 2 miles west and north of Godfrey Bridge Campground. Once you pass Godfrey Bridge, the road gets a little rougher; then, after the right turn onto Hawkin Bridge Road, the final mile and a half descends a loose, sandy road. A high-clearance vehicle is a must for this section of road, and four-wheel-drive isn't a bad idea, especially if the terrain is wet. Use extra caution after heavy rains. This is a campground where you definitely won't have cars zooming by your sites in the middle of the night.

Hawkin Bridge campground is a mostly open, level area dotted with hardwood trees. Outhouses and a water pump provide the extent of camp luxuries, so this is definitely an area for the more adventurous camper. Of the 9 family sites, campers would be wise to opt for one of sites 4–9, which are surrounded by some shrubbery and provide a bit of shade and a bit of privacy. Sites 1–3 are spacious enough (as are all of the sites), but they're closer to the road and are quite open.

The campground's namesake bridge spans Tulpehocken Creek and is about a quarter mile farther down the road from the camp. It's an easy walk from camp, and the abundance of trees along the river makes it an ideal place to head for some cool shade if the campground gets warm in the heat of the day. Characteristic of all of the rivers in the Pinelands, the waters of Tulpehocken Creek that flow beneath Hawkin Bridge are stained a dark tea color. The coloring indicates both a high iron content in the water and tannic acids that leach from the region's characteristic flora, particularly the Atlantic white cedar trees.

The Wading River, which Tulpehocken Creek joins about a quarter mile downstream from Hawkin Bridge, between Speedwell and Beaver Bridge, is one of the easiest, most scenic, and popular canoe routes in New Jersey, and there is no shortage of outfitters ready

KEY INFORMATION

ADDRESS: Hawkin Bridge Road, Chatsworth, NJ 08019

OPERATED BY: New Jersey State Park Service

CONTACT: 609-268-0444 (Atsion Office) or 609-561-0024 (Batsto Office), njparksandforests.org/parks/wharton.html; reservations: camping.nj.gov

OPEN: Year-round

SITES: 9, plus 4 group sites

EACH SITE HAS: Picnic table, fire ring

WHEELCHAIR ACCESS: None

ASSIGNMENT: First-come, first-served or by reservation (minimum 2 nights)

REGISTRATION: Obtain permit at Batsto Office (31 Batsto Road, Hammonton, NJ 08037) or Atsion Office (744 US 206, Shamong, NJ 08088)

FACILITIES: Water, vault toilets

PARKING: At campsites; 2-vehicle limit

FEES: New Jersey residents, $3/night; nonresidents, $5/night; $5/night pet fee

---

RESTRICTIONS:

PETS: On leash, all sites, 2 pets/site; pet permit and proof of current vaccinations required. See njparksandforests.org/parks/pet_friendly_camping.html for more information.

FIRES: In fire rings only

ALCOHOL: Prohibited

VEHICLES: No RV hookups

OTHER: Quiet hours 10 p.m.–6 a.m.; 14-day stay limit; 6-person/2-tent site limit; check-in at noon

to supply canoes and transportation. The closest canoe livery to Hawkin Bridge, in addition to the one at Wading Pines Camping Resort (609-726-1313, wadingpines.com), is Mick's Canoe Rental (609-726-1380, mickscanoerental.com CR 563 in Chatsworth. Remember that you must plan ahead to camp, because Hawkin Bridge and the other Wharton campgrounds require that you first secure a permit from either the state forest's Atsion or Batsto Office. Popular overnight trips include Oswego Lake or Hawkin Bridge to Bodine Field and Speedwell to Bodine Field or Chips Folly. The float downstream from Hawkin Bridge to Godfrey Bridge is about 3.5 miles long.

Boat rules are the same at Hawkin Bridge as they are at Godfrey Bridge. Campers can put in and take out canoes from Hawkin Bridge. Noncampers and those renting boats are prohibited from using the site and must use the access points designated by the local canoe outfitters.

Swimming is not permitted in Tulpehocken Creek or the Wading River, but there are guarded swimming areas at Atsion Recreation Area on US 206 and at Lake Absegami in Bass River State Forest. Man-made structures are also present in Wharton State Forest— take a tour of Batsto Village to learn about some of the Pinelands' industrial past.

The 1.1 million acres of the New Jersey Pinelands National Reserve account for approximately 20% of New Jersey's land (some sources say a little more, some a little less), covering an area larger than either Yosemite or Grand Canyon National Park. It's no surprise that it is home to a diverse array of flora and fauna, including 43 endangered species. UNESCO designated the Pinelands in 1988 as an International Biosphere Reserve for its diversity of ecosystems of natural and scientific interest.

Keep your eyes open as you canoe the rivers through the Pinelands or hike its trails. Several hundred species of birds have been identified in Wharton State Forest. A birding pamphlet, available at the park offices in Batsto and Atsion, lists 218 of the more common species in the forest. That handout and a nice guidebook can lend themselves to a very nice couple of days of bird-watching, especially along the rivers. You'll notice, as well, an abundance of sphagnum moss growing on the trees. During the Civil War, it was used as a wound dressing when cotton bandages were hard to come by.

Underlying the Pine Barrens is the Kirkwood-Cohansey Aquifer, which contains more than 17 trillion gallons of fresh water, only a fraction of which is visible in the streams throughout the region. That's a lot of water—enough, in fact, to cover the entire state in 10 feet of water, according to the New Jersey Pinelands Commission.

Wharton State Forest: Hawkin Bridge Campground

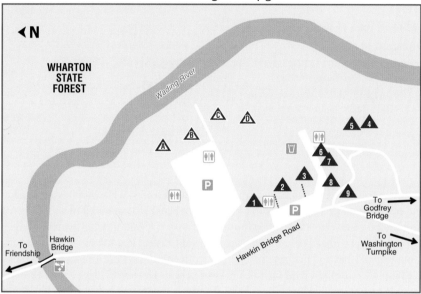

GETTING THERE

You must first register at either the state forest's Atsion Office or Batsto Office; the Batsto Office is more convenient to the campground from points east. Heading southbound on the Garden State Parkway, take Exit 52 for New Gretna. Turn right on East Greenbush Road, and drive 1.1 miles. Turn left on Stage Road, and drive 0.4 mile; then keep left to continue onto Leektown Road/County Road 653, and drive 2.7 miles. Just before the bridge over the Wading River, bear right to continue on CR 542. In 8.8 miles, turn right on Batsto Road and, 0.3 mile farther, turn left to reach the park office. Or, heading northbound on the Garden State Parkway, take Exit 50 for US 9 North/New Gretna. Continue onto US 9 North and, in 0.9 mile, turn left onto CR 542. In 11.7 miles, turn right on Batsto Road and then left to reach the park office.

After you register, backtrack to Batsto Road, turn left (north), and drive 6 miles. (Along the route, Batsto Road becomes Washington Turnpike and then Godfrey Bridge Road.) Turn left (north) onto Hawkin Bridge Road; the campground is 1.6 miles farther, on your right. A short distance beyond the campground is Hawkin Bridge over the West Branch Wading River.

GPS COORDINATES: N39° 42.743' W74° 33.853'

Wharton State Forest:
LOWER FORGE AND MULLICA RIVER CAMPGROUNDS

Beauty ★★★★ / Privacy ★★★ / Spaciousness ★★★★ / Quiet ★★★★★ / Security ★★ / Cleanliness ★★★

Bring your canoe, horse, or mountain bike—or your own two feet. Motorized vehicles aren't allowed.

Lower Forge and Mullica River Campgrounds are inaccessible by design: motor vehicles of all sorts are prohibited. So bring your horse, your mountain bike, your canoe, or just your own two feet if you want to camp in one of these wilderness sites. Lower Forge has no drinking water, which makes it the less desirable of the two sites to those who don't like to carry their own supply. On the upside, campers here are guaranteed a primitive experience with no likelihood of intrusion by neighbors unwilling to rough it.

   Distances take on a new meaning when petrol power has no relevance. Lower Forge Campground is a half-mile hike from the nearest road, but the easiest way to get here is to come by canoe, carrying your gear in a waterproof bag. Still, it's no short trek: expect to paddle

One of the old wooden structures that form the display at Batsto Village

KEY INFORMATION

ADDRESS: Wharton State Forest, Atsion Office, 744 US 206, Shamong, NJ 08088

OPERATED BY: New Jersey State Park Service

CONTACT: 609-268-0444 (Atsion Office) or 609-561-0024 (Batsto Office), njparksandforests.org/parks/wharton.html; reservations: camping.nj.gov

OPEN: Year-round

SITES: 9 at Lower Forge; 10 at Mullica River; all are loosely defined areas rather than discrete campsites

EACH SITE HAS: Fire rings

WHEELCHAIR ACCESS: None

ASSIGNMENT: First-come, first-served or by reservation (minimum 2 nights)

REGISTRATION: Obtain permit at Batsto Office (31 Batsto Road, Hammonton, NJ 08037) or Atsion Office (744 US 206, Shamong, NJ 08088)

FACILITIES: Water at Mullica River; vault toilets at both Lower Forge and Mullica River

PARKING: At sand lots—hike or canoe in

FEES: New Jersey residents, $3/night; nonresidents, $5/night; $5/night pet fee at Lower Forge

---

RESTRICTIONS:

PETS: Prohibited at Mullica, permitted at Lower Forge: on leash, all sites, 2 pets/site; pet permit and proof of current vaccinations required. See njparksandforests.org/parks/pet_friendly_camping.html for more information.

FIRES: Prohibited

ALCOHOL: Prohibited

VEHICLES: Prohibited

OTHER: Horses permitted; 14-day stay limit; 2- to 6-tent/6- to 12-person site limit at Mullica; 2-tent/6-person site limit at Lower Forge

for 3 hours from Hampton Furnace. The same number of hours will get you and your canoe from Atsion to Mullica River Campground. Set up your tent where you please within the boundaries of either area, and enjoy the rare opportunity to be away from engines of any sort.

Lower Forge Campground sits alongside the Batsto River, while Mullica River Campground is perched next to its namesake. Both the Batsto and Mullica canoe routes are popular with day-trippers. Unmarked sandy roads that lead to river-access points are busy with canoe livery trucks—watch out for traffic if you are hiking and are more than a half mile from camp, where cars are not prohibited. Advance permits are required for camping here, so there is no danger of day-trippers making impromptu overnight stops.

Both rivers are scenic, easy to paddle, and popular with beginners as well as experienced paddlers. Both can also be navigated by kayak. The Mullica River has open terrain and is more easily accessible, while the Batsto is more varied and even secluded, taking canoeists through cedars. Pinelands Adventures (609-268-0189, pinelandsadventures.org) and BelHaven Paddlesports (609-965-2628, belhavenpaddlesports.com) service this section of Wharton State Forest.

Hikers are also well served in this part of the Pinelands National Reserve. The flat, accessible 50-mile Batona Trail, which traverses the forest from Brendan T. Byrne State Forest to Bass River State Forest, passes at its halfway point just south of Lower Forge Campground. No horses or mountain bikes are permitted on Batona Trail, except where it follows existing roads. Those preferring a shorter hike can hike from Atsion to Lower Forge via Springer's Brook and the railroad, for a total distance of 7.9 miles.

The 9-mile Mullica River Trail parallels the Mullica River, connecting Atsion and Batsto. Mullica River Campground is in the middle, 4 miles from Batsto and 5 miles from Atsion.

Keep your eyes open for deer, beaver, and birds. The trail passes through wetlands and under pine and cedar trees. From Batsto to Constable Bridge, be alert for trucks towing canoes. You'll pass several appealing beaches as you hike along the Mullica; remember, however, that swimming is prohibited.

Both rivers and the Mullica River Trail pass through Batsto Natural Area, a 10,000-acre area reserved for forest communities that border the Mullica and Batsto Rivers. With its savannas, open marshes, dry soil, and tea-colored rivers, the Batsto Natural Area is like the Pinelands National Reserve in miniature.

Immediately south of Batsto Natural Area is the once-industrial, now-historic Batsto Village. For 100 years, Batsto Village thrived through various industrial trends. First, it was the site of an iron furnace. After the decline of the iron industry, Batsto became the site of a glass-production operation: the iron-rich soil of the Pine Barrens also contains the ideal combination of sand and water for making glass. Joseph Wharton, a businessman from Philadelphia, purchased Batsto in 1876. He continued buying surrounding lands and at the time of his death in 1909 owned 96,000 acres of southern Jersey. Fortunately for the population of New Jersey, Wharton's plan to utilize the pristine watershed in a moneymaking endeavor did not come to fruition. Instead, Wharton inadvertently helped future conservation efforts, preserving the area's wilderness and its fragile watershed for future generations.

The state of New Jersey acquired Wharton's land in the 1950s, adding to it another 15,000 acres over the years. Today, Wharton State Forest is the largest forest in the New Jersey State Park System, stretching from near the Jersey Shore to Philadelphia. Lower Forge and Mullica River Campgrounds are the only two sites in the system that are inaccessible by motorized vehicle—and that makes them unique treasures in this unusual natural environment.

Wharton State Forest: Lower Forge Campground

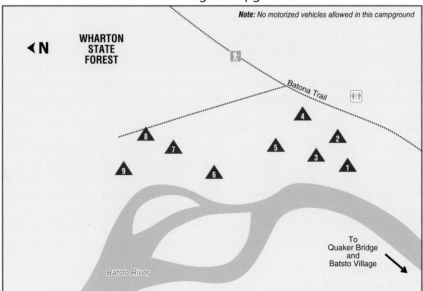

Wharton State Forest: Mullica River Campground

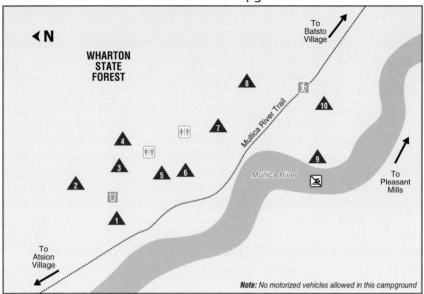

GETTING THERE

You must first register at either the state forest's Atsion Office or Batsto Office; the Atsion Office is more convenient to these campgrounds from points south. To get there from the Atlantic City Expressway, take Exit 28 for NJ 54 North, and head north on NJ 54/Bellevue Avenue, which becomes US 206. About 10.5 miles from the exit, the Atsion Office will be on your right, just after the intersection with Atsion Road/Quaker Bridge Road.

From the park office on US 206, backtrack to the intersection with Atsion Road/Quaker Bridge Road, and take the sand road on the left (Quaker Bridge Road; look for the sign for Grace Baptist Church at the turn). After about 2.2 miles, turn right (south) on Mullica River Road, and drive about 2 miles farther to an unofficial sand parking area on your left. From here, hike south on the yellow-blazed Mullica River Trail for about 1 mile to reach Mullica River Campground.

To reach Lower Forge Campground, drive east on Quaker Bridge Road about 1.9 miles past the Mullica River Road turnoff above, crossing the Batsto River on Quaker Bridge. Just after the bridge, turn left (north) on Lower Forge Road, and drive about 0.8 mile to an unofficial sand parking area located where Bulldozed Road heads right. From here, hike about 0.5 mile north on the pink-blazed Batona Trail to reach the campground.

There is helpful signage in both areas in case you get off-course. Please obey all signs indicating points past which vehicles are prohibited.

GPS COORDINATES:
LOWER FORGE: N39° 43.318' W74° 40.312'
MULLICA RIVER: N39 41.424' W74 40.515'

APPENDIX A

CAMPING EQUIPMENT CHECKLIST

Camping is more fun when you can enjoy it at a moment's notice. You never know when the opportunity may arise to head for the woods, and when it does, wouldn't it be nice to be able to pack your car with all the essentials drawn from prepacked boxes carefully cleaned, resupplied, and stored after your last trip?

COOKING/KITCHEN STUFF

Bottle opener
Bottles of salt, pepper, spices, sugar, cooking oil, and pancake syrup in waterproof, spillproof containers
Bowls
Can opener
Cooking pots with lids
Cooler
Corkscrew
Cups, plastic or tin
Dish soap (biodegradable), dishcloth, and towel
Dutch oven and fire pan
Fire starter
Flatware
Food of your choice
Frying pan and spatula
Fuel for stove
Lighter, matches in waterproof container
Paper towels
Plates
Pocketknife
Stove and fuel
Strainer
Tablecloth
Tinfoil
Trash bags
Wooden spoon

SLEEPING GEAR

Pillow
Sleeping bag
Sleeping pad, inflatable or insulated
Tent with ground tarp and rainfly

MISCELLANEOUS

Bath soap (biodegradable), washcloth, and towel
Camp chairs
Candles
Day pack
Extra batteries
First aid kit (see page 5)
Flashlight/headlamp
Lantern
Maps (road, trail, topographic, etc.)
Moist towelettes
Saw/ax
Sunglasses
Toilet paper/wet wipes
Water bottle(s)
Wool blanket
Zip-top plastic bags

OPTIONAL

Barbecue grill
Binoculars
Books
Camera
Cards and board games
Field guides on bird, plant, and wildlife identification
Fishing rod and tackle
Frisbee
GPS unit

APPENDIX B

SOURCES OF INFORMATION

APPALACHIAN TRAIL CONSERVANCY

Mid-Atlantic Regional Office
4 E. First St.
Boiling Springs, PA 17007
717-258-5771, appalachiantrail.org,
atc-maro@appalachiantrail.org

NATIONAL PARK SERVICE

Delaware Water Gap
National Recreation Area
570-426-2452, nps.gov/dewa

Gateway National Recreation Area,
Sandy Hook Unit
718-354-4606, nps.gov/gate

New Jersey Pinelands National Reserve
609-894-7300, nps.gov/pine,
nj.gov/pinelands/reserve

THE NATURE CONSERVANCY IN NEW JERSEY

tinyurl.com/natureconservancynj

NEW JERSEY AUDUBON

908-204-8998, njaudubon.org

NEW JERSEY CAMPGROUND OWNERS ASSOCIATION

New Jersey Campground & RV Park
Official Vacation Guide
campnj.com (click "Guidebook")

NEW JERSEY'S GREAT NORTHWEST SKYLANDS

njskylands.com

NEW JERSEY STATE PARKS, FORESTS, AND HISTORIC SITES

General Information
800-843-6420, state.nj.us/dep/parksandforests

Camping Reservations
camping.nj.gov

NEW JERSEY TOLL ROAD/BRIDGE INFORMATION

Delaware River Joint Bridge Commission
drjtbc.org (click "Toll Bridges")

Delaware River Port Authority of
Pennsylvania & New Jersey
drpa.org/travel/bridge-fares.html

E-ZPass New Jersey
ezpassnj.com

New Jersey Turnpike Authority
njta.com/toll-calculator

The Port Authority of New York &
New Jersey
panynj.gov/bridges-tunnels/tolls.html

South Jersey Transportation Authority
sjta.com/acexpressway

NEW YORK–NEW JERSEY TRAIL CONFERENCE

Darlington Schoolhouse Headquarters
600 Ramapo Valley Road
Mahwah, NJ 07430-1199
201-512-9348, nynjtc.org

RAILS-TO-TRAILS CONSERVANCY

railstotrails.org/our-work/united-states
/new-jersey

APPENDIX C

SUGGESTED READING AND REFERENCE

Alden, Peter, Brian Cassie, et al. *National Audubon Society Field Guide to the Mid-Atlantic States.* New York: Alfred A. Knopf, 1999.

Brooks, Christopher and Catherine. *60 Hikes Within 60 Miles: New York City, Including Northern New Jersey, Southwestern Connecticut, and Western Long Island.* 3rd ed. Birmingham, AL: Menasha Ridge Press, 2013.

Brown, Michael P. *New Jersey Parks, Forests, and Natural Areas: A Guide.* 3rd ed. New Brunswick, NJ: Rutgers University Press, 2004.

Chazin, Daniel, and the New York–New Jersey Trail Conference. *50 Hikes in New Jersey: Walks, Hikes, and Backpacking Trips from the Kittatinnies to Cape May.* 4th ed. Woodstock, VT: The Countryman Press, 2014.

Genovese, Peter. *New Jersey Curiosities: Quirky Characters, Roadside Oddities, and Other Offbeat Stuff.* 3rd ed. Guilford, CT: Globe Pequot Press, 2011.

Lurie, Maxine N., and Marc Mappen, eds. *Encyclopedia of New Jersey.* New Brunswick, NJ: Rutgers University Press, 2004.

McPhee, John. *The Pine Barrens.* New York: Farrar, Straus and Giroux, 1978.

New Jersey Atlas & Gazetteer. 3rd ed. Yarmouth, ME: DeLorme, 2005.

Parnes, Robert. *Paddling the Jersey Pine Barrens.* 6th ed. Guilford, CT: Falcon Publishing, 2002.

Sceurman, Mark, and Mark Moran. *Weird N.J.: Your Travel Guide to New Jersey's Local Legends and Best Kept Secrets.* Reprint, New York: Sterling Publishing, 2009.

Scheller, William G. and Kay. *New Jersey Off the Beaten Path: A Guide to Unique Places.* 9th ed. Guilford, CT: Globe Pequot Press, 2011.

Westergaard, Barbara. *New Jersey: A Guide to the State.* 3rd ed. New Brunswick, NJ: Rivergate Regionals Collection/Rutgers University Press, 2006.

INDEX

(*Italicized* page numbers indicate photos.)

ABOUT THE AUTHOR

Photo: Cynthia Kasales

Matt Willen is a writer, explorer, and photographer. He spends much of his time exploring little-known and remote places around the globe, most recently in areas above 50 degrees north latitude and below 50 degrees south. Matt is also the author of *Best Tent Camping: Pennsylvania* and *60 Hikes Within 60 Miles: Harrisburg,* both for Menasha Ridge Press. He lives seasonally in Pennsylvania and Nova Scotia.

DEAR CUSTOMERS AND FRIENDS,

SUPPORTING YOUR INTEREST IN OUTDOOR ADVENTURE, travel, and an active lifestyle is central to our operations, from the authors we choose to the locations we detail to the way we design our books. Menasha Ridge Press was incorporated in 1982 by a group of veteran outdoorsmen and professional outfitters. For many years now, we've specialized in creating books that benefit the outdoors enthusiast.

Almost immediately, Menasha Ridge Press earned a reputation for revolutionizing outdoors- and travel-guidebook publishing. For such activities as canoeing, kayaking, hiking, backpacking, and mountain biking, we established new standards of quality that transformed the whole genre, resulting in outdoor-recreation guides of great sophistication and solid content. Menasha Ridge Press continues to be outdoor publishing's greatest innovator.

The folks at Menasha Ridge Press are as at home on a whitewater river or mountain trail as they are editing a manuscript. The books we build for you are the best they can be, because we're responding to your needs. Plus, we use and depend on them ourselves.

We look forward to seeing you on the river or the trail. If you'd like to contact us directly, visit us at menasharidge.com. We thank you for your interest in our books and the natural world around us all.

SAFE TRAVELS,

Bob Sehlinger

BOB SEHLINGER
PUBLISHER

FOL

SEP 1 5 2023